ACTIN

THE SCREEN

Acting for the Screen is a collection of essays written by and interviews with working actors, producers, directors, casting directors, and acting professors, exploring the business side of screen acting.

In this book, over 30 show business professionals dispel myths about the industry and provide practical advice on topics such as how to break into the field; how to develop, nurture, and navigate business relationships; and how to do creative work under pressure. Readers will also learn about the entrepreneurial expectations in relation to the internet and social media, strategies for contending with the emotional highs and lows of acting, and money management while pursuing acting as a profession.

Written for undergraduates and graduates studying screen acting, aspiring professional actors, and working actors looking to reinvent themselves, *Acting for the Screen* provides readers with a wealth of first-hand information that will help them create their own opportunities and pursue a career in show business.

A two-time Emmy Award-winner, **Mary Lou Belli** has been directing television for over 30 years, with credits including *NCIS: New Orleans*, *Bull*, *Station 19*, *Monk*, *Legacies*, and *Dynasty*. She is the Co-chair of the Women's Steering Committee at the Directors Guild of America, where she also serves on the Western Directors Council and the Leadership Council Political Action Committee. Mary Lou is an honorary board member of the Alliance of Women Directors, an advisory board member of Women in Media, and a longtime member of Women in Film. This is her fourth book.

PERFORM: Succeeding as a Creative Professional

Series Editor: Anna Weinstein

The PERFORM series aims to offer engaging, uplifting, and expert support for up-and-coming artists. The series explores success in the arts, how we define success in artistic professions, and how we can prepare the next generation of artists to achieve their career goals and pay their bills.

The books in this series include practical advice, narratives, and insider secrets from industry professionals. Each book will include essays by and interviews with successful working artists and other professionals who represent, hire, or collaborate with these artists.

Ultimately, the goal of this series is simple: to illuminate how to make a living—and a life—as an artist.

Directing for the Screen
By Anna Weinstein

Acting for the Stage
By Anna Weinstein and Chris Qualls

Writing for the Screen
By Anna Weinstein

Acting for the Screen
By Mary Lou Belli

For more information about this series, please visit: https://www.routledge.com/PERFORM/book-series/PERFORM

ACTING FOR THE SCREEN

EDITED BY MARY LOU BELLI

Routledge
Taylor & Francis Group

NEW YORK AND LONDON

First published 2020
by Routledge
52 Vanderbilt Avenue, New York, NY 10017

and by Routledge
2 Park Square, Milton Park, Abingdon, Oxon, OX14 4RN

Routledge is an imprint of the Taylor & Francis Group, an informa business

© 2020 Taylor & Francis

Library of Congress Cataloging-in-Publication Data
Names: Belli, Mary Lou, editor.
Title: Acting for the screen / edited by Mary Lou Belli.
Description: New York, NY : Routledge, 2019. | Series: PERFORM : succeeding as a creative professional
Identifiers: LCCN 2019009441| ISBN 9781138311619 (hardback : alk. paper) | ISBN 9781138311640 (pbk. : alk. paper) | ISBN 9780429458729 (ebook)
Subjects: LCSH: Motion picture acting—Vocational guidance. | Television acting—Vocational guidance. | Motion picture actors and actresses—Interviews. | Television actors and actresses—Interviews. | Motion picture producers and directors—Interviews. | Television producers and directors—Interviews. | Acting teachers—Interviews.
Classification: LCC PN1995.9.A26 A267 2019 | DDC 791.4302/8—dc23
LC record available at https://lccn.loc.gov/2019009441

ISBN: 978-1-138-31161-9 (hbk)
ISBN: 978-1-138-31164-0 (pbk)
ISBN: 978-0-429-45872-9 (ebk)

Typeset in Adobe Garamond Pro and Avenir
by Swales & Willis Ltd, Exeter, Devon, UK

To my dear family: Charlie, Maggie, and Tim. You are my world.

CONTENTS

FOREWORD

Anna Weinstein

If success were as simple as drawing magical pavement art and jumping across it to the comfort of our fantasies, life would certainly be simpler. There's a reason we appreciate the opportunity to escape into fantastical stories. Perhaps it's the same reason we were drawn to the arts to begin with – because in the worlds we create, anything is possible.

All of us humans, young and old, need to believe that *possibility* is a reality – that dreaming is believing. At least to some degree. It's what we call "hope." With hope, the world looks sunny.

At the same time, we do need to find a healthy balance of dreaming big and living small. This is especially true for artists. If we ignore the many realities of the arts business and focus solely on the dream, it's unlikely we'll find success – whether critical or commercial. And we might even inadvertently sabotage our success (think, for instance, of getting into unmanageable debt because we just know that we'll one-day-soon be wealthy). On the other hand, if we were to live too squarely in the harsh realities of the industry, we'd all likely give up on the dream – convince ourselves that it's unreasonable to pursue work as an artist.

Thus the need for the professional artist to find that balance.

And then there's that pesky term "professional" and its ambiguous association with "artist." What exactly does it mean to be a "professional artist"? Is it possible to be a professional even if we don't make money from the work? What if we make some money but not enough to pay the bills? What if our goal isn't to make money at all and instead to simply – and perhaps more nobly – make *art*?

These are the types of questions all artists ponder from time to time. This book series was born out of the notion that years working feverishly in dedicated commitment to a dream is in fact the definition of "professionalism." *Merriam-Webster*'s first definition of the term is the "conduct, aim, or qualities that characterize or mark a profession or professional person"; it's the second definition that discusses "for gain or livelihood."[1]

This is an important distinction, of course, because few artists generate enough income from their art to make a living. The pavement artist asks for no remuneration for his artwork, but still, he says, his cap "would be glad of a copper or two." If the artist works consistently, though – committed to the regular practice of creating – he is making a *life* as an artist, isn't he?

Over the past several years, exploring questions and answers about working in the arts, particularly the performing arts, has been a deeply rewarding journey for me. Through the development of this book series, I have had the opportunity to connect with actors, writers, and directors I've admired for decades, reconnect with longtime friends I haven't seen in years, and make new friends and colleagues who are working toward many of the same goals that have consumed my creative energies all of my adult life.

Connecting with Mary Lou Belli has been one of the many gifts I've received in the years since I started this journey. I am indebted to my friend Toni Kalem for introducing me to Mary Lou. When I mentioned that I was searching for an editor for this book, someone with significant expertise in screen acting as well as experience in publishing (a very tall order!), Toni's recommendation was immediate and enthusiastic. Here we are some 18 months later, and I can't imagine a more knowledgeable or energetic person to have shepherded this volume from concept to publication. Not only is this one of many books Mary Lou has published about working in the business, she is also an Emmy Award-winning director, writer, and producer with a wealth of industry experience. She has directed more than 150 episodes of television and has served as an acting coach in Los Angeles for decades, teaching some of our most celebrated screen actors.

Mary Lou's passion and insider insight into the profession is threaded through every essay and interview in this volume. The conversations with working screen actors shed light on the often surprising realities of working in the industry – everything from engaging in social media marketing to adequately preparing to be on set to the ins and outs of working with directors. These Q&As explore every corner of the industry, from features to television series to commercials to audiobooks. Mary Lou has curated breezy, markedly readable content in this book. It's enlightening (and empowering!) to learn the many ways screen actors go about navigating this business.

Quick reads, for sure, but these are chapters you will want to savor. There are so many pearls of wisdom in these pages, you'll undoubtedly return to this advice many times in the years to come. The essays are equal parts pragmatic and inspirational, offering interesting takes on how to approach an acting career with optimism and intention. What a gift to read first-person perspectives from actors like Jason George (*Grey's Anatomy*), Tania Gunadi (*DC Superhero Girls*), and Toni Kalem (*The Sopranos*). So rarely do we have the opportunity to learn about successful actors' careers through their own words – and it's especially rewarding to find out how these performers have adapted and grown over the years. They are a model for how artists can nurture longtime passions while at the same time discovering new aspirations. A reminder that we are always evolving.

I hope you enjoy losing yourself in these pages as much as I have. I can't think of a more engaging way to learn about building a career as a screen actor.

Thank you for taking this journey with us. Here's to wishing you the very best in your career . . .

Anna Weinstein is series editor of PERFORM: Succeeding as a Creative Professional. *She is a regular contributor to* Film International *and teaches screenwriting and film studies at Auburn University.*

Note

1 "professionalism". Merriam-Webster.com. 2019. www.merriam-webster.com.

ACKNOWLEDGMENTS

Special thanks to Isabella Way, Toni Kalem, Tim Grey, Lucia Accorsi, Colin Morgan, Andrew Melvin, Stephan Smith Collins, and Stacey Walker . . .

all the articulate contributors and the photographers who allowed us to use their images . . .

and, most especially, Anna Weinstein for trusting me with a piece of her elegant vision.

INTRODUCTION

Could there be any better time to be an actor? There has never been more opportunities, product, or access in the television and film world . . . and all the other ancillary jobs that give employment to actors because of their talent, experience, and entrepreneurship. Why is it such a great time to be getting started, or sticking it out, or finding success, or getting ahead, or starting again? You will get the answers to those questions in this volume.

And a bonus will be that you'll find that discovering your unique journey will inform who you are as an artist and empower you in ways you never imagined. And you have the potential to make a *lot* of money . . . much more than you ever would on stage.

If you're an actor and you're looking at Figure 0.1, you'll see the cyclical nature of the acting business . . . a profession that allows you to create and adapt and recreate to meet the needs of the fast-changing, fast-paced market. The saying in Hollywood is you are only as good as your last job.

But you might say, "I just want to act. I'm not good at the other things. I'm not good at getting the job." Then we will say to you that you need to find a detour around just that. Or get good at it.

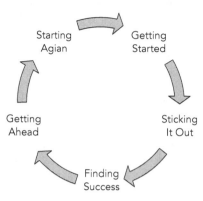

Figure 0.1 The acting business

Our experience has been that you don't get anything for free. You must give value to get value. Can you find someone who is better at the business than you are? How about finding or cultivating a circle of friends to support you at what you are good at, and give them an opportunity to do what they are good at? Sometimes you just have to know where to look and what to offer others in return for what you want or need.

Show business loves creative people who think out of the box. But you can't ignore the fact that it's show *business*. Well, you can, but there will be equally talented, more focused actors who want success more than you do who will find success ahead of you.

Here is the one truth about acting for the screen that you need to realize. Because of the nature of doing multiple takes, only one of which gets put up on that screen, the talent level of actors differs wildly. But a good director knows that he or she only needs one good take, so the way talent is judged for the screen is different from the way it is judged for the stage. So part of your job might be finding a niche . . . and targeting the kind of shows for which you may be right. So that means analyzing the market is part of your job.

It flabbergasts me when an actor who wants to work in the business says to me, "I don't watch TV." Is there someone else who he or she thinks is going to watch for them? Is there someone else whose job it is to know the market better than they should? You might say, "Well, yes, my agent or manager – they are the one selling me." I argue that you can't expect someone who only gets 10% of your job income to do 100% of your work.

You will learn how social media has changed the business. If someone isn't giving you a job, or giving you access to meeting the person who can give you the job, you can create your own job, or just bypass them completely. The person who gave me my first job in Hollywood told me, "There are no roadblocks . . . only detours." That has never been truer.

And once the industry knows who you are, there are more jobs than ever on the screen, be it film, TV, or streaming:

> Never before in the history of the medium have there been so many scripted original series to be watched and analyzed . . . Consider these statistics from FX Networks Research: in 2010 there were 216 scripted original series. By 2015, that number had shot up to 420. It kept rising, hitting 454 in 2016. And just when you thought the networks and streaming services couldn't possibly produce more content, FX Networks CEO John Landgraf announced [. . .] there could be nearly 500 scripted original series by the end of 2017.[1]

How to Use This Book

This book is about the business of acting for the screen. There are other books that reinforce craft, the tasks associated with developing your skills and talents as an actor. But this book is specifically about the work involved with becoming a professional actor.

You don't have to read it cover to cover. It won't benefit you necessarily to read the essays and interviews in order – although there's certainly nothing wrong with that approach. But the book is structured so that you can pick and choose what to read when, at the pace that works best for you. Flip through the pages and browse the interviewee introductions and contributor bios. This will give you a glimpse of the personalities, successes, and individual perspectives on building a life as an actor on the screen.

What you'll find in this book is insider insight into the day-to-day life of an actor. What is it like to be a struggling actor? What is it like to be a working actor? What is it like to hop from series to series?

You'll hear from a range of actors, directors, producers, professors, and career coaches, a casting director, a manager, an executive director of creative development of a streaming network, and a lot of hyphenates (actor-director, actor-writer, etc.), in this book. You'll read stories about people who create their own content. You'll read about overcoming or redefining what you want from your film career. You'll learn how you can have an enriched personal life while still pursuing your life as an artist and a professional who treats his or her life as a business.

The range of advice, wisdom, and stories you'll read in this book is meant to give you perspective. The essays and interviews are grouped thematically, exploring the broad ideas of Getting Started, Sticking It Out, Finding Success, Getting Ahead, and Starting Again. These groupings, however, do not indicate that what you'll find in each chapter is a logically ordered list of how-to advice. You won't!

Some interviews include topical questions and responses about how to approach specific goals and situations as a film, TV, commercial, or voice-over actor, and others take a broader exploratory approach, with the interviewees sharing personal narratives or opinions about some of the more intangible aspects of the career. The same is true of the essays and conversations. You'll find a range of scopes, from direct advice and calls to action to interview snippets with multiple working actors.

The key is this: don't look for advice alone. Look for insights. Look for new ways of approaching challenging aspects of the career. Look for information about the realities of the business. Above all else, look for a deeper understanding of how to celebrate the *pursuit of* success as well as the *result of* success.

You'll find that discovering your unique journey will inform who you are as an artist and empower you in ways you never imagined. Enjoy your trip!

Note

1 Champagne, Christine. 2017. "Peak Technique". *Emmy Magazine* 2: 17. www. emmys.com/news/features/peak-technique.

CHAPTER I

GETTING STARTED

Y ou've learned the craft of acting, been in countless stage productions, done a couple student films – one is an official selection at a film festival. You don't have an agent. You have no connections. No free ticket to Los Angeles (LA) and no place to stay if you did pack your bags and make the trek. Or maybe you are in high school and know you are destined for the screen but don't know where to start. So, what comes next? This chapter will walk you through practical steps you can take to get started on your journey to becoming a working screen actor. Do you move to New York or LA? Or a smaller market? How do you make yourself into someone an agent or manager wants to sign? How do you put together a reel? Why do you even need a website? This first chapter will answer these questions and more!

All of this "getting started" business begins and ends with the passion you have and the decisions you make about where you would like to begin. And then taking that first important step from wherever you are now. That first step might be the hardest. But if you are an artist with a dream, you know you must take it. It is a special and rewarding path to choose. This book will help you each step along the way.

Here's what we're going to address in this first chapter:

- How to assess your strengths and weaknesses as an actor and to see if you can be competitive with other professionals already in the marketplace.
- Establishing realistic goals and pursuing them with passion and common sense.
- How to form a business plan.
- Information about reels, head shots, and websites, including tips from multiple sources!
- Deciding whether to go to college, and if you do, what program might best suit you.
- Making sure you are a confident actor who has a sense of self-respect and is a friendly, warm, and vibrant person with whom others enjoy associating.
- What factors go into knowing your "type."
- How to build your website.
- The difference between film and stage acting.
- Getting a manager's take on how to set yourself apart by making your characters come alive.

So set your path. Take the steps we suggest. You are so fortunate that so many experts generously contributed their words of wisdom for your benefit and specifically to get you started. They want to inspire you, guide you, demystify the process for you. So read on . . .

MOVING TOWARD A CAREER

Some Basics

▶ A Q&A with Grant Kretchik

Grant Kretchik is the Associate Director of the School of Performing Arts at Pace University and he created and directs the school's BFA (Bachelor of Fine Arts) Acting program. Grant has appeared Off-Broadway as well as in film and television. His projects have premiered in festivals around the world, including Cannes, Austin, Mumbai, Santa Fe, Boston LGBT, Honolulu, London. His latest project, *America*, which he executive produced, has been seen at Rosebud, Julien Dubuque, the Women's International Film and Arts Festival, the Glendale Film Festival, and the Sapporo International Short Film Festival.

Figure 1.1 Grant Kretchik

Photo: Jessica Osber Photography

Grant assisted director Michael Grief on the first national tour of *Next to Normal*. Other directing credits include: *The Parade* at the Provincetown Tennessee Williams Theater Festival; *Scottish Sperm* at the Edinburgh Festival Fringe (world premiere); and Zoofest and Just for Laughs in Montreal, Canada. Grant has worked as both director and an actor at La MaMa Experimental Theatre Club. As an actor, he has appeared Off-Broadway in *The Servant of Two Masters, Einstein, I Knock at the Door* and *Pictures in the Hallway*. His film/television credits include: *Law & Order, Guiding Light, As the World Turns, Broken, Man on the Moon*, and *When Harry Tries to Marry*. He is a proud member of the Actors' Equity Association and the Stage Directors and Choreographers Society.

Grant is a contributing expert for *Backstage* magazine and he contributed to *The Ultimate Musical Theater College Audition Guide: Advice from the People Who*

Make the Decisions (Oxford University Press). In 2019, Grant was recognized in Washington, DC as a recipient of a prestigious Jefferson Award in public service.

Grant (Figure 1.1) holds an MFA (Master of Fine Arts) in Acting from the New School University.

Do you think actors need training before they enter the work place?
Yes, but not just for the reasons you might think. There are obvious reasons, such as learning the fundamentals and developing nuance to your craft and analytical skills. Beyond that, I think it's important that actors feel both accomplished and have a sense of confidence in their abilities. When you are collaborating with knowledgeable, professionally trained actors, it's empowering to know you you've prepared properly to be in that room. There is an expectation of what a professional actor should know and should be capable of, and it's through training that you gain permission to expand your capabilities.

Of course, an actor can enter the workforce or book a gig without having training. It happens, but one job does not equal a career. Often actors cannot sustain themselves. This can happen to any actor, but when it does, the trained actor never says, "I wish I hadn't spent time training," whereas the untrained actor might say, "I wonder if I should be better prepared." Either way, a smart actor will always take a class because savvy professionals should remain curious about expanding themselves. Actor training can never be taken away from you, even if a job is. Training is not only where you expand yourself but where you develop relationships that cultivate your network of collaborators, which leads to sustainability.

The last thing I'll say about the merits of training is that it's both the beginning of your artistic development and a springboard that can lead to your first professional meetings; agents managers, and other such professionals are more likely to take a risk on investing in you. Training is the first indication that you have made a commitment to learn and invest in both craft and yourself as you endeavor to be a professional actor. People are more likely to take a risk on someone whose resumé signals they aspire to be educated.

So why a BFA? or BA? Or any other college degree? Is one better?
There is a difference, but one is not necessarily better than the other. I find that college hopefuls, some parents, guidance counselors, and mentors have a tendency to overly glorify a BFA and falsely devalue a good BA degree.

A BFA can be associated with a liberal arts program where you are responsible for taking university general education courses. However, a BFA can also be a conservatory with little or no university general education coursework. A BA (Bachelor of Arts) can be slightly less acting-focused and has the upshot of being more flexible while incorporating more liberal arts and humanities courses. The BA often provides students with an opportunity for minoring or double-majoring in other disciplines. I'm speaking in broad generalities – it is important that you research and understand each individual program's intricacies, strengths, and expectations.

Determining if one is better than the other is certainly a challenge. In a BFA program, you'll receive a more well-rounded actor training experience. Such programs are singularly geared toward the student who endeavors to have a more profound understanding of acting as a multidisciplinary approach. A BFA likely incorporates any number of sub-disciplines, such as voice, speech, movement, stage combat, and improvisation as well as additional history and text analysis.

Some BA programs run the risk of being dated or tired. They may lack direction and rigor, often serving the university's enrollment goal rather than the devoted student. Do your homework and be sure there is mentorship and opportunities within the BA program (or BFA program, for that matter). A BA program is an ideal venture for students who have a desire to study acting while also being unsure if it's solely the career they want. A good BA program provides curious students with an excellent education and unique opportunities. There are any number of really exciting BA programs that have developed unique experiences for the actor in training.

As a professional who created and runs a BFA, I have to admit that I am curious by those applicants who self-identify as a "BA only" applicant. This student may understand something greater about his or her self, about the kind of storyteller they want to be, the kind of career opportunities they are open to. Ultimately, I think, they want a broader experience and seek to bring that to their process as a creative artist, which is compelling.

My concern is that an applicant might feel a stigma around a BA as being less valued and so their application to a BFA is solely motivated by fear. Fear that they won't be taken seriously if they are not accepted into a BFA. This is a very dangerous way to think and is totally false. A BFA, quite simply, is not for everyone.

It should be mentioned that there are also some associate degree programs that are worth evaluating. While you can find a good associate degree with great faculty and training, many of these are based on a for-profit business model where volume supersedes quality. I wouldn't rule these out, but I would advise being cautious and diligent in your research.

Lastly, should you choose to study something other than acting as your college degree, there's always the opportunity to pursue professional classes while simultaneously studying a different field. Professional classes, given the right teacher and the right mix of students, can be rigorous and impactful. It is important to make sure your teacher has training of his or her own as well as professional experience. You want to know that your professional teacher understands how to conduct a course and deliver content in a meaningful and effective manner. Be certain that it's a course with defined objectives and training goals, not just coaching. It's important that you are learning craft and developing technique. Coaching is another discipline and frequently isolated, focusing on the individual. True actor training involves, at a minimum, a partner or partners and, ideally, a small ensemble of talented and dedicated individuals.

I've heard arguments for going to a small school where I will get to do everything: write, direct, act, and shoot with or run a camera. And others where they say you should go to a school even where the acting pool is big and competitive. Do you think one is better?
The traditional ideology holds that an actor should train solely as an actor. I still think there is merit to this: you do need focus. Being a dilettante isn't necessarily the best road to success. However, we are experiencing a revolution where an avalanche of technology is changing how and what actors are capable of producing. So, while actors have a responsibility to fully dedicate and commit themselves to training, there is also an added responsibility to embrace the tools technology offers, using them to complement your ability to tell stories and establish your unique brand.

"You're seeking to be a trained actor, but ultimately, familiarizing yourself with these other skills can expand your creative collaborations while you're waiting to book your next gig."

It's always been naïve to assume you will be hired for your talent alone. Now, it is irresponsible not to develop additional skills that make you more well-rounded in the industry. All professions evolve and expand; why should acting be any different? Absolutely, train as an actor and let that be your primary focus, but if you want to be a more compelling collaborator, traditional "actor training" is only one element. Seek out understanding and knowledge of how to write, produce, direct, and operate a camera. You're seeking to be a trained actor, but ultimately, familiarizing yourself with these other skills can expand your creative collaborations while you're waiting to book your next gig. The opportunities to create your own work and take control of your brand are far greater than they have ever been. Actors can either fight it or embrace it.

It's critical to understand the difference between large and small schools and the opportunities that are provided or limited as a result of the size and scope of the curriculum. When choosing a university, it is important to be curious about what you respond to and what environment you'll thrive in. You might want an intimate environment with a strong ensemble base. Here, you'll be held accountable to standards that are monitored by faculty and staff to ensure your success. Or, perhaps the autonomy found at a larger school might appeal to you, allowing for self-expression with fewer eyes upon you.

I can't stress enough how important it is to know what excites you, where you thrive, what inspires you as an individual. Ultimately these are questions you have to answer for yourself. To answer these, visit a variety of campuses to find out if you like urban, rural, or country settings. Meet students, talk to them, listen to them interact with each other; can you imagine yourself as one of them? See the work of the students in production or rehearsal. Sit in on classes if you can. Meet the faculty, and ask yourself: "Am I inspired?"

Is there a difference between stage and screen acting?
Yes! This has been a debate for as long as I can remember. The answer I was always told during my training was no. But I disagree. Certainly, at the core, they're not that different. They have the same fundamental principles (such as actions and truth), but in regard to preparation and execution, I believe they are fundamentally different.

Historically, training in the American theater was for the stage in a time when regional and repertory theaters thrived. Institutions didn't seem interested in including film and television acting courses in the curriculum. It makes sense: equipment was expensive and challenging to operate, and even good acting teachers didn't have experience with film and television courses themselves. So the solution was to leave well enough alone. The system didn't appear to be broken. There were plenty of theater jobs, or alternatively, if you worked in film and television, you could learn on the job. Gradually, institutions started to include a wider range of courses, but even then, the strategy was to just put a camera in the room and film theater scenes. It's only recently that progressive and respected programs have started to incorporate really strong film and television training in their curriculum. This is largely due to the aforementioned technology revolution, the boom in cable and streaming television productions, and institutions' access to expanded facilities and equipment. A world which was once so foreign and specialized has suddenly become accessible, making it impossible to ignore. Now it is possible to break in and create film content. Subsequently, it's possible for institutions to develop meaningful curriculum and experiences in the film and television space.

All of this has allowed, or perhaps forced, training programs to acknowledge the differences between stage and screen acting. I believe this is critical as they are wholly different exercises. The evidence is displayed when actors who work predominantly on camera attempt to transition to theater or vice versa. Often, performances don't translate. Of course, there are exceptions, but the evidence is still there. Let's say that acting is like an arm muscle that must be exercised: stage acting is the biceps and screen acting is the triceps. Each require a different movement and different apparatus in order to be defined. In some ways, film and television acting can even be the "unlearning" of good stage technique. For the stage, we devote a good deal of time training an actor to live in an exaggerated, yet authentic, version of a character's journey. For film and television, you still need that authenticity, but actors must get away from that exaggerated gesture and trust what's more natural. Often, this leaves actors feeling like they are not "doing enough" and that sense can lead actors to draw on their stage technique and the result can appear false through the lens of a camera.

Preparation/Rehearsal

Preparing for your theater role is typically a collaborative process with other actors and a director. It requires a kind of exploration that takes time and repetition of the process in order to adequately express the start and end of a character's journey through their circumstances. You develop the endurance to sustain the arc of the character because live theater happens in only one take. You walk on stage at the opening and live that full arc that your rehearsal has prepared you for. You tell that story all at one time and then repeat it, nightly, with renewed energy.

Preparing for film is often a chaotic process with various creatives around you working simultaneously to convey the expression of the piece through multiple elements. There is often little or no rehearsal, and depending on the size of the role, you may be expected to be performance-ready when you arrive to set. The performance doesn't happen in real time since film is shot out of sequence. There is no time to ease into the journey of a character's circumstances, and so your analysis of the script and role must be exceptional. For example, you might have to film the climax on the first day (and you will not have had the benefit of the preceding sequential scenes to support that arc). The opportunity to discover through the rehearsal process, and let these discoveries impact your performance, is limited.

Location/Space

The difference between a theater and a film set is central to what makes acting in one medium different from the other. It is also what makes the transition between the two mediums most difficult. When theater actors work in front of a camera they often hear, "Too big! Too loud! Too much!" When screen actors move to the stage they often hear, "We can't see you! We can't hear you! Be bigger!"

In a theater, there is space that separates the spectator from the actor. Every spectator has a different vantage point from which they hear and see circumstances unfolding. Therefore, the conceit is that the actor must be louder, broader and bigger so that the circumstances can be revealed sufficiently to all while the action and dialogue are understood. There is a certain artifice to stage technique, and actors train so they can perform truthfully within the heightened gesture of the theater realm. It is this same artifice that may betray the theater actor when they work on camera. The camera robs the actor of distance while exposing what might work in the theater as false.

Expression/Voice

Because of the space available on stage, actors express outwardly, often using their whole body. There is more freedom of movement to support the action. The movement, gesture, and expression – even a subtle one – must be full-bodied to reach the back of the house. Likewise, this is also true of the actor's voice.

> "In film, so much of what would be expressed outwardly in theater must be internalized and made more simple. Actors must take their emotions and express them through their eyes or tone or a simple gesture."

In film, so much of what would be expressed outwardly in theater must be internalized and made more simple. Actors must take their emotions and express them through their eyes or tone or a simple gesture. The camera not only eliminates the space, it also serves as a magnifying glass while the microphone acts as a bullhorn.

Film minimizes freedom of your body movement while also amplifying the task of hitting your marks. In theater the actor is required to "find their light." While this requirement is something to be understood, the physical area of light available to the actor on stage still creates a larger playing area. In film, on the other hand, the equivalent of "find your light" would be to hit your mark. The consequences of not hitting your mark can be detrimental to your performance. You run the risk of being out of frame. The good news for film acting is that retakes are always possible, but they cost time and money.

Interaction/Solitude

"Communion" is the unbroken communication between actors, which is meant to captivate the audience and communicate the drama that exists between the characters. By the very nature of live performance, actors come together in a given space to tell the story. The actors are stimulated by each other's dialogue, tones, and expressions and the setting in which the action is taking place. This all contributes to the storytelling. Developing and demonstrating real "communion" is a calculated and cohesive process that creates the world of the play.

Film, on the other hand, can be isolating. As previously mentioned, there is often limited rehearsal. Once the wide shots have been captured and you are filming a close-up, they might have to imagine and create the stimulation that contributed to the performance they just gave in the wide shot. While requiring the power of imagination, filming can be isolating from the experience of communion.

Often, this leads actors to self-generating emotion as they seek to recreate their performance for their close-up. The beauty of film is that, with enough coverage through multiple shots, editors control time and space, making it possible for the actor to appear present in every moment.

Historically, many actors get their start in the theater and later make a transition to film. With training and good technique, your experiences as an actor in one medium can translate to the other. However, it is imperative to understand the specific features that distinguish the crafts of acting for the stage and acting for the screen.

Outside of learning my craft, what should I do before graduating to prepare myself for the business?

There are excellent actor training programs across the country. Some good programs can be found in New York and LA, while others are peppered in-between. No matter the location, the best programs aim to develop the talents of their aspiring artists and produce quality actors. Good actors are not produced overnight: the end of training marks the beginning, not the end, of development. I want actors to think like artists and train as such, but I also work to equip them with the tools needed to navigate the evolving climate of our industry. You can be an "artist," but if you plan to pursue a professional career, your job will be that of an entrepreneur who is ultimately responsible for your own business.

The following are some of the things to keep in mind and prepare for beyond graduation.

Preparing for Working in the Industry

First of all, you need to know that you will and should continue to take classes. A show dog doesn't stop being groomed when the competition is over . . . neither should you. Honing your craft will continue beyond any program you graduate from.

A good program should provide you with strong industry and "business of acting" courses that result in an industry showcase. The all-important senior showcase is the graduate's debut to the industry, essentially the college actor's equivalent of a bar mitzvah, a debutant ball, or First Communion. While showcase certainly is the exciting culmination of the training experience, because it marks the end of one chapter, there is an overwhelming, and unnecessary, anxiety that surrounds what is intended to be a joyous rite of passage and a new beginning for the young actor.

Headshots and Resumés

It's not cheap, but actors are required to have a professional headshot. You will need two, maybe three. First, a commercial headshot usually features a smile with easy colors and bright lighting. A theatrical or "legit" headshot is where an actor can communicate their type. Headshots must look like you; it must look like your "brand." How disappointing is it when you swipe right on Tinder only to have your date walk in looking nothing like their photo? This is what agents, managers, and casting directors go through regularly except, in this case, you've wasted their valuable professional time and yours. Also, *never* let your parents select your headshot. Seek advice from those who know you closely and have seen your work and what you bring to that work. If you are the "girl next door," avoid wearing a leather jacket with the collar popped just because you think it's "sexy." This might be useful as a third headshot (an out-of-the-box headshot), but if you are the "girl next door," *be* "the girl next door."

> "It can be an easy temptation to lie or falsely boost your credits to make yourself look more professional, but *do not* do this."

While there are some format variations, the typical resumé shares a number of similarities. It is very easy to Google "actor resumés" so you can compare a few and follow the format. It can be an easy temptation to lie or falsely boost your credits to make yourself look more professional, but *do not* do this. You're just starting out. The industry knows this; it's part of your appeal. To you, it might feel like your lack of professional credits might be a drawback, but it's way more interesting than lying. Including college credits is important in the beginning but list them as "University Theater." Just because your university might perform in a regional theater does not mean the production you were in can be considered regional. Leave off high school productions.

Clips and Reels

During school breaks or post grad, start creating content and auditioning for student films. You'll want to have digital content to pull together a few clips of your work. Traditionally, the standard was for an actor to have a 90- to 120-second reel of their work on camera. It's still great to have this in your arsenal, but now it's more common for an actor to have clips that reflect a variety of styles and genres (to name a few: comedic, dramatic, episodic, procedural drama). When you are starting out, it might be difficult to have a wide range of clips of those specific styles. So start with easy ones like comedic and dramatic. Having single clips versus an entire reel will make submitting for projects much easier.

Websites

Your website is the next stop for anyone who responds positively toward your headshot, resumé, or submission. The industry wants to know more about you and that you have the ambition to keep a clean and updated website. After all, your site is the digital face of your brand. It says a lot about an actor who responsibly manages their image. It helps the industry understand that you are working at a career versus just "putting yourself out there and seeing what happens." Be sure the website is easy to navigate and avoid letting your creative nature get in the way of it being straightforward.

A good website should include the following:

- A landing page with your headshot.
- A bio balanced with professional and appropriate personal context.
- A resumé and a button to download it.
- A "news" or "what's up next" page.
- A few additional headshots.
- A photo gallery of stills from projects that you have been in.
- A video gallery for your reel and clips.
- A link to your most-used social media platforms.
- A contact page (avoid using your home address; consider setting up a Google voice account instead of your personal cell number, and if you have representation, use the contact information that they provide).

Social Media

Whether we like it or not, social media is a tool that makes it easy for people to find you and for you to reach people. The current thinking is that if you don't have followers, it's more difficult to book jobs. While there might be some truth in that for some jobs, it isn't entirely true. Spielberg, Hanks, Bigelow, and Oprah don't need you to have followers to sell their projects. If you have Meryl Streep or Viola Davis in a project, it's unlikely the producers are concerned about your followers. Smaller projects might seek to benefit from your having both followers and, more importantly, a social media presence that demonstrates the kind of brand they want to associate with. This is why social media should be your branding tool and not a place for you to vomit up your careless thoughts and moments or ugly criticisms. Use it wisely. Don't dilute your brand. Meaning, find one or two platforms to master versus having a weak presence on every platform.

Actors Access

While talent representatives actively submit their clients, casting directors can also choose to release the breakdowns on Actors Access, where actors can view jobs and self-submit. On Actors Access you can also save your headshot, resumé, and video clips for easy submission. It's important to note that submissions with clips are viewed more favorably and moved to the top for review.

Lastly, keep current. Read the industry's trade papers and websites to be aware of what's happening. Who's producing and directing what, what's being cast, who's casting it, etc. You'll want to have this knowledge so that you can better position and pitch yourself to the appropriate professionals for the right projects. Additionally, you need to see plays, films, television shows, web series, etc. It's your job to know what's out there and it will likely improve your own abilities as an actor.

At some point, every actor/artist who aims to be commercially viable and successful has to start considering themselves an actor/entrepreneur. You'll need to be savvy in packaging your unique brand. Consider what it is that you are selling and what you uniquely have to offer the industry.

What should be my immediate goals after graduation?
First, enjoy the success of your accomplishments. It is important to breathe. It's unlikely you will have the opportunity to work in the same capacity again. Take a moment to reflect; it's humbling.

Second, appreciate the opportunities that you've had and thank the people who supported you through this achievement.

Third, take the long view. Too much emphasis is placed on senior showcases and what that does or does not yield. Regardless of the meetings that resulted (or didn't), it's important to remember that you have power because you now possess valuable skills and tools to navigate this business . . . even when the phone isn't ringing. If you don't get meetings after showcase, the goal should be the same as if you did: continue to work on knowing your type, your brand, and how to sell it. Collaborate with colleagues to create your own work and professional opportunities, self-submit, go to open calls, volunteer to be a reader at auditions. Read trade papers and websites, because the more informed you are, the better actor and client you'll eventually be.

Fourth, take a class! I cannot emphasize enough how important it is to keep up with training. Consider taking Improvisation, Audition Technique, Scene Study, or even a business-type course. These will keep you engaged, further your skills, expand your contacts, and help acquaint you better with the business of your developing brand. It's easy to assume that training is finished when you graduate, but realize that, like any profession, your degree alone does not make you relevant. You expect your dentist to be knowledgeable of the best and most recent practices – you should be too.

Fifth, explore what makes you happy other than acting! Anything from volunteering to painting to politics. Seek out a passion that feeds your soul and your mind in other ways. It will keep you sane, and you'll be more interesting in both meetings and professional functions.

Should I start in New York? Atlanta? Chicago? LA?

Expanding on my last point: what makes you happy in and out of the business? Climate and culture are as equally important to consider as acting opportunities because, to be successful, an actor must be comfortable with their surroundings. Yes, it might be necessary to make sacrifices for work and so you choose a location where you're not the happiest. You might give up family time or leave a lover for the pursuit of professional success, but remember: you can be an actor anywhere. Of course, location can play a huge role in the trajectory of your career. If New York makes you crazy, don't live there. If you're lonely in LA, don't live there. If you hate humidity and heat, do not move to Atlanta. If the cold bothers you, then Chicago might not be the place for you. This is a difficult career, so why make it harder on yourself? Being miserable is not a prerequisite to pursuing an acting career.

The most significant differences between New York and all of the other markets is theater. Although other markets (especially Chicago) have great theater opportunities, New York remains the central hub for casting theater. This is not to understate the significance of theater in other markets. We're prone to think LA has few theater opportunities, yet in less than six months I've had several recent alumni book LA theater gigs that have led to great reviews, extended runs, and more bookings in film and television. While LA has a vibrant theater community, it does exist somewhat in the shadows of the Hollywood lights. Beyond the plentiful opportunities theater provides in New York, there are nearly 30 television shows regularly filming there (more than at any other time in history.)

> "The industry revolves around these two major cities, which means a high concentration of projects but also a high concentration of actors trying to be seen."

Beyond the two traditional entertainment capitals, second cities offer film incentive programs that are drawing large Hollywood productions. As far as the television and film industry in smaller markets goes, the major difference is frequency of opportunities.

The larger markets of New York and LA have an abundant amount of projects being cast year-round. The industry revolves around these two major cities, which means a high concentration of projects but also a high concentration of actors trying to be seen.

In smaller markets, new projects are less frequent, so while you might be more likely to be seen, you might be limited to fewer opportunities. It can be easier to get acquainted with casting directors in smaller markets, and with less competition you can often earn your Screen Actors Guild-American Federation of Television and Radio Artists (SAG-AFTRA) card more easily.

The bottom line is if you're working regularly and that makes you happy, trust that. The industry will find you. A dear friend of mine left New York after many years of the grind. She moved to Minneapolis, where the Coen Brothers discovered her and put her in *A Serious Man*.

New York City and LA will always reign supreme as the ultimate destination for actors. They are not being overthrown any time soon and so they will be there waiting for you. Remember that you deserve to be happy. If you're happy in one of these major cities, you're likely thriving, likely feeling more ambitious, and likely possess the energy and time needed to put into successfully pursuing your career objectives.

IS THIS PATH RIGHT FOR YOU?

What Is My Actor Readiness? A Self-Evaluation

▶ By Peter Cocuzza

Peter Cocuzza is a professor in the Department of Theater and Dance at Southern Illinois University Edwardsville. He holds an MFA degree in Performance from Ohio University's Professional Actor Training Program. For the past 30 years he has taught a variety of acting-related classes, such as Acting for the Camera, Acting as a Career, Comedy Styles, Period Styles, Auditioning, Voice & Movement, Mask Characterization, Stage Dialects, and Stage Combat to all levels of performers from beginner to advanced. He also has directed over 40 theater productions at and/ or outside of the university. As an actor Peter (Figure 1.2) adapted the book *Town Hall Tonight* into a one-person show which he toured. He acted with the Three Rivers Shakespeare Festival's Shakespeare-in-the-Schools Program, toured children's theater with Saltworks Theatre, and performed in dinner theater, tent theater at Hartwood Acres, and summer stock theater at the Monomoy Theatre on Cape Cod, as well as in industrial films, television commercials, and voice-overs in the Pittsburgh market. These varied and numerous experiences enabled him to teach, coach, and advise the careers of hundreds of students over the years.

Figure 1.2 Peter Cocuzza

Photo: South Illinois University Edwardsville Marketing

An actor is someone who creates and performs a role for an audience either on stage, television, or film. Each year thousands of new and "wannabe" actors move to the big city to begin their screen careers. Perhaps your friends, family, teachers, and coaches have all said you should be in the movies or on television, and made you wonder "what if."

Earning a living wage as a film actor is not easy and not for everyone. So how do you know if this path is right for you? Consider first these four axioms that I believe successful actors have in common and see if they apply to you:

1. You should have some kind of *training* in theater and/or film, both to assess your strengths and weaknesses as an actor and to see if you can be competitive with other professionals already in the marketplace. No one is going to pay you substantial sums of money without reassurance that you can do the job well.
2. Your *talent* alone is not enough. You may be one of the greatest actors in the world but if no one knows who you are then your dreams will eventually sputter and dry up. Do something every day to make new contacts and meet people.
3. Your *goals* should be realistic, attainable according to your skill level, and pursued with passion and a dose of common sense. Wanting something with all your heart is no guarantee you will get it, so you need a business plan to promote yourself. Dream big but take small, manageable steps.
4. You must be physically *healthy* and emotionally balanced. Actors sustaining themselves in this industry all understand the necessity of staying mentally sharp and physically ready when opportunity comes calling.

In addition to these four axioms, there are a number of other questions to ask yourself before deciding if this career is for you. Here are a few to give you an idea of what it takes to succeed in this industry.

Are You Aware the Odds Are Against You – Every Day?

If you have not heard the sad statistics of how many actors work on any given day you should ask your teacher/coach, go to the SAG-AFTRA website, or, better yet, talk to someone who is a professional actor. Most actors starting out likely earn less than $15,000 per year from their actual film work. That's hardly enough to live on – waiters make much more and eat better. If you have a fallback plan then go and do that now and save yourself the time, money, and effort. Do this work because you love it and can't imagine yourself in any other profession.

Are You Now in Good Enough Physical Health?

Do you have the stamina to perform your duties as an actor? Film work can be intense, demanding, and draining on your body. Getting back and forth to auditions can be stressful. Even shooting a 30-second commercial might take all day to finish. Do you tire easily during the day or are you able to pace yourself with good energy, especially on a long day of filming? You are expected to do no less than a full and complete performance each time the camera is rolling.

Remember, too, that you are hired to do a job and expected to attend all callbacks, rehearsals, and filming with focus, energy, and stamina. Calling in sick is not an option once you are hired to the job. Are you ready to meet this challenge?

Do You Have a Support System?

You excitedly moved to a new city but still haven't gotten an audition! You didn't find an agent today and life seems hard. How would you feel if you went to 20 auditions and were rejected at all of them? Rejections are going to follow you throughout this career and happen much more often than successes. Many actors even find themselves in therapy because they can't handle the constant rejection. Disappointment one day can be followed by elation the next. How will you handle this emotional roller coaster? Finding friends or family to help support you during both the high and low points of your journey is a must. If not, it will be easy to become despondent and give up. Surround yourself with people who genuinely care about you. A friendly face and a few words of understanding and encouragement may be all you need to keep you on track.

Do You Have Healthy Self-esteem?

Do you blame others when you don't get cast, or do you challenge yourself to be better and more prepared for the next audition? A film career can be both wonderful and horrible all in the same day. In the course of your day, you are going to meet people desperate to get cast, people who have soured on the business, people who can't seem to get their lives together, and people who will just want to put you down so they can feel better. The negative energy from these kinds of people can be infectious and may drag you down as well, unless you have good self-esteem.

A healthy self-esteem keeps you positive, upbeat, and proactive about your career. These actors are confident in themselves and their ability, have a sense of self-respect, and are friendly, warm, and vibrant people with whom others enjoy associating. This seems like a much better way to go through life as well as increasing your odds of success.

Have You Ever Been on Camera and Are You Knowledgeable about the Industry?

Learning the vocabulary and protocols of the screen are the first things done in a camera class. Are you confident you know the terminology used on a film set and what to do if you got cast? You can't be expected to play any game well if you don't know the rules. So make it your mission to learn the language of the screen world and who does what. If you got your dream job tomorrow, do you feel confident in both your ability and knowledge or do you still need additional training? Be honest, and if you do, then go get it. There are many ways to gain experience as you work your way up to a professional. Work as an extra. Act in a student film project. Take classes. Seize every opportunity to gain more screen time.

If you already have substantial film experience, then that's great. Are you now aware of the current trends, the names of the movers and shakers in the business, new works being developed, or the names of the hot new directors? You don't need to be an encyclopedia of film lore, but a little knowledge gives you an edge over the competition in an interview or can help you decide where to put your energies as you make decisions concerning your career.

Is Your Acting "Technique" Reliable and Repeatable?

Every actor has a personal way of working and getting through a shoot on those days when they are not "feeling" the part. Trusting your natural instinct is not enough. Hopefully, you learned technique during your training. Film technique includes knowing where to stand and look, knowing how a shot is being framed or directed, blocking awareness, mastery of voice, economic and precise body movements when needed, connecting to an emotion, understanding your character's objective, and the ability to repeat the same performance take after take. It is the craft part of performing. Find the artist within you but be an artisan.

Are You Always Running Late for an Appointment, a Class, or a Meeting, or Do You Get There Just Barely on Time?

There are lots of reasons why we are, on occasion, legitimately late for something. Typically we apologize, give our reasons, and are forgiven by our dear friends. However, chronic lateness may get you a reputation which your friends may accept, but in the professional world regularly showing up late will likely get you fired and replaced.

The adage "Time is money" is never more true than in the film industry. Professional film shoots can cost at minimum tens of thousands of dollars a day, and work on a very tight shooting schedule. Being tagged with the reputation of not showing up on time may put a black mark next to your name as "that person" who is not dependable. The casting director, your agent, and your fellow actors will begin to wonder if they can trust you to be in their project.

That said, take heart: any habit can be changed and new habits cultivated. Start today. Try to be the first to get to class. Be early to your next meeting or audition. If nothing else, you give yourself time to prepare your notes, look over the script, or center yourself. There are plenty of books and articles online to help you make better choices to arrive on time (or better yet, early) to your next appointment. No one was ever condemned or scolded for always being early.

Are You a Team Player with a Good Work Ethic?

Do you enjoy being around people or are you a loner? Can you graciously take direction? Do you have the patience to sit and wait for long periods of time as a shot is being set up? Can you follow, remember, and repeat simple directions? Any film or television project requires a small army of variously skilled people. Just look at the credits that run after your favorite movie. Sure, there is a chain of command to follow and someone needs to be in charge, but it nevertheless remains a team effort. Super-talented, famous people may exhibit diva-like behavior and get away with it, but for most of us, no one wants to work with a whiner, an egotist, or someone who exudes bad energy (at least not by choice).

The Golden Rule applies: "Do unto others as you would have them do unto you." You need to remember that all these people are here to make you look good and after a project is over they talk to each other regularly. Actors who were friendly, easy to work with, and who get the job done leave a good impression. Good reputations will get you rehired. Bad ones are hard to change and may get you blacklisted. It is a small world and the screen world is even smaller. Help your colleagues remember you in a good way by having a good professional work ethic and attitude.

Do You Know Your "Type"?

Your "type" is how a casting director, agent, or even your friends see you. We type people every day in life in order to know how to talk to them. We may call them introverted, kind, outgoing, loud, serious, fun-loving, or confused. You, too, will be labeled with some kind of descriptive when someone meets you for the first time. A casting director may see you as the evil genius type, the funny best friend, the quiet soft-spoken librarian, the over-achiever in the office, etc. How do you see yourself? Are you the athlete or the nerdy, artsy kid in the band? Do you look like a punk rocker or police cadet? Your height, weight, age (or at least how young/old you look), face, body structure, and personality all contribute to your type and the kinds of roles for which you will most often audition and be cast. If you don't know, then ask ten people you trust to be objective to give you a list of five words they would use to describe you. Compare the lists and see what words/phrases are in common. This will get you thinking in the right direction.

Are You an Out-of-the-Box Thinker with an Imagination?

Close your eyes. Can you imagine you are on the *Titanic* as it starts to flood and have the thought of never seeing your loved ones again? Do you cry or laugh? Or perhaps you are freezing as you climb Mount Everest? Do you ponder your mortality and give up, or find your courage and push on to the summit? These choices come from your imagination. While many films are shot on location, there are plenty of scenes filmed in a studio in front of a green screen where you have to imagine you can see things or people that are not really there until the computer fills in the background later. Even when on a realistic set, there is an entire film crew often in full view and you have to imagine they don't exist as you commit to being in the moment.

Are you afraid to try something new because you may look foolish? Finding interesting yet appropriate ways to perform simple things marks you as a creative, imaginative actor. Learn to say, "Yes, I'll try," and have an adventure, rather than "No, I can't," and shutting yourself off. Keep all your doors open since you never know who (or what) will step through.

Do You Have a Specific Plan to Promote Yourself?

What kind of screen work offers you the most personal satisfaction? Commercials? Sitcoms? Feature films? Documentaries? Voice-overs for cartoons? Part of creating the right strategy is to be very specific about your goals. Wanting to be an actor on television is too general. If, on the other hand, you know you want to work on a specific soap opera, then you can begin to research the show, find out who the casting directors are, and format a plan to submit your materials. Knowing exactly where you see yourself ultimately saves time, money, and a lot of unnecessary grief. This clarity does not mean that you will never audition for other projects or accept parts in other venues when offered, but it does give you a plan to work on every day. Write down your specific goal in one sentence and look at it every day. List all the little, seemingly unimportant steps that will ultimately help you get there and don't be afraid to let other people know what your goal is, as you never know who can help.

> "Notes of what you spend going to an audition, comments on who you just met, etc., will not only help you at tax time but also to remember names for any future meetings."

Being this specific, however, also means you must have an excellent way of keeping records to stay organized as you track your progress. Notes of what you spend going to an audition, comments on who you just met, etc., will not only help you at tax time but also to remember names for any future meetings. Making this a business as well as an art requires you to be diligent. There are wonderful resources online as well as many books for actors offering tips to wade through the business and marketing side of the industry. In this business you are the product, so figure out how to sell yourself.

Do You Know Your Personal Performance Dos and Don'ts?

Be very clear about your moral and ethical limits. Today, cable television and film constantly push the limits of what is comfortable for some people to watch. Will you ever appear in a nude scene? Are you willing to cut your hair or shave your beard for a part in a movie? Will you smoke if you are a nonsmoker? Gain or lose a lot of weight? Are you willing to be "intimate" with a co-star you don't know or someone of the same sex? Does the actual story of the movie make you uncomfortable or feel opposite to what you value? Think about what you will and will not do. It may mean you have to turn down a job offer because of your ethical beliefs, and while you may lose this particular role, you will retain your personal integrity and likely earn the respect of others because of it.

Do You Like an Urban Lifestyle?

If you really want to find great success in this profession, you are going to have to move to one of the bigger cities and adopt an urban way of living. It may mean moving away from family and friends. Yet these cities are where the greatest number of films and television shows are made. City living has its perks and drawbacks, and they also come with big living expenses. You may need a roommate or roommates to help defray living costs, or a car to get to auditions. Yet cities are brimming with the arts and full of adventures and opportunity that you can't find elsewhere. If you are not a big-city-type person, then many midsize cities will still have film opportunities in the form of industrial/training films, local commercials, and the occasional feature film. Your choice!

Are You Currently in a Committed Relationship?

Okay, maybe this last question is a bit unfair since people fall in and out of love every day and a relationship for today's millennial is not what it once was.

However, think about the special considerations that need to be discussed and understood ahead of time with a potential life partner, especially if having a family is important to you. Consider that an actor's life is rarely stable, especially in the early going. How will your significant other react when you have to kiss someone else in a movie or play an intimate love scene in bed?

If your partner is also an actor/artist, will there be jealousy if one of you is constantly working while the other struggles for an audition? Will your significant other support your career choice, including the many hours' time away from home? Will your partner understand the necessary cash outlay you need to get headshots, resumés, demo reels, audition attire, and classes to continue training? While love can conquer all, better to think twice about what type of relationship offers you fulfillment as well as how another person fits into your career picture.

Okay, time to tally up. As you already have guessed, the point of this unscientific quiz is simply to give you a greater understanding of yourself as a person and the challenges that await you as an actor. So, while there are no right or wrong answers, if you believe you are actor-ready, then "Standby . . . and Action!"

TRAINING. DETERMINATION. ORGANIZATION: A NY ACTING TEACHER'S PERSPECTIVE

Getting Started

▶ By John Howard Swain

Figure 1.3 John Howard Swain

Photo by Mary Ann Halpin

John Howard Swain is a veteran actor, director, and teacher. As an actor, John guest-starred in dozens of network television shows, ranging from the legendary *Hill Street Blues* to the current *Law & Order: SVU*. He also starred in the acclaimed mini-series *Family of Spies* and *Blind Faith*. His film credits include *Best Seller, Angels in the Outfield*, and *The Tenderloin*. In addition to his film and television work, John has directed more than 25 plays in various venues across the country, including productions in New York City, LA, and San Francisco. As a film director, he has directed four films: *Whose Life, Uncommon, Stand By*, and the multi-award-winning short, *A Younger Man*. John (Figure 1.3) taught at Santa Clara University and was the founder of one of the country's most prestigious television/film acting programs, Full Circle Productions, in San Francisco. Currently on staff at the Terry Schreiber Studios in New York, his students can be seen on Broadway, in episodic television, and on the big screen. His book, *The Science and Art of Acting for the Camera* (Routledge, 2017), is considered to be the quintessential guide for actors working in film and television.

Figuring out how to get started in show business is just as difficult as it is in any other business. Ask a hundred actors how they got their start and you'll get a hundred different answers. Some will say they got their big break doing a show, or an agent got the ball rolling for them, or their reels opened doors, or having a dynamite headshot, or . . . the list goes on.

A question I think every actor should consider before diving in is, "Why do I want to get into this business?" For those of us who have this particular "bent" to our personalities, we want to be actors for different reasons; some self-serving, others more altruistic.

Years ago, I took a workshop and the leader asked, "If it wasn't for the fame and glory, how many of you would be doing this (pursuing a career in show business)?" I'm embarrassed to say but as I watched the hands go up around me I thought, "*Really? There's another reason for doing this besides getting famous and being adored.*"

Fortunately, I came to realize there are loftier goals – like interpreting and communicating important ideas; being a conduit so a group of people, the audience, could experience emotions they might otherwise avoid; and perhaps most important, being the torchbearers who illuminate what is going on in our society, giving ourselves and each person in the audience the ability to peer into his or her own soul.

Over the course of time, our criteria of what we hope to gain and how to manifest it changes. I'm not the actor I was when I took that workshop; nor am I the only actor who ever thought, "Hey, this is all about me." Just as there are many different ways to get started, your goals and how you see yourself in the business are bound to change as well.

Over the last 40-plus years – having worked as an actor, director, producer, and teacher – I've come up with a few guideposts I feel will help you grapple with that all-important question: how do I get started?

Training

Our craft, what we do, demands discipline, and if you aren't working at it, exercising those muscles, it will slip away. It's like going to the gym. You can't walk in on your first day and bench press 200 pounds. Nor can you, after you've been working out steadily, take three months off and expect to lift the same weight you were lifting when you stopped. Same with acting: if you don't nurture the craft, continue to work at it, those acting muscles won't be there when you need them.

A wonderful thing about our craft is that as you continue to grow as a human being, as you continue to meet life's challenges, as you gain more life experience, you have more and more material to draw upon. I remember being in class with Nikos Psacharopoulos. One day, a very young and very dramatic actress was crying because she felt her scene hadn't gone well. She said to Nikos, "I want to be a great actress. What should I do?" And Nikos (in his very thick Greek accent) said, "You want to be a great actor? I'll tell you what you need to do to be a great actor." He paused and every person in the class leaned forward – like in one of those old E.F. Hutton commercials. We thought, *"Here it comes. He's going to reveal the secret that will unlock the mystery of acting."* "You," Nikos continued, "have to live. You have to live a life."

I remember leaning back in my chair, thinking, *"That's it. That's the big secret."* Later, I realized it was *the biggest secret.* In essence he was saying, "You being you is much more important than you trying to be someone else. And if you live a full, authentic life, you will have all the material you need to be a great actor."

> "Once you've studied with a teacher and mastered what that teacher has to offer, move on."

I share this story because one of your primary goals should be to find the right teacher. You need to work with someone you respect, someone who will challenge you, someone who will insist that you do your best. Nikos was a demanding sometimes-not-the-most-pleasant-person-in-the-world but he was a great teacher and helped me and hundreds of other actors develop our craft.

And once you've studied with a teacher and mastered what that teacher has to offer, move on. None of us, myself included, have all the answers. Hopefully, one day you'll get to the point where you'll be working so much that "being on set" is your classroom. But if you aren't ready for opportunities when they come your way, if your craft isn't in tip-top shape, that will never happen.

Determination

When you're first getting started, having someone say no is like being stabbed in the heart. But if a no at any phase of your career is going to stop you from going after what you want, get out of the business now!

I tell prospective students that if there is anything else they'd be even remotely happy doing, do that. Rejection is a huge reality in our business. People are going to say no to you a long time before they start saying yes. This business will test you on a daily basis until you – and I don't want to get all *woo-woo* here – let the Universe know you're serious and you aren't going to let the no's stop you.

We all know how to handle life when things are going our way but it's how we handle life when things aren't going our way that matters. If you're going to crumble when a casting director says no or an agent says they don't want to represent you, do something else. But if you keep getting up after getting knocked down and you keep letting the Universe know you aren't going away, that you're in it to stay, *no* will eventually turn into *yes*.

I didn't move to New York until I was 30 years old. I knew I wanted to be an actor when I was 8 but I either let myself or someone else talk me out of following my dream. Finally, after trying a lot of other things, I rallied my courage and dove headfirst into the "business." I didn't have a fallback position. It was either make it or . . . well, I don't know what. Fortunately, I didn't have to find out.

When I got to New York, I made the rounds, went to the auditions, did the showcases in crappy Off-Off-Broadway theaters, scrambled to get meetings with agents, whatever it took. I got rejected a lot but somewhere along the way the Universe got that I was serious, and doors started to open. This has been my experience throughout my career, and now that I teach, I see it happening all the time with my students.

Recently, a young actress in my class was struggling to express certain emotions. Week after week, for months, she failed but she kept plugging away, working on her craft. Not too long ago, she had this amazing breakthrough in class and the things she had been working for fell into place. And the Universe responded, *"Okay, I see you're serious, and because you're serious here's your reward."* She was cast as a lead in a SAG feature film. Who knows where this role will lead, but the doors, at least that door, opened for her.

This doesn't mean things won't change or you can't be flexible but if this, being an actor, is what you want to do, you have to keep striving toward your goal, letting the "rejections" bounce off of you until you start to get the acceptance, the yeses, you want.

Organization

When I was getting started, all you needed was a decent headshot, some post-cards, an answering service, and a good pair of shoes. *Shoes?* In New York, it was cheaper to walk to the agencies/casting directors' offices and hand-deliver my headshots and resumés than it was to mail them.

It's harder now. You still need a dynamite headshot and postcards but now you also need a cell phone, a reel (both commercial and legit), a website, a social media presence, and the wherewithal to self-tape. Having and keeping all these things current is time-consuming. Couple all of that with a full-time job or two part-time jobs, an acting class, family obligations, and auditioning, and it's easy to get overwhelmed.

> "Make sure you prioritize your day – know what needs to get done that day and do it."

Being organized, no matter whether you're just getting started or you've been at it for a while, is highly personal and everybody has a different way of doing it. What is paramount, however, is that you find a system that *works* – a method that allows you to do the things you need to do to keep yourself afloat (pay the rent, put food on the table, etc.) and also gives you the time to work on your career.

Make sure you prioritize your day – know what needs to get done that day and do it. Along the way, you will have to make some sacrifices. If that involves getting up an hour earlier or staying awake two hours longer, or not going out drinking with your buds, it's a small price to pay in order to be able to make your living doing something you love.

You have to put in the time. A lot of things that used to be done in person are now done electronically, but you still have to put in the time. Don't forget that "show business" is two words – and in order to do the *show* you have to take care of *business*.

So, what do you need to get started?

Headshots

Whether you hand your picture to someone or submit it electronically, your headshot is packed with information about how you see yourself. Make sure you are presenting yourself in the best light.

First of all, make sure you hire the right photographer. Look around and see who shoots your type (people who look like you) well. Once you've found two or three or four photographers that are good at capturing your type, set up an interview and meet them. Make sure you have a connection. There's no sense in investing your time and money with someone who doesn't "get" you. They don't have to be your new best friend, you don't need to invite them over for dinner, but there needs to be a simpatico vibe.

Your headshot needs to look like you on a good day. Not you overly made-up, or overly lit, or overly re-touched. Not how you looked two, three, five years ago but how you look now. Don't shoot with a photographer who is more interested in showcasing his or her talents than showcasing you. It's how you look, how you come across, that's important. I had to fight with the guy who took my last headshots. He wanted to airbrush out every line in my face. I told him, "Hey, I earned those lines, they're part of me. Leave them in."

Reels

If you are interested in doing film and television, you must have a reel. Make sure it is short and well edited, and that you're the star of the show. It's okay if other actors are in it but your reel needs to be you-centric. Make sure your reel is current. Don't use footage from 10 years ago. If you're new to the business and just getting started and don't have any "professional" footage, check with the local colleges and universities; see what their film departments are doing and how you can get involved. Don't forget the students in those schools are film-makers of tomorrow.

Websites

You probably know more about creating a website than I do. It doesn't have to be complex. It needs to be functional and easy to navigate, and should contain (at a minimum) your headshots, resumé, and any reel work you have.

Social Media

Whether it's Facebook, Instagram, Twitter, Snapchat, or whatever is tomorrow's newest thing, you need to be on it and be active with it. More than ever, actors, at every phase of their careers, need to promote themselves and their work, and social media is an essential tool for doing that.

Self-taping

The ability to self-tape is imperative. More and more projects are being cast this way – even theater projects. You don't need a lot of equipment, but you do need some. If you have a smart phone, it will probably be good enough, but you should also have a basic lighting package, a tripod, and a neutral background. If you don't have the equipment, find someone who does. And when you shoot, use a medium close-up shot (mid-chest to the top of your head) unless specifically directed otherwise.

Diplomacy

Be nice to everyone. *Everyone.* Sometimes it's hard, because there are jerks in the business. Nevertheless, be nice; be kind. The secretary you're dealing with today could be a producer tomorrow; the casting assistant, the next hot director. Everybody has to start someplace, and it pays to be nice to everyone we encounter along the way.

Being nice doesn't mean compromising your values or your principles. Don't let anyone take advantage of you, but treat people, even the jerks, the way you would like to be treated. And when you run into someone who is "out of harmony with the world" and is acting like a bozo, remember what Plato is believed to have said: "Be kind, for everyone you meet is fighting a hard battle." We rarely know the difficulties other people are facing, so treat everyone with kindness and respect.

The Prize

If you're looking for the pot of gold at the end of the rainbow, you will be sorely disappointed, because no matter how successful you are, it will never be enough. You will constantly be longing for more. But if you come to understand that the process, what you learn about yourself at every phase of the game, is the real prize, then no matter where you end up, you will have succeeded.

Don't let the fear of getting started keep you from getting started. Remember: everyone starts somewhere. Everyone was a rookie at one time. So, muster your resources and dive in.

BEFORE COLLEGE, IF COLLEGE . . . WHERE DO I START?

It Starts with a Dream . . .

▶ By Judith Patterson

Figure 1.4 Judith Patterson

Photo: US Performing Arts

Judith Patterson, along with her son Craig, is the Co-founder of US Performing Arts (USPA), the country's premier summer instructional programs for teens in the performing arts and digital media. As President and CEO of USPA since 2002, she has helped shape the course for thousands of teens interested in a life on stage, in front of the camera, and behind the lens and scenes. As an associate professor, she has taught theater and dance as well as having chaired those college departments. She is not only an instructor in the arts but has produced and directed as well. Judith began her career as a child actress on the national stage and in television. She danced with the New York City Ballet and taught at the San Francisco and Marin Ballet Schools while simultaneously producing television for television shows and a Christmas special for the A&E Network. With her father David M. Sacks and husband Charles Patterson, along with their friend and colleague Bing Crosby, Judith (Figure 1.4) helped found Experience Productions, which produced permanent multi-media city tourist attractions for the visitor entertainment industry, such as *The San Francisco Experience, The New York Experience, The Hollywood Experience, and The Christmas Experience*, among others.

It starts with a dream, and then the question, "Is it a 'calling?' How do I make it reality?" You hear your inner voice saying, "I want to do this. I *can* do this." But then the doubting voice says, "I don't know where to start!"

The journey from aspiration to fulfillment takes many paths. The starting point is right where you are. It starts with your dream, your "calling," and moves to your craft. It is the tools of your craft that will enable you to tell stories that capture and engage audiences. Your craft will enhance and nurture your ability to tell stories that entertain and motivate and even educate.

So, what is craft? In our case, craft is a professional activity that requires skill and training. It's not a one-time course or class that you will take that anoints and certifies you as an actor. It is on-going training and honing that perfects your craft and builds your skill. Just like the journeyman craftsman builds his tool belt, you too are assembling the tools you will need to use in creating your character, collaborating with your director, and working with your crew members. As you become more proficient, your ability to know which tool to "grab" will become more innate and organic, and you will find that you are creating and telling story with ease. Once you have gained that proficiency, you are on your way to becoming an artist and it is at that point you will have realized your dream.

An artist is many things to many people and *Merriam-Webster* gives us many definitions, but many synonyms have to do with being a performer: *actor, singer, dancer, musician,* and so on. We can also add to that list: *filmmaker, writer,* and other media talents.

However, an artist is more than a category. In fact, the word "extraordinary" is what we think of in connection with a true artist. An artist is an extraordinary craftsman. You can also think of an artist as being fearless. They break new ground. They challenge themselves to do more, learn more, and to constantly express their insatiable passion.

Some artists, past and present, that come quickly to mind are Robert Duvall, Tom Hanks, John Lithgow, George Lucas, Steven Spielberg, Meryl Streep, Ella Fitzgerald, Maria Callas, Yo-Yo Ma, Bobby McFerrin . . . the list goes on. Each of these artists comes to thought because of their fearless ability to step out of their comfort zone and break new ground as an artist and discover new passion.

> "Remember: acting is acting. So, even if your goal is to act on screen, take advantage of every opportunity you can."

So, for the young craftsman and burgeoning artist, where do you start? The first steps are in the classroom and the rehearsal studio. You deserve the very best classes you can afford. Take the classes your school offers, but don't stop there. Do your research. Find a workshop with an acting coach who not only has a resumé of acting you admire, but has teaching experience and has exhibited a desire and ability to pass on the craft. Look for professional companies that offer workshops in acting for the stage and camera. Find a class that is peopled with others who share your passion and focus and is outside your comfort zone. Talk with people who have taken the class or workshop, and be sure to audit them at least once.

Remember: acting is acting. So, even if your goal is to act on screen, take advantage of every opportunity you can. Audition for plays and musicals that are presented by your school and your local and regional theater groups, but don't allow rehearsing and presenting plays to be your only outlet. While rehearsing and being in front of an audience is rewarding, every actor needs the structure of the classroom to try new things and risk it all in order to grow. Don't limit yourself to school plays either. Branch out. Take the leap and audition for regional theater and Equity-waiver companies in your area. Just the need to develop audition pieces will push you to a new level. Get to know the filmmakers among your friends and let them know you're willing and able to be one of their actors. Utilize that camera in your phone, or on your computer, as a constant tool to review, hone, and supplement your work. It'll be a new experience for you, and you will be able to begin to collect footage for your reel.

Start thinking about your "next." As your life experience grows, the time will come to decide what to do next to embark on the pursuit of your dreams. Are you ready to leap into your craft as a professional, or do you need more time to hone your skills? If you go to college, will you major in acting and will it be acting for stage and screen, or just for the stage, or only the screen? Do you need to make that decision immediately?

There is a right, progressive next step for you. It has nothing to do with age. It has all to do with success and longevity in this business we all love, and there are many paths to it. There is only one *you* and you want to be the best *you* you can be. The world is waiting. For some of you, it will take a traditional path. You will thrive in college, nourishing your mind and soul with proven academics and creative endeavors. For others, you might enter a conservatory or take workshops while you pursue work. Still others of you may opt for creating your own content directly for the internet. The opportunities are vast and you will learn and grow by doing. Whatever your journey, stay focused on the goal of becoming the best artistic craftsman you can be.

For those of you who choose the college route, there is a right college or training program for everyone and it's important to discover that right one for yourself. You're the one who will be attending the classes, doing the work, and reaping the reward.

When is the right time to begin your college search, you ask. If you are asking the question, it's time to do it! It's really never too early to begin to think and plan for the future. Gathering information is the first step. Think of it a little bit like planting a garden. First you till the soil. Then you sow seeds. Next you weed out unwanted growth, and then you reap the harvest!

Gathering information and breaking it down is like tilling the soil. You can begin that as early as middle school and certainly by freshman or sophomore year in high school. When you think about it, it's so easy to do, and fun. You can start by asking older friends and family about their college experience. Get to know universities and where they're located. Find out about their performing arts and digital media departments. Keep a journal and a file about the things that interest you. Figure out what part of the country you think you'd be happiest living in. You can even take a virtual tour of most universities. You'll want to start with this general information because selecting the right theater, film, or digital media program is more than just being a part of the smaller arts community. To use another analogy, the department is like being in a suburb of a major city. You are part of the larger community too.

There are many tools out there for you to use. A great step toward learning about the performing arts and visual media departments within the university can be done by attending the National Association for College Admission Counseling Performing and Visual Arts College Fairs. These annual fall fairs connect students and departments. They have material to hand out and will gladly answer questions. There will be one close enough to you to make it possible to attend. Start early in your high school years and attend several years in a row. (Sow your seeds.) Each year you can narrow down your choices (weed your garden) so that by the time you reach your senior year you're really ready to hone in on the schools to which you plan to apply. Soon you'll be ready to reap your harvest!

Here are some questions you should be asking yourself, along with some steps to take in finding the answers that are right for you.

Do You Feel at Your Most Comfortable with a Balance of Liberal Arts Courses to Supplement Your Acting Classes?

By all means research colleges and universities nationally and internationally. Use every resource at your fingertips and don't forget to talk with previous students from your school who attended those institutions in your field of interest. If you're able, take a tour and see the work that their students are doing. Ask questions! Find out the philosophy of the department. Don't be mesmerized by the reputation of the university or department. Remember: it's the curriculum of study that is offered now that's important to you, not the reputation of a department long ago. It isn't what *was* but what *is* that should define the program for you. Find out how long the dean and chairs will be remaining in their positions. They shape the excellency of the program, so if it's *today's* program that is speaking to you, make sure that it will be same program during your four years of study.

Are You at Your Best in a Conservatory Setting Where You Work with Your Peers All Taking the Same Coursework and Classes Together until You Graduate?

If so, it's probably a BFA conservatory-style program of study you are interested in pursuing. That can be done at a degree-granting independent conservatory or within a traditional academic college/university. Professional schools exist in both environments, from public institutions to private schools. One is not necessarily *better* than another and both are worthy of your investigation. You can even hone your craft and receive an accredited degree in a school within an active film studio lot! Again, it's important to visit the campus when you can. These types of schools tend to be more collaborative in nature and some blend the education of live performance with film and media. On the other hand, some are *very* traditional and classic in their approach to the craft. The journey from stage to screen can take a different path for each one.

Are You Confident That You're Ready to Step into the Profession Now without Formal Academic Study?

You may already be a working actor and your career path is on the brink of taking hold. You may want to continue your education, but this isn't the time to concentrate on that aspect of learning. Fortunately, you live in the digital age. There are many avenues for continuing your accumulation of knowledge; so important to any creative artist. You have to know about the world and understand its effect on the human condition before you can effectively tell the story and move an audience. There are so many wonderful online courses available to supplement your work as an actor and to move your journey forward as you work. There is the opportunity to apply to college and defer enrollment by taking a gap year. Or, take the gap year to explore and then apply at a later time. No matter what you decide to do, enroll in that acting workshop and build relationships as you audition for work.

> "Find a reputable college audition workshop to learn more about the procedure; preferably a workshop that will allow for mock auditions and even present a panel discussion with college adjudicators."

No matter which direction you embark on, you're going to need a resumé. Start preparing it now and continue to edit and update it. Find someone who can show you what a good professional-looking resumé is. *Professional-looking* is different than a *professional* resumé. No one looking at it will expect you to have more experience than you are truthfully showing, but they will want it to look professional. Take headshots. Keep them current. Start with someone you know and branch out to a professional photographer when you are ready. If you are going to be auditioning for colleges, begin to prepare your audition material. Make sure it is age-appropriate and stay abreast of what various colleges will want to see and how they will want it presented. Find a reputable college audition workshop to learn more about the procedure; preferably a workshop that will allow for mock auditions and even present a panel discussion with college adjudicators. Auditioning for college is very different from auditioning professionally. This type of workshop will give you the confidence you need to succeed.

So, for our next generation of artists, I say embrace your passion, learn your craft, get in front of the camera, develop a hunger for new frontiers, and thus honor your profession with becoming an artist.

A TALENT MANAGER'S GUIDE TO DISTINGUISHING YOUR WORK

Initiating a Sustained Connection to Your Character

▶ By Marilyn R. Atlas

Marilyn R. Atlas is a talent/literary manager and producer. She has long been committed to diversity and the portrayal of strong female protagonists. She's the producer of the HBO Sundance Audience Award-winning film *Real Women Have Curves*, and *The Choking Game* on Lifetime, among other films. Marilyn (Figure 1.5) also produced several plays, including the award-winning *To Gillian on Her 37th Birthday* and Ashman and Menken's *God Bless You Mr. Rosewater*, as well as *Real Women Have Curves* at the Guadalupe Theater in San Antonio, among other plays. She has spoken at numerous writers' conferences throughout the US and Europe. She's currently developing projects based on diverse characters, such as the Gary Phillips books and the award-winning book series *The Code Busters Club* for television, as well as co-producing a limited series in conjunction with a Chinese-based company. She is the co-author of a relationship-based screenwriting guide called *Dating Your Character* (Stairway Press, 2016).

Figure 1.5 Marilyn R. Atlas

Photography by Devo Cutler-Rubenstein

Not everyone has the knack to gain ready insight into their character's internal life. To be able to portray a character with bracing honesty, a true understanding, and an enduring connection throughout your performance is an enviable talent.

In the end, any actor or writer needs to know their character's core essence. Orchestrating that authentic connection at the deepest level with your character requires a personal and idiosyncratic approach. This is especially vital if you're having trouble igniting your passion for character creation.

Ideally, that will spark a recognition not just of your shared similarities, but how you're different, too. Inhabiting a character who would process an experience that both of you shared, but with a distinct point of view from your own, shows subtlety. Mastering your craft also means being able to bring a "comfortable specificity" to your performance that will set you apart.

Writers who conceive characters with great complexity or depth facilitate this task for the actor. But truly embodying a character requires a striking amount of ownership and creativity. Even early in the audition process, you have to have the confidence to fly away from the rough character outline you may have to intuit.

So, How Do You Bring Your Character to Life?

It's not only the willingness to experiment with physicality, attitude, gestures, and vocal articulation. You must take a psychological inventory of why she's the way she is. Whether you have five minutes before a cold read or a day to prepare before an audition, it's important to gain access to her hidden recesses. Such a pointed analysis lets you see your character as more than the drama she presents, but as someone with her own internal temperature, her own code of ethics, and different levels of driving motivation.

The series of choices you must make in regard to her internal conflict relies on your instincts. As an artist, you're probably sensitive, sympathetic. But, in heeding the contradictions that arise, some actors immediately attempt to incorporate their own desires. Resist the temptation to quickly subsume yourself in her experience. Draw a line between you and her.

Why Would You Want to Forestall Imprinting Yourself onto Your Character?

While "method acting" has an invigorating integrity about it, forcing you to be able to draw upon all your cumulative experience, it also has the tendency to reduce the knowability of your character to only that piece of you that can relate. That effort of imaginatively projecting onto the character reinforces a narrow kind of empathy at the root of the unintentional bias many of us may not be aware we carry around. It's the inability or finite ability to see the world from someone's – or some other group's – POV that leads to a failure to connect and misunderstandings.

> "An actor has to know himself, to borrow from his own psyche and experience, while being able to listen to what his character is telling him."

One way to transcend any boundaries limiting your perspective is to tap into an alertness akin to Stanford Meisner's technique of "the truth of the moment." Being available forces you to listen to the clues the world offers you. That core idea was expanded on in my co-written book *Dating Your Character*, which was conceived with screenwriters and all kinds of creative professionals in mind. Instead of being dependent on what you bring to a character, if you cordon off some space to grow your awareness, your character will begin to inform you.

I feel exploring character is a case of being consciously observant. That it's all about forging a relationship between you and the character. One way to do so is to round out your initial ideas through trial and error. To be palpable, this intimacy requires a kind of give and take. As I've observed as both a manager and a producer, a writer's ego can get in the way of fostering a genuine connection with his character; an actor has to know himself, to borrow from his own psyche and experience, while being able to listen to what his character is telling him.

Forming a Relationship with Your Character

You're going to have to get used to the notion that her life doesn't start and stop the moment you come into the room . . . she "exists" when she's not with you. She doesn't just "switch on." Recognize that by thinking of her "in the present" and always "being" in the present you're allowing her to breathe and being mindful of her downtime.

"Downtime" away from you and the specific scenes in which she features can be instructive, because she's less guarded. Because she doesn't expect to be judged. She'll be going through life, not necessarily going into battle every second of every day, even if she's the lead. At least, not before the end of Act II, when she buckles in and totally commits; and certainly not before she even *decides* to change in Act I.

Think about the people who know you most intimately: your friends and family. They know what you like, what makes you laugh, what moves you, and all the things that make you *you*. They understand your essential philosophy, though they might not use that exact term. Because, when you're in your natural element, spending time with those in your circle, relishing where you are in life and what you still have to learn, you feel free to dream . . .

What Are Your Character's Inner Thoughts?

A great way to start figuring out your character's personal priorities is a commonplace acting tip that involves mapping out where a character's been just before a scene starts. That simple shortcut can only yield so much insight, however. She's not a fossil waiting for her DNA to be sequenced so she can roar to life like one of the dinosaurs in *Jurassic Park*.

Go further, go deeper, commit. Try seeing her moving through the world in her own timeframe at the same time you are in real life. Where does she go? What does she like to do? Is there anyone else around? Does she adhere to a set routine? When she's totally relaxed and alone, what does she choose to do? What is she preoccupied with?

An outgrowth of knowing who your character is on her downtime is that when incorporating a vocal or physical detail, you don't feel self-conscious while doing it. It's not something that you've tried on once or twice for a few minutes for the sole purpose of energizing your sides; it's not artificial, but something that can naturally elevate your performance. Spend an afternoon trying on your accent or practicing your limp. This should not be a brief attempt, but something you can embrace and let settle inside you. A trait or a behavior you've managed to incorporate that aligns with what you feel you already know about the character.

As an example, a young developmental client of mine was auditioning for a role about a teen mom who was thrown out of her parents' house and was going to a job interview. The client took the time to get into the character's headspace. She wrote a couple of diary entries and chose to bring in a doll to the audition, as a substitute for the character's baby. There was no direction in the scene that the character had brought the baby to the job interview. I believe she booked the job because of her talent, character research, and the effort she demonstrated. And all this was for a guest-star role!

I don't endorse mind games or character sketches as an immediate way to launch into a layered portrait, but as a way to fumble toward a deeper and more sympathetic understanding of who your character was, before she evolved into the creature before you; and who she will have to become if she wants to triumph . . . There are many means of jumpstarting the creative process: journaling, sketching, even list-making, though I frown on that last one because people seem to infer a finality in the "answers" they come up with. As if they can't be improved, massaged, or completely turned on their head, once truth slivers start to pierce your consciousness.

How Do You Get a Sense of How Your Character Is Feeling in a Specific Scene?

Remembering your first automatic response to her is paramount. Consider how she makes you feel, as a person, apart from what she's dealing with in the scene. Then, once you have a baseline, tease out the particular strains of worry so you can section out their subtext. Realize that with the same degree of drama swirling about, someone else, another character, would react to those elements differently. In the classic action film *Lethal Weapon*, if the Danny Glover character Roger Murtaugh was the more dominant personality in the partnership, how would he have taken charge and led the investigation soberly instead of in the careening style of Mel Gibson's Martin Riggs?

While in the midst of using tools to analyze your acting assignment, the mind still has to meet the heart. Depending on the character and the situation in which you find her, that may not always be an equidistant point. After all, some scenes are more visceral spectacle than others. So, on the heels of any investigation that you do, spend the time grounding those discoveries in your body – in your posture, your gait, your sense of active agency. Save what you've excavated about your character's drive in a nook somewhere along your spine. Let that personal knowledge push you, as you work through a scene.

What Is the Emotional Temperature in the Scene versus Your Character's Private, Internal Temperature?

By asking yourself that, you'll isolate what the external stakes are for most of the other characters in the scene, in contrast to the individual level of adrenaline she's experiencing. Now, start to get a basic measure of her capabilities. In situations that are less fraught, would she be more likely to succeed? Less likely? Does she in fact thrive under pressure or when she's in danger?

There is probably a logic to the hierarchy of emotion coursing through her. Find an internal need for why she's trying to accomplish "that thing." What other goal-oriented priorities is she trying to balance? Does anything in the scene surprise you about what most unnerves her?

Next, focus on what focuses her. What she purposely draws a bead on and what calls her to attention. Does another character in the scene have an outsize pull on her? Like real-life people, characters have a certain amount of push–pull in them. Wanting to do something, but pulled to do something else. What could that person's influence over her be? Why is that? And more fundamentally, what's tempting her to make everything so complicated for herself?

How Does Threading Your Way Back to the Beginning of Your Character's Interior Life Enrich the Resolution of Any Scene or Sequence?

At first glance, regressing the character's arc back to when she was happy and well-adjusted (if there ever was a time) isn't likely to provide much drama. Most teachers and acting guides focus on the negative – on everything that is pushing the character to change her habits in order to adapt to the crisis she's facing. But what do you gain if your first acknowledgement in your character work is everything she'll be giving up? As mentioned earlier, being able to root down as deeply as possible can only contribute to creating a more indelible character.

> "By brainstorming backstory for your character, what you're really doing is strengthening your ability to pick and choose among seemingly throwaway details for one or two salient touchstones."

What is normalcy like for her? What does it take to pull this character off her axis? What would have to go really wrong for her to abandon *everything* in order to go after some epic goal? What if she can't articulate that goal to herself yet? It's up to you to see how far and wide you need to go. But, whenever you're missing behavior components in the material you receive, the tips I've shared (based on my experiences working with writers and actors) should help jump-start an inner dialogue between you and your character.

By brainstorming backstory for your character, what you're really doing is strengthening your ability to pick and choose among seemingly throwaway details for one or two salient touchstones. Refining this ability to connect with your character will sustain you in the long run, whether you're trying to establish a career or face the daunting task of lasting the length of an extended theater run or perhaps multiple renewals of a popular television series.

CHAPTER 2

STICKING IT OUT

This chapter is all about tenacity. What does it take to break in as an actor? How do you hear "no" over and over again and not let it cripple you? As an aspiring actor, a big part of your job is holding onto hope that your hard work, networking, and hours of scene study and on-camera classes will give you a network of fellow actors who will be your support system and share information with you. Your job is to stick it out for the long haul. Your job is to create opportunities for yourself and increase your "luck factor." In this chapter, we'll discuss realities about slowly building a career as an actor. We'll share some very personal, moving stories. Finally, we'll inspire you so that a co-star becomes a guest star and then you get your sights set on a series regular.

In the film *Tootsie*, an agent, played by the director of that same film, Sydney Pollack, tells Dustin Hoffman's character Michael that no one will hire him. This is the inciting action for the entire film, and Michael goes to great lengths to get his next job. If you've never seen this film, please do. It is a gem. It also illustrates a point that is sometimes the elephant in the room. People hire people they want to be around. It is a business of relationships. And it is very personal.

So as you read the wonderful wisdom and moving personal stories in this chapter, ask yourself how can you not only stick it out, but how can you become that person who casting directors, directors, and producers want to spend time with. Start by being nice. Always be prepared. And get a life to accompany your career.

Here's what we're going to address in this second chapter:

- The simple secret to being prepared for an audition is to practice.
- How, as an actor, you're essentially running your own business . . . and you're the CEO . . . and so much more.
- How social media figures into your career goals.
- Why staying patient is essential.
- That respect will take you places money won't.
- That you must find the solution to the desperation which may seep into your demeanor, if all you're focused on is booking.
- How to not lose any impact as you "contain" your performance for the screen.
- Why it is important when you get an audition to research the director, writers, and producers.
- When to hire a coach and how to maximize your investment of time and money with his or her guidance.
- How visualizing your life as a life less ordinary, and the opportunity to make a life as an actor, are gifts.

You can stick this out. You will do it your way. And the choices you make will define who you are as an actor and the quality of life you have pursuing it. So continue . . .

GROWING A SUCCESSFUL BUSINESS CALLED YOU

Be the CEO of Actor, Inc.

▶ By Gilli Messer

Figure 2.1 Gilli Messer

Photo: David Muller Photography

Gilli Messer is a writer, performer, and, unfortunately, a millennial. She is a summa cum laude Phi Beta Kappa (that's Latin and Greek for "nerdy") graduate of Barnard College, Columbia University, where she studied Anthropology (super useful!). She grew up in LA by way of New York City and Tel Aviv, Israel. Most recently, Gilli developed and scripted a musical comedy series, *Camp Curtain Call*, for AwesomenessTV; wrote a freelance episode of the popular podcast *Imagined Life*, narrated by Virginia Madsen, for the podcast network Wondery (*Dirty John, Dr. Death*); and was a comedy writer for the 2018 CBS Diversity Sketch Comedy Showcase. She was a finalist for the 2019 Sundance Episodic Lab, the 2019 Sundance New Voices Lab, the 2018 21st Century Fox Writers Lab, Film Independent's Project Involve 2018, and the American Film Institute's 2017 Directing Workshop for Women, and a writer for both the 2016 and 2015 ABC Diversity Showcases in LA and New York. *The Drunk Lonely Wives Book Club*, a web series set in the early 1960s that Gilli created, wrote, and starred in, was directed by Emmy Award-winning Mary Lou Belli and is now screening in film festivals nationwide. Gilli's romantic comedy short film *Dog Park* is also currently on the festival circuit, garnering such awards as Best Comedy Short at the Nice International Film Festival in France. *Meme Queens*, a female-driven comedic digital series that Gilli (Figure 2.1) co-wrote and starred in, was picked up for distribution by Elizabeth Banks' comedy site, WhoHaha. Gilli's humor prose has been featured on McSweeney's Internet Tendency, and she is a regular contributor to Stephanie Laing's female-driven humor site PYPO. As an actress, Gilli's network television credits include roles on *Jessie*, *2 Broke Girls*, *American Housewife*, *About A Boy*, *Ryan Hansen Solves Crimes on Television*, and *How to Rock*. For more info, mediocre puns, and dog photos, check out www.gillimesser.com, @GillsGoneWild on Instagram, and @NetflixandGil on Twitter.

Becoming a working film, television, and commercial actor isn't a sprint. It's a marathon. Scratch that . . . it's an ultra-marathon. In Death Valley. Uphill. In 100-degree heat. If that doesn't intimidate you, read on!

> "Luck is the intersection of opportunity and preparedness."

Sure, we've all heard those success stories about actors who seemingly walked off of a Greyhound bus and onto a soundstage, but that is the exception, not the rule. Unless your narrative is one of those fortuitous anomalies, you're going to have to put in the work, both the creative and the logistical.

Luck is the intersection of opportunity and preparedness. You can have all of the talent, training, presence, and passion in the world, but if you neglect the business side of your acting career, you may never get that precious opportunity. And on the flip side, if you focus only on the logistical portion of your career, you may get some opportunities, but you won't be prepared when your craft isn't up to par once you find yourself in that room that can possibly change your life.

Most actor training programs are focused on developing and honing your craft, and rightfully so. Your craft should always take precedence over all else. However, since it's clear that you need many different pieces to succeed in cracking this crazy puzzle, you must also find time to address the business side of your career. This is show *business*, not simply *show*, after all.

As an actor, you're essentially running your own business. Think about it: you have the potential to grow a successful company . . . even a multi-million dollar one. As with any entrepreneurial endeavor, building your business takes time, energy, strategy, patience, effort, laser focus, organizational skills, and a thick skin. The good news is that you have some level of control when it comes to this aspect of your career, often unlike the creative side. Now more than ever, we have plenty of tools to take ownership of our businesses, from social media to our own projects that we can easily execute with a smart phone. There's always something you can be doing to further the logistical side of your acting career, whether you're at the startup level or are a full-fledged company that employs many people. This is one of the most competitive industries on earth, so you need to go above and beyond to truly break in.

In your business of being an actor, you have multiple positions. Obviously, *you* are the product itself, so welcome to the business of selling . . . you! Behind the scenes, you're the CEO – congrats! – and you're the janitor, too. It's daunting, but it's also empowering. You have the freedom to establish your best business practices and the way you run your company. You get to define your process and build something that is uniquely yours. Let's take this metaphor a few steps further by going over the key players, departments, and actions you can take to grow your business.

Mission Statement

Most companies have one, and you should too. What's your mission as an actor? Is it to tell a certain type of story? Work in a particular genre? Create your own work as a hyphenate? A mission statement is an active phrase that can carry you throughout your career and remind you why you pursued this life in the first place. This affirmation can also guide you through which projects to take on and how to use your platform to be a positive force of change in the industry and beyond.

Human Resources

In addition to being the CEO and face of your company – you're the product, remember? – you're also your company's Manager of Human Resources. So build your team! You're in charge of hiring them, keeping them excited to work for you, and even firing *them* sometimes. It's easy for actors to forget that agents and managers work for them, and not the other way around. So, remember that when you have meetings with reps, it's your chance to interview *them* too.

Your representatives literally represent you, so it's important to put together a team that you believe in and that believes in you. Once you have reps, make them want to keep working for you by holding up your end of the bargain of being proactive and professional. They get paid 10% commission, so you should be doing 90% of the work.

> "Your team does not only include your reps: it also includes your mentors and eventually mentees, too. Think of them as the board members of your company."

Your team does not only include your reps: it also includes your mentors and eventually mentees, too. Think of them as the board members of your company. CEOs rely on their board members for guidance and expertise, as should you. Make it a point to accumulate some trustworthy "board members" in your actor life who can inspire you, be your sounding board, and point you in the right direction through your career. (Guess who's on my board? Mary Lou Belli!)

How and where do you meet these board members? At acting classes, networking events, on sets, at panels . . . anywhere, really! The best way to recruit a mentor is to offer to help them in whatever way you can. Do they need an intern? An assistant? The best mentorship relationship is one that is mutually beneficial, and contributing in whatever way you can will prompt others to help you. Also, do not be afraid to ask questions. That other actor, director, or writer whom you admire? Ask them for their insight. The worst thing that can happen is that they say no.

When you've been at it long enough, do your part to mentor younger actors and share your experiences with them. This is a difficult and often lonely path, so why not help others along the way?

Branding

Though using this buzz word to describe an actor sort of makes me cringe, there is something to be said for establishing your brand as a performer, and so you must be your company's Brand Consultant. Sometimes, actors want to be so versatile that it's hard for them stand out. The expression "typecasting" has such a negative connotation when, in fact, being a type can be an asset to you, especially early in your career. Casting directors get hundreds or even thousands of submissions for roles, so being a type can help you help them in making the decision to bring you in to read. You can worry about breaking out of being typecast later on down the line! Actors who have a strong brand are also easy for others to refer, whether it's on a small or big scale. Actors talk, and actors are also friends with other key players in the industry. If someone asks them if they know an actor who can play a certain type, the performer who is memorable because of their branding is easy to refer and pitch. And how does one become memorable? Through. . . .

Advertising and Publicity

Once you start your business, you need to make sure people know about it. Move over, Don Draper, because *you* are in charge of your company's Advertising and Publicity department. This includes but is not limited to curating your head-shots, website, social media presence, and marketing. If you've been a good Brand Consultant, then these materials should look and feel cohesive for the brand you've established.

Secure Investors

The venture capitalist in this scenario is your day job, side hustle, survival gig . . . whatever you want to call it! You have to spend money to make money by investing in your career and, of course, to live. Making a living as an actor takes time, and it requires spending money on typical life expenses as well as on materials, classes, a car, and the like. You don't want to *want* an acting job because you need it to pay your rent. This is not the right frame of mind with which to go into an audition room. Therefore, as part of your actor business, you need to secure outside financing by working in what-ever type of side job works best for you and your situation. There are many creative ways to make some income during the hours when you aren't audi-tioning and working besides the classic actor-slash-waiter trope: tutoring, dog walking, working for a sharing-economy-type app, and even role playing as a fake patient for medical students (seriously, that's a thing!). You can also think about exploring smaller markets – Atlanta, aka "Y'allywood"; Austin; Albuquerque; Chicago – if you aren't financially ready to invest in living in LA or New York. Now that self-tapes are the norm, you can audition from pretty much anywhere.

Research & Development

Any strong company has a solid R&D team, and congrats again . . . you're the head of this part of your company as well! To truly be a part of the industry, you've got to *know* the industry. This means reading the trades, learning who the key players in the industry are, and always being in the know. During pilot season, read as many pilots as you can get your hands on. During episodic season, work on current material from shows that are casting then and there. And this is my favorite part: watch television and movies! Seriously. Your homework is to watch television and films. That is the coolest homework in the history of homework! As you watch, make note of which shows would be a good fit for the product that you're selling (aka you!). I'm not talking about the series regulars; I'm talking about the costars and guest stars on that show. Do *you* show up on that show, week after week? If so, you need to make a point to target that show's casting office.

Training

I know I said this was all about the business side of acting and not the creative, but part of running your business includes allotting time and money to stay in shape with your craft. As Training Manager, ensure that you're regularly taking different types of acting classes, coaching for auditions, and performing live, if that's your jam. You can even get some actor friends together to do a table read. The amazing thing about acting is that you never stop learning. I took an acting class recently with a working series regular, and I was so inspired by the fact that she still showed up to class and was excited to work on her craft. Being a lifelong student is par for the course when you're an actor, and that's true for many other professions. Would you want to have surgery with a surgeon who wasn't up to speed with the latest technologies? I'm guessing not. How about flying on a plane whose pilot was totally out of practice? Nope. Would you want to elect a president with no political experience who refused to learn the ins and outs of the job? No way. Wait a second . . .

> "Do whatever it is you need to do to maintain your look, whether that's hitting the gym, not hitting the gym, cutting and dying your hair, combing your beard (or whatever it is that hipsters do to keep their beards so coifed), and having clothing that suits the type of roles you regularly audition for."

Cleaning Crew

Did you think I was joking when I told you that you were also the company janitor? I wasn't. Your appearance is an enormous part of your company. We cannot pretend that it's not. Film, television, and commercials are visual mediums. Do whatever it is you need to do to maintain your look, whether that's hitting the gym, not hitting the gym, cutting and dying your hair, combing your beard (or whatever it is that hipsters do to keep their beards so coifed), and having clothing suits the type of roles you regularly audition for. This is an ongoing process, because you'll usually get auditions last-minute, and when they do come in, you want to work on the material and not have to go shopping to find the right outfit. The Cleaning Crew should work very closely with your Branding and Advertising and Publicity departments, since your brand determines your look, and your marketing materials should represent the way you look day in, day out. Just like customers aren't happy when the product they bought doesn't look as appealing as the picture on the box, casting directors tend to hate it when an actor comes into the room looking nothing like his or her headshot.

Clients and Acquisitions

Business owners will tell you that customer loyalty is the key to success. As with any business, it's better to have a few loyal, long-term customers or clients – who, in your world, are casting directors, directors, producers, show runners, and executives who are fans of your work – than a bunch whom you don't know well at all. Make sure you maintain the relationships you've made over time by keeping track of who calls you in, who hires you, and who advocates for you. Then, consistently follow up with them. Don't annoy them, but update them on your progress so that they can root for you. And finally, stay patient. This is the hard part. Most of the time, you won't see immediate results, and it can be tempting to spin your wheels. Remember that this a marathon – sorry, ultramarathon – and not a sprint, and the seeds you plant can take some time to blossom.

Recruiting and Partnerships

This role is different from Manager of HR. As Head of Recruiting and Partnerships, it's your job to find people outside of your business to connect, create, and commiserate with. Since I've likened this career path to an ultramarathon, think of it as finding some running buddies to keep you going when you think you can't go any further, and vice versa. I don't know if that's how running works, because the longest race I've ever run is a 5K, but you get the idea. I'm saying find your community: your "people." Being in the trenches together creates a bond unlike any other. Now I'm mixing metaphors, but you're still with me, right? You all rise together and there is room for all of you. Plus, with the advent of smart phones and editing software that even the most technophobish among us can use, you can create with these people. And not just other actors . . . I'm talking writers, directors, editors. It's a tough industry for those in front of and behind the camera, and collaboration can be an amazing way to get content for your reel, make friends, and learn. Don't forget that this is a collaborative industry!

Track Your Performance

As with any business, you should do a quarterly and annual review of your performance – not of your acting, but of your accomplishments! – to get a sense of your progress and to identify areas you want to improve in. To do so, you need to keep track of your work and stay organized. I recommend the software Performer Track, which, if used properly, can be a one-stop shop for all of your contacts, auditions, bookings, and expenses. You can also keep track of these items on your own, be it on a spreadsheet, in a notebook, or in some other regard. Get specific so that when you look back at your last few months or year, you can identify what is and isn't working. For example, if you see that you consistently do not book commercials and/or projects that have you improvise for the audition, perhaps you should consider taking an improv class. Or if you see an increase in auditions once you began using new headshots, then you know for a fact that these are effective pictures. Once you've weighed your wins and losses, you can set goals for yourself moving forward. There's a lot we as actors cannot control in this business, but we *can* control our work ethic and our will to succeed.

> "Building your business is a grind, and it's important to unwind and unplug from it from time to time so that you can come back refreshed and recharged. Plus, there's nothing that helps you book a job more than buying a nonrefundable plane ticket!"

Vacation Allowance

Even CEOs take vacations, so make sure you give yourself permission to take time off throughout the year. Building your business is a grind, and it's important to unwind and unplug from it from time to time so that you can come back refreshed and recharged. Plus, there's nothing that helps you book a job more than buying a nonrefundable plane ticket!

I hope you've found this extended metaphor helpful. Maybe I should've mentioned this earlier, but everything I've just told you is both true *and* untrue. There is no one way to "make it" as an actor in this industry. But chances are, thinking of running your acting career like it's your own entrepreneurial endeavor can't hurt!

A SERIES REGULAR SHARES HER JOURNEY
Welcome to the Numbers Game
▶ By Shalita Grant

Shalita Grant's career continues to evolve with diverse and challenging projects, nurturing an impressive body of work encompassing theater and television.

Shalita recently starred on the hit CBS drama *NCIS: New Orleans* as Sonja Percy, a whip-smart ex-ATF (Bureau of Alcohol, Tobacco, Firearms and Explosives) agent who prefers working alone and struggles to adapt to working alongside the NCIS team. She also starred in the highly anticipated PBS Civil War drama series *Mercy Street*, about doc-

Figure 2.2 Shalita Grant

Photo: Sam Lothridge

tors, nurses, contraband laborers, and Southern loyalists in Union-occupied Alexandria, VA, during the Civil War. "Shalita Grant, giving the show's most memorable performance" (*Washington Post*) is just one of many rave reviews for Shalita's portrayal of freed slave Aurelia Johnson. Her other television credits include *Search Party*, *The Santa Clarita Diet*, *The Good Wife*, and *Bones*.

Segueing effortlessly between television and theater, Shalita garnered a Tony nomination for her work in the Broadway show *Vanya and Sonia and Masha and Spike*. The *Los Angeles Times* called Shalita a "stand-out" for her portrayal of Cassandra, a sassy voodoo-practicing housekeeper. Shalita (Figure 2.2) returned to the New York stage in the summer of 2017, starring in the Shakespeare in the Park production of *A Midsummer Night's Dream*.

Head in hands, tears streaming down my face, the bleak revelation dawned on me: *This is how LA kills your dreams.* I was 26, a Tony-nominated actress, and I had just been rejected for the 43rd project I had auditioned for in eight months. Little did I know I was a mere 12 rejections away from booking my first job.

So, You've Had Some Success

During my last year at Juilliard, we had to take a class called Real World. Actress Kathleen McNenny taught this class and we learned many important lessons for our life after graduation, like: Open Your Mail, Your Full-Time Job Will Be Looking for a Job, and Every Person "Hits" at Their Own Time. That last lesson was the one I anxiously scoffed at because I was going to graduate and immediately become a Hollywood starlet. I couldn't imagine a reality that wasn't that. And if I didn't immediately become a Hollywood starlet, wouldn't I just die a miserable anonymous death somewhere in Jersey?

Needless to say, I didn't walk across the stage and right into a hot Hollywood career. However, three years after graduating, I learned that I could survive nine months of unemployment and become a Tony-nominated actress. The Wednesday after losing to Judith Light, as I walked into the Golden Theatre I thought, *"What now?"* I decided I would move to LA and focus on television because, hey, I wasn't an anonymous wannabe anymore, right?

According to LA, wrong.

LA is where I began my education on the business. For me, New York was much easier than LA. I had a community of actors, theaters, and casting directors who knew me and knew my work. New York is a small town in that way. New Yorkers have a lot of the same frames of reference. Certain words convey levels of experience and connote ability. On my resumé I had words like "Juilliard," "Lincoln Center," and "Broadway," to name a few. I never had the experience of a New York television casting director who didn't understand what those words meant. Therefore, what I was taught about the business while at school, my experience in New York confirmed. There was a clear cause and effect: audition enough times for one casting director, I'd book a show, and then when I have enough shows, I'd book *the* show. LA was a different animal, mainly because it's a completely different town. For starters, it's huge! Not just in terms of space but also in terms of money, work, and the number of A-, B-, and C-list actors. The offices in Hollywood have a storied turnover rate. The assistant in an office can become an associate producer then executive in no time. What that means for an actor is that the assistant to a casting director, or the person most likely putting your audition on tape, may not know what your resumé means and they most likely won't have to because they have their sights set on an office with a view. When I started auditioning in LA, I would have casting people look at my resumé and say, "Broadway . . . but can you do regular acting?"

> "The person most likely putting your audition on tape may not know what your resumé means and they most likely won't have to because they have their sights set on an office with a view."

After those first few months in LA, I asked my manager if my time in New York was a waste. I had "tested" within a month of being in LA and was regularly getting callbacks, but when I was rejected because I didn't have enough experience, I seriously questioned whether my time in the theater was more of a set*back* than a set-*up*. And that's when she gave me the sobering truth I thought I could escape: this is a numbers game and, unfortunately, no one will ever be able to tell me which number will be mine.

Welcome Back to the Numbers Game

As an actor your full-time job is looking for work; employment is your vacation. If acting is your career, it is vitally important to stay in the reality of this career: it is often hard and comes with a lot of unsolicited "time off." Don't forget, even the most famous and successful actors go years at a time without working. The only seeming difference is that they don't have to work another job to support themselves in the interim. For those of us who have gone through the employment/unemployment process a few times, you may understand all of this intellectually but are still experiencing an emotional revolt. If you are currently in an audition phase that's "taking too long," or what I like to call "active unemployment," you could go through the motions of resentment, anger, fear, desperation, or even fatalism.

Eight months into living in LA, when I was crying on my sofa, I had run out of money again and needed a loan from my manager to pay my rent. I felt so much shame and embarrassment that I couldn't take care of my basic needs, and it was hard for me to hear "But you're in the zone" and "You got another network test" when I had about three dollars in my checking account. Not everyone on the business side appreciates or respects the craft of acting and what we have to do to get to that audition. I've had three auditions in which a director or producer either put their heads down as soon as I walked in the room, or spent my entire audition on their phones. I beat myself up afterward because my performance didn't inspire them to look up. However, the hard truth is if you bring that into your next audition with you, you certainly will not improve your situation. Even when your personal and financial life isn't dire, there are still hard emotions to wade through: entitlement and frustration can be a couple of emotional stumbling blocks.

When I went through "active unemployment," I had to remember daily why I was doing this in the first place. Is it because I'm a masochist? Probably, but I'm working on that. Is it because I want all the money and all the fame? Yea, but that's not all of it. Is it because I could do something else with my life but all I really want to do is this and I'm willing to risk not doing it for the opportunity? [Finally.] Yes, that's the reason!

Change Your Relationship to Rejection

Take a moment and say these words to yourself 10 times: "Rejection is a part of life." You only create misery by trying to avoid rejection. However, changing your relationship to rejection helps with the bitter truth.

It turned out my magic number was 57. I was rejected for 57 projects before I booked my first television job in LA. Understand that those 57 rejections were not cut and dry. For any given project, I could be seen upwards of four times before they pulled the plug on my dream. The roller coaster of emotion: the high of getting to the point where there are only three other people to the swift crushing low of not getting picked. It's more than anyone can stand, and luckily most people only experience that ride a few times in their lifetime, whereas we experience several periods of that roller coaster. One must achieve Yoda levels of self-awareness and self-care to withstand the constant highs and lows.

> "Rejection is a part of life. You only create misery by trying to avoid rejection. However, changing your relationship to rejection helps with the bitter truth."

However, when you're in the throes of disappointment and desperation, you lose sight of what auditions are for actors: a job, as well as a job opportunity. Every time you are rejected, use the feedback from the room to fail better next time. Victor Williams, an actor from the long-running sitcom *King of Queens*, told me he began looking at his auditions as his one opportunity to act that day. His approach to the audition material was to act as if it were the first day of rehearsal. When you aren't working and you're given an opportunity to audition, that time is the chance you are given to do what you love. That attitude adjustment is not only good for the caliber of your work but also your attitude in the room.

That's what I had to do. When I realized that this was a numbers game and recognized all of the pitfalls therein, i.e. my hard emotions and money trouble, I began to have gratitude for every opportunity I was given. I looked forward to "period" projects in which I would experiment with different hairstyles. I began to pay attention to my thoughts and attitude before, during, and after auditions. I also changed my attitude to my callbacks as well. I went from "Ugh, they're just setting me up to knock me down again" to "Wow, I was really on to something in that first audition! I'm glad that I can trust my instincts." I looked at every rejection as one piece of information that could bring me closer to booking a job, because auditioning and not being chosen isn't nearly as bad as not even making it into the room.

Walk in as if You Are Worth the Risk

"If you use every rejection and the feedback you get from the room to help figure out what makes you seem less risky, then when you meet someone who's open to someone new or unvetted for a role, you have a better shot."

For the people with the money and the risk, taking a chance on someone who hasn't done television (which was my case when I got to LA) or has drama credits but no comedy (or whatever the mismatch of experience) is scary.

Fear is an emotion that motivates a lot of people in Hollywood, believe it or not. No one wants to make a mistake, so really, part of the numbers game is the luck of meeting someone willing to take a risk on you. If you use every rejection and the feedback you get from the room to help figure out what makes you seem less risky, then when you meet someone who's open to someone new or unvetted for a role, you have a better shot.

As actors, we're used to approaching the role artistically. However, this is a business, and if you want to save yourself some pain, start thinking like a producer. When you get an audition, research the director, writers, and producers. Watch some of their projects and get a feel for their style. While you may not book the job with this information, you could be called back because you "get" the project. Making it to a producer/director session goes a long way with the casting director's office, your management, and your ego. Doing some simple research could inform your choices for how you dress and wear your hair, and these things also go a long way in making you seem like you could potentially be a great fit.

Take Your Eye off the Ball

Show business is hard, and being an actor can often feel powerless. If you are having real-life struggles like money, a relationship ending, etc., it's hard not to make rejection personal. God bless us. This is why it's incredibly important to be kind to yourself in this process. Find things that fill up the time when you're not working and make you feel like, even without work, life is worth living.

This is a great time to insert a ubiquitous baseball metaphor: the saying "Never take your eye off the ball" doesn't apply to pitchers. Most pitchers bring their arms over their heads, momentarily blocking their view before delivery. Others take a step back right before the wind-up and look to the side to counterbalance. Right before delivery they inevitably lock in on their target and release the ball with speed and accuracy. This principle can apply to actors when in "active unemployment." Our job is to convey life, but how do you convey life if you don't have one? I was consumed with getting a booking. If I wasn't auditioning, I was bartending, or crying. I had no life, and until someone shared that baseball metaphor, I thought meticulously obsessing over every detail of my auditions was the right thing to do.

"If all you're focused on is booking, desperation seeps into your demeanor and could eventually bleed over into your performance, robbing you of nuance."

If all you're focused on is booking, desperation seeps into your demeanor and could eventually bleed over into your performance, robbing you of nuance. Find something that you love and invest in that. Reading, writing, family, papier mâché . . . anything that replenishes you while you are doing the hard work of getting yourself work. There is some truth in the old actors' adage: if you want to book a job, go on vacation.

Project 58 was a guest star. It didn't change my life; in fact, the show itself was canceled after 12 episodes. Nonetheless, I treated that job as an opportunity to build a good reputation for myself. I showed up on time, was a team player, was on top of my work, and showed that I was compliant with direction. On set, I didn't try to center myself in conversations. I also didn't shrink away. I was self-confident but not obnoxious or arrogant. After that guest star was over, I realized that my life likely wouldn't change and that I needed to keep up that attitude and work ethic. Every other month I either booked a job or worked a job or tested (for HBO, no less) until five months later I booked my first series-regular position.

A VETERAN SHARES WHAT GOT HER AND KEEPS HER DOING IT

A Q&A with Anne DeSalvo

Figure 2.3 Anne DeSalvo

Photo: Alan Weissman Photography

Anne DeSalvo's Broadway credits include *Gemini* (Obie Award Showbusiness Award for Distinguished Performance) and *Safe Sex* opposite Harvey Fierstein, and Off-Broadway Durang's *The Nature and Purpose of the Universe*, Innaurato's *Transfiguration of Benno Blimpie*, Ashman and Menken's *God Bless You, Mr. Rosewater* (based on Vonnegut's novel), *Sorrows of Stephen* (Public Theater), and *Girls, Girls, Girls* (Public Theater). She wrote/performed *Mamma Roma*, an Anna Magnani solo show (Cherry Lane Mentor Project). Her regional credits include: *The Miser* (Yale), *Gemini The Musical* (Barrymore Award nomination for Best Actress), and *Lend Me A Tenor* (Best Actress, Pasadena Playhouse). Her film roles include *Arthur*, *Stardust Memories*, *My Favorite Year*, *Perfect*, *Compromising Positions*, *Taking Care of Business*, and *Burglar*. On television she starred in USA's *Dead in the Water* with Teri Hatcher, HBO's *Hi-Life* opposite Charles Durning, *Ordeal of Patty Hearst*, *Almost A Woman* (Masterpiece), *Jane Doe, Citizen Jane*, and the Emmy Award-winning *The Last Tenant* as Lee Strasberg's daughter. Series include *Two Broke Girls*, *The Closer*, *Monk*, *CSI: Miami*, *Entourage*, *Sex and the City*, *Judging Amy*, *Chicago Hope*, *The X-Files*, and recurring roles in *L.A. Law*, *Taxi*, *Cheers*, and *Wiseguys*. Anne (Figure 2.3) was also a series regular in *The Man in the Family* opposite Ray Sharkey. Anne produced/wrote/directed/starred in *Women Without Implants* for Lifetime

(Cable Ace nomination for Best Actress). She wrote/directed *The Amati Girls* with Mercedes Ruehl and Cloris Leachman (Best Film/Best Director/Best Screenplay, Marco Island Film Festival; Award of Excellence, Heartland Film Festival; Award of Excellence, Film Advisory Board; Best Film, LA Italian Film Festival). She is a USC Film School professor.

With your wide experience as both an actress and teacher as well as an award-winning writer/director, will you talk a little about juggling it all?

The entertainment field is a business of reinvention and more reinvention . . . and then more reinvention. There was a time in New York that, as an actor, I was being offered a play, a television movie, and a feature all at the same time. It was when I was young and very sought after. Through the years, things changed in that there was more of an ebb and flow as my career continued through the years. When I got in my fifties, I still worked but not as often. When I did a film directed by Diane Keaton, I so admired watching her branch out into so many creative arenas, since roles for women her age were becoming quite spare. She told me to start thinking about getting behind the camera as well because there'd come a time when things would slow down for me too. Soon after I took a film course and wrote a short called *Women Without Implants* (difficult to cast in LA, ha-ha). I called some actor friends and produced, wrote, directed, and performed in it. I shot it in my house and a couple other locations. Long story short, it played at festivals around the world. Lifetime saw it at the Hampton Film Festival and bought it for their Women's Film Festival and I was nominated for Best Actress. Glenn Close won . . . but not bad company. After that, I wrote a feature, *The Amati Girls*, which was sold and played at the Beverly Connection here in LA. It starred Cloris Leachman, Mercedes Ruehl, and Lee Grant. It won a slew of festival awards, including Best Writer, Best Director, and Best Film, as well as an Award of Excellence from the Film Advisory Board. Since then I've just continued writing. I wrote a one-person play called *Mamma Roma* about the legendary Oscar-winner Anna Magnani. It was picked up for a New York production at the Cherry Lane's Mentor Project. I penned a TED Talk called "Blending Feminism and the Feminine in the 20th Century." A couple of weeks before we were to shoot it, it was canceled, [amid claims that] it was "too controversial" because it celebrated gender differences instead of the current topic of "neutering genders." I am now writing a book on the subject. I also teach at USC Film School and the Strasberg Institute. Teaching has been so valuable in helping me keep in check with the important principles of acting. When I go to an audition . . . I'm ready for it! Instructing also gives me the opportunity to inspire others. To see the light turn on in a young person's eyes when they feel like they're getting the wonder and beauty of acting . . . makes my heart sing. I juggle it all because I love being creative. I remember hearing someone ask Paul Newman, "Why did you do so many 'so-so' movies?" He answered, "I did the best of what was around." He was smart. He wanted to stay creative, so he juggled what was available for him at any given time. Good for him. That is my philosophy. Stay the course. Churchill said, "Never give up. Never. Never. Never."

Is there one thing you do that you like more than the other?
Yes, I have to admit that acting is still my first love. I'm currently doing a play . . . and it feels great to be on stage and to fly in a good role. I also love writing and teaching but acting is still my life's blood.

> "Creativity feeds creativity. The source is all the same . . . the imagination."

Do your various creative projects feed each other?
Absolutely. It's all a continuum of the creative process. It's all working from imagination. If I am redoing my house and buying antiques, I find a creative way of placing them so they can relate to each other in an inventive way. Also, when I teach, I love testing the imagination of my students as well as my own . . . always pushing the boundaries. Creativity feeds creativity. The source is all the same . . . the imagination. That magic also is at the heart of my writing or any inspired endeavor.

Do you have hobbies that are not showbiz-centric?
I love to garden. Planting a seed or a bulb and seeing it grow into a flower can make my day. It also teaches me about life. Different flowers grow at different times and in different seasons. That is all out of my control. It teaches me surrender and warms my heart by putting me in touch with the miracle and order of nature in a humbling way. Gardening allows me to be in touch with design, which is also a form of creativity. I also like to study languages. I was getting near-fluent in Italian and also studying French, but not as diligently. I adore reading and I started a book club with close friends. I love being current on recent books and new ways of thinking. I've become interested in starting to paint again. It was my major in college and I'd like to start doing some landscapes. I also like to do volunteer work at different charities. Giving service is a blessing. You always get more than you give.

Can you please talk about casting and auditioning and any hints you might have from being on both sides of the process?

Merriam-Webster defines "auditioning" as "a trial performance to appraise an entertainer's merit."[1] It can be a brutal experience or an inspiring opportunity. It's a craft unto itself and constitutes a major part of an actor's artistic endeavors. People want to see an actor's A-game. They're not interested in seeing tame, unsure choices. To audition well, you need to have focus and vision for your character. The casting director is looking for talent and confidence. I'd say that confidence is one of the key elements in an audition. No one knows what makes this business work . . . really. It's all based on creative "hunches." If I put this person in this role and then put that person in that role . . . will it be for the best outcome for the project? So creative people are all on the line, including actors, directors, casting directors, and producers. For an actor, confidence can be gained by practicing, practicing, practicing. I even rehearse my scenes in different rooms, so no matter where the audition is held . . . I'll be able to adapt to any space because my fix on the character will be unshakeable. Be early or on time. When you enter the room, look people in the eyes. Smiling helps. Dress with the flavor or hint of the character. If it's a television show . . . get familiar with it on YouTube or wherever. Relaxation is also crucial. Do whatever gets you there. For me, I go to the gym and then meditate. I stay present and turn my nerves into enthusiasm. At the moment of auditioning, you are essentially simulating your work experience. Be great! Not . . . "Oh, I'll just give them an idea of what I can do."

> "Relaxation is also crucial. Do whatever gets you there. For me, I go to the gym and then meditate. I stay present and turn my nerves into enthusiasm."

I cannot stress enough the idea of preparedness. Casting directors love prepared actors who make the casting directors look good. Sometimes directors don't really know what they want . . . they are waiting for someone to come in with something interesting or exciting. I've gotten roles by putting a twist on things. Risk taking is a good habit to develop but it's got to be a risk that the character might take . . . not just any random risk. Remember this is a "referral business." People don't want to work with people who stir things up or make trouble. Be great to work with but always hold your ground.

How big is too big for the screen?

In my first film [*The Last Tenant*], I played the daughter of teaching legend Lee Strasberg. My very first scene was with Lee. I was washing dishes and putting them in a drainer. When I did the master, I was fine. But in the close-up . . . I was not containing my movements in the now tighter frame, so through the lens the cinematographer was getting a large swish of my head. Lee said, "Just contain your movement more 'cause we are in closer now." It was an easy adjustment and taught me the intimacy of the camera. I enjoy making strong character choices. If the character is really angry . . . I get really angry. As long as I am not flailing my arms around like a zombie. I allow myself to be very authentic in the intensity of the rage a character might be feeling as long as it is true to the circumstance.

Was there ever a time when you wanted to throw in the towel? Do something else? What is the secret to your longevity?

My secret is my passion for acting. I love it! It will always be first in my heart. I also love directing, producing, and writing, but acting, for me, is the most visceral and personal. To be so in touch with your own humanity and create through the instrument of your own body . . . out of thin air . . . the breath of life of someone new with a different circumstance, point of view, heart and soul . . . is an extraordinary experience.

KEEPING CENTERED, EVEN WHEN THINGS AREN'T GOING YOUR WAY

Against the Odds

▶ By Bob McCracken

Bob was born in Philadelphia, but his father's lifetime of military service kept him on the move. He attended elementary school in Philadelphia; Bay Ridge, Brooklyn; and Largo, Florida, and graduated from Antilles High School in San Juan, Puerto Rico. He worked his way through college at West Chester University in Pennsylvania, receiving a BA with a major in Theater. He immediately began working in Philadelphia area theaters: The Pocket Playhouse, Hedgerow Theatre Company, and The People's Light and Theatre Company, as well as forming his own theater company, the South Street Theatre Company. He also toured in productions for Rick Trow Productions, eventually becoming a director there. A production of *Sexual Perversity in Chicago* moved him to New York in the summer of

Figure 2.4 Bob McCracken

Photo: Michael Helms

1981. In the fall of 1981, he moved to LA to begin what would be so far an almost-40-year career acting in and directing television, film, and stage. He has directed plays in New York, Philadelphia, and LA, and several in Dublin, Ireland. After a personal setback in 2003, Bob escaped LA and moved to Ashland in Oregon, spending the 2005 season at the Oregon Shakespeare Festival. He returned to LA in the fall of 2005 with a renewed appreciation for the craft, joy, and gift of acting and actors.

His IMDb page lists 59 titles, the most recent being guest-starring roles in *NCIS: New Orleans, Hawaii Five-0, Bosch, The Exorcist,* and *Here and Now* and five seasons recurring as Brendan Roarke, an "Irish King," in *Sons of Anarchy.*

His television directing credits include several episodes of both *Any Day Now* for Lifetime and *Judging Amy* for CBS. Look for Bob (Figure 2.4) as Pastor Barnes in the soon-to-be-released film *The Last Champion.*

Each section of *Acting for the Screen* has a bearing on "sticking it out." Even before "getting started," anyone seriously wanting a career as a film and television actor should do the research necessary to understand what the rewards and perils are of what seems to be a very glamorous way of life. I keep a book filled with quotes that have inspired me or just made me laugh or reflect. Some of these quotes have attribution and some I've picked up along the way in conversation. There is one I usually keep close at hand and sometimes post on my chalk board in my garden. It helps keep me centered when things aren't going my way. "Expectation is the root of all sorrow" is most often attributed to Shakespeare, but it is not found in any of his writing. The closest Shakespeare comes to that quote is in *All's Well That Ends Well* (Act 2, Scene 1: 141–143). Helen says: "Oft expectation fails, and most oft there where most it promises." This is an even better thought to keep in mind while beginning and pursuing a career in any artistic endeavor: "there where it most promises" certainly applies to a successful life as an artist.

You have a gift, and I don't mean you're "gifted" as an actor. I'm not really sure you can define "gifted" in that way. The gifts you have are the gift to visualize your life as a life less ordinary, and the opportunity to make it happen. Nicholas Kristof and Sheryl WuDunn, in their book *Half the Sky,*[2] say about life's opportunities, "Talent is universal, opportunity is not." Out of all the millions of people in the world, you have access to a life of your choosing. That gift should be respected every day in everything you do. For me certainly, acting was never a job or occupation or career or lifestyle – acting is a life like no other. If you've done your research on the economics of this career, the numbers can be very discouraging. The percentage of SAG-AFTRA members who work at all in a given year, let alone the number who actually make a living acting, is alarmingly small. There is certainly no guarantee of owning a house with the perfect partner, kids, and a new car every few years. Hopefully, you'll be among the lucky few who make a life of acting, but if you enter this life with the "expectation" of wealth and fame, you'd be better off doing something else because you almost certainly won't be able to "stick it out."

Expectations can be very high for a young actor, especially if they have spent several hundred thousand dollars getting an MFA from a prestigious graduate program. This is when practical experience quickly tamps down those expectations. The good news for those who didn't get an MFA is that film and television is quite a bit more democratic – some will say random – than that. More research: just go down the list of top box office names in the last few years and see for yourself how many stars never went to college; some never even finished high school. I don't recommend this approach but only point it out to demonstrate that there is no clear path to this life, so expectations are useless and disheartening or "the root of all sorrow." Do that research for yourself: read about the careers of Mark Wahlberg or Jennifer Lawrence and a few others on the list. I think you'll be surprised.

I started acting in school plays in elementary school. St. Patrick's Elementary in Bay Ridge, Brooklyn, is where the Dominican nuns taught me tap dancing three times a week after school. One of those lovely sisters would hike up her habit and show us a time step or "Shuffle Off to Buffalo." I never became much of a dancer, but being around kids finding pure joy in a common pursuit made me extremely happy, and that's what acting continues to do for me almost 60 years later.

> **"It is not just a matter of how much you're making as an actor but also how you spend and plan."**

Growing up without much money or material things prepared me for this life much better than if I had a privileged childhood. One of the biggest challenges in this business is financial. This is a life that shouldn't be chosen lightly, because there are consequences for every aspect of your life, from whom you partner with to when and if you'll have children. Remember: it is a "life less ordinary." If, after doing your research and coming to terms with the reality of an actor's life and being honest about how prepared you are for the financial sacrifices involved, you still feel you would be happy in this life, you just may have a chance of "sticking it out."

It is not just a matter of how much you're making as an actor but also how you spend and plan. We all know the stories of famous actors who go broke after making millions. Almost every actor I know has had or currently has another means of income. Even after getting established a little you may still have to occasionally find another source of income. Financial responsibility is a crucial part of an actor's life. During the writers' strike of 1987 there was no work and no end in sight. I got a job delivering Chinese food in Beverly Hills. I spent the night of my 36th birthday driving a Dodge Colt with a painting of a fire-breathing dragon on the side, speeding up and down the Hollywood Hills dropping off Kung Pao chicken to Milton Berle, Sammy Davis Jr., and other famous names. Financial maturity means doing what is necessary to keep doing your art. That means paying your bills and planning ahead. When you do get that gig that pays well, don't rush to change your car, address, and wardrobe. Remember the times you were dead broke; make a plan for the down times. You may not be taking the same great vacations as some of your friends or driving the car of your dreams, but if you're lucky you may get to look back on a life well and honestly lived, filled with great memories and wonderful friends. This will prove to be the most challenging part of "sticking it out." Very little disposable income at times and a lack of security is what makes most would-be actors throw in the towel. This is definitely a case of forewarned is forearmed.

> "You owe it to your gift of opportunity to take your time before quitting altogether and see if there is a way to 'start over' and 'stick it out' one more time."

Actors who have stuck it out have most likely "started over" or at least regrouped, sometimes more than once. An actor's life includes the same trials and tribulations of everyday life. Illness, divorce, and financial setbacks happen to actors just like everyone else. You may have to pause or stop at some time and reflect on whether this life is still for you. This is when your initial research and decision-making process comes into play once again. Go back to what worked for you in the beginning. Make sure you're honoring the gift of opportunity you've been given. Read plays, go to plays, return to a theater company you may have worked with before. Go back to square one and humble yourself, no matter how far you've come. In my late forties, just as I was beginning what looked to be a promising television directing career, I had to deal with a personal setback that made me question everything I had been through and accomplished in the previous 20 years. It took a while to get back on my feet, but I eventually went back to the very beginning of my career, hoping to recapture that feeling I had as a boy being taught to tap dance by nuns. I sold everything I had except my dog and moved out of LA and moved to a place where I could get back on stage and be in the company of actors. You may not have to go that far, but you owe it to your gift of opportunity to take your time before quitting altogether and see if there is a way to "start over" and "stick it out" one more time. You may need to pause and take care of the business of living your life, and when it is time to get back, you'll have more knowledge and tools available to "stick it out."

When I returned to LA determined to "stick it out," I read for every part I was right for in every play and every theater where I could get an audition, even if I wasn't sure I could do the play. Auditioning is a chance to act in front of strangers . . . it is, in effect, a free acting class. Get in touch with producers, writers, directors, and anyone else you have had a personal relationship with and let them know you are back and what you've been doing, and that you're ready to get back to work. Today, it may not be getting back to the theater and plays – there are so many other ways to be seen and create. Websites like Stareable and No Film School can get you in touch with other actors making their own films and web series. Get back to being a part of the creative community. Make sure you do all the things that helped you carve out a career in the first place. Take care of your health, your money and your relationships. Be honest: one of the most annoying things about being in Hollywood or New York, or almost anywhere now really, is hearing someone announce that they are an actor. Well, an actor acts or is preparing to act every day. It is a title you earn by doing, not by talking, and most definitely by "sticking it out." As Polonius says to Laertes in *Hamlet* (Act 1, Scene 3: 79): "This above all: to thine own self be true." By "sticking it out" you may be rewarded with a life lived on your own terms. Maybe not with a large financial reward, but with a much deeper meaning when you look back. From the first chapter of Henry David Thoreau's *Walden* comes another one of my favorite quotes. I doubt this is true, but my mother says I looked up and repeated this to her when I was 8 years old: "The mass of men lead lives of quiet desperation."[3] A life as an actor may help you avoid such a fate. I wish you luck and stamina.

MAKING THE MOST OF WHEN SOMEONE GIVES YOU A CHANCE

A Q&A with Daryl "Chill" Mitchell

Figure 2.5 Daryl "Chill" Mitchell

Photo courtesy of CBS Broadcasting Inc.

Daryl "Chill" Mitchell first came to public attention as a member of the rap group Groove B. Chill. The Hudlin Brothers, who directed one of the group's videos, cast the group in the feature film *House Party* in 1990, where Daryl had the opportunity to work alongside Martin Lawrence, Tisha Campbell, and other prominent actors. He found the experience so enjoyable that he decided to turn his focus from music to a full-time acting career.

He followed *House Party* with appearances in the feature films *Boomerang*, *House Party 2*, *Sgt. Bilko*, and *Home Fries*. His more recent films include *The Inside Man* opposite Denzel Washington, *10 Things I Hate About You*, *Galaxy Quest*, *Lucky Numbers*, *Black Knight*, and *The Country Bears*.

On television, Daryl was a series regular on *The John Larroquette Show* and *Veronica's Closet*, and appeared on *The Fresh Prince of Bel Air*, *Law & Order*, *The Cosby Show*, *Here and Now*, *The Suite Life of Zack and Cody*, and *I'm With Stupid*. Additionally, Daryl made guest appearances on *Desperate Housewives*, *Wizards of Waverley Place*, *The Game*, *The Cleveland Show*, and *See Dad Run*.

In November 2001, Daryl was sidelined by a motorcycle accident that left him paralyzed from the waist down; however, it never halted his forward momentum. Once he was in control of his wheelchair, he went back to work and signed on as a series regular for the role of Eli on the series *Ed*, a role which became the basis for the pilot titled *Eli*. Eli's character gave Daryl one of his favorite phrases, "Roll or fold," which encompasses his take on life. Continuing his acting career in television, he starred in and produced the series *Brothers*.

Daryl (Figure 2.5) was born in the Bronx and raised in Wyandanch, Long Island, NY, with his five brothers and three sisters. Currently, he resides in Atlanta with his wife and three children. Follow him on Twitter @DarylChillMitch and Instagram @DarylChillMitchell.

You've had a career that has spanned decades. Can you talk a little about getting into the business?

I always say there's no set formula to getting into the entertainment industry. When people ask me how did I get into the business, I always reply by saying, "You don't get into the business – the business gets into you." I started out in the three-man rap group known as Groove B. Chill. My main focus was to become one of the biggest rap artists of all time. But as fate would have it, I met two brothers by the name of Reginald and Warrington Hudlin, who had nothing better to do so they sat down and inked out a movie called *House Party* and put me in it. LOL – if only it was that easy. From this movie, I became known to the movie and television industry as this new comedic actor. So I tell people, "Leave yourself open, and the industry will dictate to you what it is you're supposed to be doing in the game."

Did you have any formal training?

The only training I can say I had was doing drama in high school, and then the Hudlin Brothers had an organization known as the Black Filmmakers Foundation where they did workshops, such as improvisation. But did I go to any college or acting school? No, I did not. Sometimes I get a little embarrassed to even say that because of my extensive resumé. But what I can say is I had a hell of an on-the-job education. I had the opportunity to work with some of the best actors in the industry and some of the greatest directors, such as Mary Lou [Belli], but they knew I was a raw talent and they knew how to smooth out the edges, and they also knew how to work to my strengths.

What was your most important early job?

House Party starring Kid 'n Play.

Do you believe work leads to more work?

Oh definitely, especially if you're doing a project that the industry is watching. I'm currently doing a television series known as *NCIS: New Orleans*, and now I'm also doing a recurring role on *Fear the Walking Dead*. While doing *Fear the Walking Dead*, there was some interest in me playing a recurring role on a HBO series that I can't mention at this moment because it hadn't come together at this time. So the answer to your question is yes, it definitely does.

> "It's almost like a brotherhood or fellowship. When you get to the next set, everybody is in place, and everybody knows what they are doing, so when you show up, you don't have this nervousness of meeting a new group of people. You're just ready to go."

What's the best part about doing television series, and does it have its downside?

The best part about doing a television series, especially if it's successful, is you are constantly working that muscle, and that's the best part about doing the series, that consistency of work – not only your mind but your physical being are put to constant work. When I started doing *Fear the Walking Dead* at the same time I was doing *NCIS: New Orleans*, when I got on that set it was as if I had been on *Walking Dead* since it started, because you know your way around. It's almost like a brotherhood or fellowship. When you get to the next set, everybody is in place, and everybody knows what they are doing, so when you show up, you don't have this nervousness of meeting a new group of people. You're just ready to go. But now the downside is the amount of time that you have to sacrifice to put in the work. Call it, then, the equivalent to being a soldier away from home: you can't be weak, all worried; you have to stay strong and remember to live, but you can go to sleep and wake up and years went by and you don't know where it went.

You seem to move seamlessly from comedy or drama. Do you approach the two genres any differently?

No, I do not approach the two differently. I was taught by a great actor: whether it's a drama or it's a comedy, tell the truth. That's it. Tell the truth.

You work in many markets – LA, New Orleans, Atlanta. What city is your SAG-AFTRA local? Do you work as a local hire in any market?

Atlanta.

Had you had any slumps in your career and, if so, how did you deal with it?

Well, yes, I have had slumps in my career but one thing I've learned to do is to build my career around my life, so that I have other things moving in my life to keep me motivated. I have my religion, my faith. I think that's one of the things that we are lacking in this world today: faith. It's like having a parent, and you know when your days are dark and long you always have a place to go back to Mom and Dad. Sometimes we need to go home and see God.

> "I got to say, the one thing people gave me, and I say this all the time, is a chance."

You have had a career before and after your accident. Besides the obvious challenges from the severe injury, did you notice any difference in the way you were treated in the business at auditions? On set?

Well, here's the funny thing. When people ask me a question, I always said that I was doing extremely well in my struggles as an African American male in a predominantly white male industry as a whole, in front of the camera as well as in the back of the camera. But after I had my accident, I became black all over again. LOL. Now I had a whole new struggle that I had to fight, but the good thing about the industry . . . I learned that respect would take you places money won't. And don't forget, the same people you see on the way up, it's going to be the same people you see on the way down. I got to say, the one thing people gave me, and I say this all the time, is a chance. Disabled actors are not looking for handouts; they are just looking for a shot to show you what they can do. Just because you're in a wheelchair doesn't mean you can act. Hell, I know a lot of people who can walk who don't know how to act.

You're an advocate for actors working with disabilities. Will you talk about what changes you would like to see in the industry as we go forward?

I would like to see actors receiving chances and opportunities to audition for parts that are not even written for an actor with a disability. Most of the jobs that I received, I went in and read for one role, and ended up with another one that wasn't even written for a person with a disability. Sometimes the role wasn't even written for a man, it was written for a woman . . . but after meeting me, seeing what I could do, they decided to change the role from a white woman to a black man in the chair. So being that the role was initially written for a white woman, fully able-bodied, when they changed the role for me, all they did was change the name. The action remained the same, and the chair was never mentioned.

> "There's no such thing as a horrible set. You can always learn, even if it's how not to conduct yourself."

What advice would you give to an actor just starting out?

You have to remember this is a business. It's just like opening a grocery store, a clothing store, a car repair garage. You have to treat it as such. You have to do inventory. You have to do maintenance. You have to do checks and balances, and know your audience. Sometimes you need to go watch bad movies so you know what not to do. There's no such thing as a horrible set. You can always learn, even if it's how not to conduct yourself. And remember: you're not there to love anyone or to be loved; you're there to respect and be respected.

What advice do you have for an actor who is mid-career?

I say if you're mid-career you should have had some success emotionally and financially. You should be in a place where you can now surround your career around your life. Let's say, for instance, you had a family. You can now structure your career around your family, instead of your family around your career. The industry comes and goes; it's built on a very fragile foundation. I believe a lot of people build their lives and relationships around the industry and then when they have to get out and deal in the world as the everyday person views it, they find it hard to deal. There's no makeup trailer. There's no place to do looping to clean up something stupid you may have said.

A CASTING DIRECTOR, INDUSTRY COACH, AND SHOWBIZ AUTHOR KNOWS WHAT IT TAKES TO STICK IT OUT

When to Hire a Coach

▶ By Bonnie Gillespie

Bonnie Gillespie is living her dreams by helping others figure out how to live theirs. As a weekly columnist for more than 15 years, Bonnie built her empire by demystifying the casting process and illuminating the business side of pursuing a creative career. The most popular of her books is *Self-Management for Actors* (Cricket Feet, 2014), which has been named one of the top 10 best books on acting ever written.[4]

She tours the world teaching curriculum based on this top-selling book at universities, actors' unions, and private acting studios. She also works as a coach to creatives eager to bring a sense of empowered joy to their storytelling journeys. When not coaching, Bonnie casts indies

Figure 2.6 Bonnie Gillespie

Photo: © Ron Goodman 2018

like the Machinima zombie smash hit *Bite Me*, which made the leap from web to television with Lionsgate in its second season. Her work on this groundbreaking series led to her membership in the Television Academy.

Bonnie (Figure 2.6) has been featured on *Good Morning America*, *BBC Breakfast*, *Sunrise Australia*, E! Online, and Yahoo! Movies, and in the *Wall Street Journal*, the *Washington Post*, and the *Los Angeles Times*. Her podcast *The Work* is available on iTunes. To hop on Bonnie's mailing list and grab your tip-filled MP3, visit BonnieGillespie.com.

If you've ever worked out, you know the challenge of getting, and staying, motivated for showing up for yourself every day to build strength, flexibility, endurance – all things required for a healthy acting career too, really. There are times when a do-it-at-home fitness routine will take care of the job. Other times, we find ourselves needing the community a fitness class provides. And when we're really trying to create change at an optimal level, we may employ the expertise of a coach.

In my workout regimen, I've found that my group classes and even my at-home exercise improve every time I work with a personal trainer – a coach for my fitness – because during our one-on-one session we're able to customize, personalize, and optimize my every move. When I work as a coach for actors and other creatives all over the world, we're doing essentially the same thing: we're taking the work they're already doing on their own and making sure it's in peak form. We're reducing bad actor habits and eliminating actor busywork. We're introducing new tactics that can sometimes revolutionize the day-to-day pursuit of a creative career.

Essential to your experience with a coach is, of course, selecting the right fit for you! Just because you hear a friend gushing about the work they've done with someone – whether a craft coach, a business strategist, a brand stylist, a media trainer, or a publicist – doesn't mean you're going to have a similarly stellar uptick in trajectory! You could meet with the best weightlifting coach on the planet and if your goal is to create a lean and toned physique, you're possibly gonna end up frustrated with both the session and the results of the subsequent work you put in.

First things first: when to hire a coach . . . There's no one recipe for success in this business and, similarly, there's no such thing as the right and perfect time to get some customized professional advice. But there is an awful lot you can learn through books, podcasts, YouTube channels, articles in trade publications, and, of course, experiences shared by other actors you encounter. When an actor comes to me for coaching but wants to spend an entire session going through headshot proofs, I'm happy to do it, but I'm also thinking, "Wow! We could've done this at the Self-Management for Actors Facebook group!"

> "Private coaching is rarely cheap, so getting clear on your goals for the session before you're in the middle of it is smart business."

Of course, if you're not interested in crowdsourcing feedback or having a workout in front of others, you may choose to meet with a coach at much earlier stages of your acting career than someone who waits until she's going through the Emmy nomination process or facing a press junket for her latest feature film! Just be sure you're investing wisely. Private coaching is rarely cheap, so getting clear on your goals for the session before you're in the middle of it is smart business. If you're meeting with a coach who — like me — has copious free and low-cost resources all over the internet, be sure you've exhausted some of the freebies before booking time in which the coach is thinking, "Yeah . . . I cover that extensively in Chapter 37 of my book." Far better to prep for the session by visiting the material that's out there, hitting a block, and then being able to say, "Okay! I'm confused by this section of your free mini-course on targeting agents and managers. What am I missing?"

Now, there is such a thing as waiting "too late" for coaching. Certainly, some actors do just fine never seeking out the support of a coach, but for those who do, getting out ahead of issues with a game plan is smart strategy. Of course, you're potentially going to make amazing things happen during and after the collaboration no matter when you get together, but some of my clients delay getting that first session on the books due to anxiety over not feeling ready enough for coaching. Thing is, we can optimize all the work they'll do outside the session during that first meeting! So while you may stress out that you're "too new" for coaching to be meaningful, consider asking yourself, "Could my solo workout be more efficient due to the advice a coach could provide?" as the fitness-oriented checkpoint for the timing.

> "When a client has prepped for a one-on-one session by crafting a list of questions and goals, we can start in on what's feeling most essential upon arrival."

One of the major benefits of working with a coach is the all-about-you focus which, of course, is missing from a class, even if Q&A does allow you to ask specific questions from time to time. The level of intimacy and specificity found in coaching can really unlock blocks that may be skimmed over due to the format of a group experience. When a client has prepped for a one-on-one session by crafting a list of questions and goals, we can start in on what's feeling most essential upon arrival (in person or using teleconferencing software, of course). Some coaches are prescriptive, meaning they check out your materials ahead of time and show up for the session with a list of fixes. Personally, I like to show up open to what might evolve out of our conversation. Sure, I've checked out your starting point, but a bit like the personal trainer who wants to see you do a few reps before correcting your form in weightlifting, I like to let you lead.

Of course, trusting that you've selected a coach who can lead you to where you want to go is key! Check out the body of work the coach has out in the world. Not just testimonials and slick photos of clients on sets or on red carpets, but actual advice that is in blog posts, on YouTube channels, in podcast episodes, or out in social media. Sure, general advice given by coaches will always be exactly that – general – but it should also give you a sense of the vibe to expect in the coaching session. And while you don't have to be best friends in order to experience the support, resources, and encouragement that a coach can provide, you do need to click!

Some actors like to work in accountability groups with one another and I think this is a great element to a healthy support system! But I have seen these groups devolve into gossipy complaint circles, so be careful. Sure, it's great to vent, but your time is valuable, and the energy you expend building up your creative career to the next tier needs to be invested wisely! Further, while a peer may have a great idea for affordably crewing up that web series you want to get off the ground, your coach is going to have worked with dozens if not hundreds of clients who have launched web series at all budget levels and that range from hugely successful hits to abysmal failures. She can be sure you avoid pitfalls your buddy might not even know to look out for. Heck, she may also encourage you to submit your series for an Emmy – and be able to tell you exactly how another of her clients won one of those by doing exactly that – so there's no telling where the expertise and resourcefulness of the right coach may take you!

One note of caution I'd like to share is that you avoid being a "guru hunter." Guru hunters seek out experts who deliver highly-opinionated advice as if it's from some Hollywood rule book (there's no such thing). There is no one-size-fits-all bit of advice that's going to work for every person's specific situation. The problem with gurus is that they give themselves very little wiggle room because it's important to their public image that they prescribe the same advice to everyone. That's what makes them gurus! Of course, part of what makes private coaching so dang valuable is the specificity to your exact situation and goals. Nimbleness is a superpower in coaching! Make sure you're working with someone who has the ability to adjust, customize, and curate other people's resources to create the overall best roadmap for you.

Now, before you charge off to meet with a coach, be sure you understand that ongoing motivation is your responsibility. When it comes to my fitness routine, I find that meeting with my personal trainer (my coach) regularly keeps me more motivated than if I go long stretches working out on my own. Ultimately, getting my butt to the gym is my work to do! But I find having quarterly check-ins with my coach – always adjusting form and re-evaluating my goals – to be the combination of resource-access and inspiration I'm looking for throughout the year.

Some coaches will offer up a contract for services, spelling out expectations and identifying benchmarks, possibly even creating a client checklist. In some parts of the world, a contract is required by law. For example, in California we have AB 1319, which regulates all corporations and individuals providing Talent Counseling Services (which includes all coaching – craft, business, or even the Q&A in casting workshops – whether conducted in person or virtually with one party in the State of California). We cannot coach any performer who has not completed an AB 1319 contract with us, and we're required to spell out the law on our website, plus hold a $50,000 bond against which you would be able to collect if we were scam artists who duped you out of your money. Similar laws protecting artists are working their way through the legislative process in several other states as I write this. The best coaches out there worldwide are already operating under AB 1319 even if they're not in places that require them to do so. It's good business to be on the right side of laws we can see coming! It also allows us to be role models for great business practices. And since you – as an actor – are running a small business of your own, your understanding of how to operate legally is only going to make you a more confident businessperson in every negotiation you face along your trajectory through to the top tiers!

I don't share that last bit to scare you. In fact, I hope you feel empowered by seeing yourself as a businessperson who must be focused on not only your craft, your talent, your ability to bring life to brilliant stories whether on stage or on screen, but also on your brand awareness, your marketing savvy, and your overall mindset for the endurance required in this phenomenal business of ours. Ah, endurance . . . there we are, back at the gym! Trust that wherever you start, you're getting stronger with every visit to that gym of yours. Keep showing up for yourself and, when you're ready, let's do some coaching!

EVERYTHING YOU NEED TO KNOW ABOUT SOCIAL MEDIA

A Q&A with Ben Whitehair

Figure 2.7 Ben Whitehair

Photo: David Muller

Ben Whitehair is a working actor in film and television, a certified business and mindset coach, and a successful entrepreneur. When not on set, Ben (Figure 2.7) is working with actors, creators, and businesses to create the life – or company – of their dreams. He is a SAG-AFTRA Board Member and Chair of the NextGen Performers Committee, Chief Information Officer of TSMA Consulting – entertainment's premier social media management and growth firm – and co-taught a graduate class at UCLA on social media and the business of acting.

Previous endeavors include co-founding a company that saved college students $30 million, interning for Congress in Washington, DC, and becoming a champion sheep and dairy cow showman. #TrueStory.

And no, his hair is not yet white.

Let him know how you're making the world a better place: @BenWhitehair on social media. For more, see BenWhitehair.com or visit https://working.actor, his online business academy for actors.

How important is it for today's working actor to have a large following on social media?

It's a misconception that most jobs are being cast based on a performer's social media following. That rarely happens, and every single casting director I know echoes the sentiment that if someone can't act they won't get hired because of their Instagram following. Casting needs to find an actor who fits the role and tells a good story. That will always be the priority.

That said, let's say in an instance that the entire casting process has concluded and it's down to two actors, both of whom are extraordinary, fit the part, and are good humans. If one has 100,000 followers and the other has a million, who would you cast?

Similarly, a large, engaged audience might support you in getting in the door. Once there, it's your job to deliver a powerful performance.

> "Social media offers an opportunity to circumvent the traditional actor path (get an agent, audition, book increasingly large roles on television) by creating your own content and building an audience on your own."

One caveat [involves] digital series and lower-budget independent films, which often rely more heavily on organic marketing. Without studio money, a performer's ability to assist in promoting the project is that much more valuable.

In addition, social media offers an opportunity to circumvent the traditional actor path (get an agent, audition, book increasingly large roles on television) by creating your own content and building an audience on your own. With vision and follow-through, you can not only grow a following and get your content seen, but also earn money over time.

Look, this entire business is based on how many people watch any given piece of content, so if you can cultivate an engaged audience that will watch your content, you have an advantage. Why are celebrities able to command so much money for a project? Because they bring an audience.

Commanding an audience matters, but know that without skill, passion, and grace it will only take you so far.

How else can an actor utilize social media?

Business – especially a business centered around an audience – is about people. And social media is an *incredible* tool for creating, maintaining, and deepening relationships.

In addition to the benefits that come with a large, engaged following, social media allows you to connect with industry professionals you would have had zero access to 10 years ago. You can follow show runners, directors, agents, managers, producers, writers, and casting directors on Twitter or Instagram, learn from them, and build a rapport.

I have booked jobs, signed with agents and managers, and met my best friend all through social media.

How? you ask. Great question, young Padawan. Here are my four keys to social media relationships:

Key #1: Listen

I think most people first think of social media as a megaphone, a way to promote themselves. My experience is that the true value of social media comes when you *turn the megaphone around and listen*.

Follow the people in the industry who are telling the stories that resonate with you, the agents and managers you respect, and the producers who are making the films you love. Find out what makes them tick. Learn about their daily lives and what's important to them.

At the very least, social media is an incredible learning tool. And you can do so directly from the people at the top of the industry.

Key #2: Engage

It's called *social* media for a reason. Like, comment, share, re-post, tag, *engage*! Take the listening to the next level and demonstrate that the people you follow are heard.

Remember, it's simply another human being on the other end of that Instagram post (Russian bots excluded). Interact with them like a normal person.

You're an actor. You are literally trained in how to listen, communicate, and create relationships. Utilize those same skills you use in a scene to engender genuine relationships on social media.

Key #3: Add Value

This is probably the #1 place where people either ruin an opportunity or thrive. We often want to act so badly that we become myopic and selfish.

Your fellow industry professionals on social media are merely living their lives, doing their best to be happy and enjoy their day, just as if they're walking through a grocery store. Imagine if a random stranger came up to you at Trader Joe's and asked you to spend 20 minutes helping them pick out a headshot. Now, imagine if *10,000* strangers did that to you. That's what happens to casting directors every day online.

Consider instead if a random stranger approached you as you were looking at the avocados (*drool*) and mentioned that they are experts in avocados and would be happy to support you in selecting the best ones. Completely different interaction, right?

When in doubt, focus out. There are *myriad* ways to support the people you're following. Express gratitude, share your own expertise, or promote *them*. The next time you're watching your favorite television show, why not look up the writer and director of that episode, and tag them in a post telling your followers how great the episode they worked on is? See an incredible short at a film festival? Find the director online and tell everyone to go follow his or her work. The casting director of your target show gets nominated for an Artios Award? Send them a heartfelt congratulations. A producer is doing a project that shoots in your hometown? Connect them to people who can help or simply share the best restaurants or places to visit while they're in town.

More than anything, this is about the mindset of adding value. There's no particular magic to it, and sometimes it's a seemingly small thing. But I guarantee that as you shift your thinking from "What can I get?" to "What can I give?" your results will dramatically improve.

Lastly, adding value also applies to the content you post. What do your followers enjoy? Post quality content that adds value to them. If you have a great sense of humor, utilize that. Have a particular eye for great photos? Share those. Have a knack for inspiring people? Do it! Add value, add value, add value.

Key #4: Turn the 2-D into 3-D (and Vice Versa)

I love social media, but nothing beats face-to-face human interaction. If you listen, engage, and add value over time you can leverage your 2-D social media relationships into in-person meetings. Maybe you build rapport then request a meeting, maybe that director posts about a panel they're speaking on, or your favorite writer is looking for people to volunteer at the animal shelter with them. Cultivate authentic relationships online, then actively seek organic opportunities to meet them in person.

Similarly, maybe you meet someone at a wedding, strike up a conversation, and learn that they're a casting director (this actually happened to me last month). Go follow them on social media! When you meet industry professionals in real life, keep in touch and keep them top of mind on social media while utilizing the same keys above.

What is expected with regard to social media from actors who are just starting out?

As with any profession today, your employers have this nifty thing called the internet. If they're going to hire you, there's a *very* good chance that they will type your name into the ol' Google and see what pops up.

What will they find? Is your online presence going to encourage or discourage them from hiring you?

Can you guess the *average* cost of a single television episode? 2.5 *million* dollars. And that's on the low end. If you were in charge of a multi-million-dollar project that only had a week to complete, how deeply would you care about the professionalism of your employees?

So if a bunch of pictures of you passed out drunk in a gutter holding a stuffed unicorn are what come up when someone googles you . . . let's fix that.

Social Media Checklist

- Reserve your handle on all significant platforms (Instagram, Twitter, Facebook, Snapchat, etc.).
    - I *highly* recommend your handle have your first and last name in it, ideally @FirstNameLastName – isn't the whole point for people to remember your name and face?
    - Even if you're not planning on being active on a platform, keep someone else from taking your name.
    - Ideally, have the same handle across all platforms.
- Add a professional profile photo to each (a headshot or something similar).
- Create a professional bio for each.
    - Prominently mention that you're an actor.
- Remove any offensive or unprofessional content.
    - This in no way means you must neuter your personality, but be mindful of the message you're sending.

What is expected with regard to social media from actors who are established and are on a series?

Increasingly, the contracts series regulars sign have requirements about posting on social media. The specifics vary greatly, but I would add that promoting the series on social media is certainly in the best interest of the actors. If the series goes away, so do their jobs . . .

How often should an actor tweet? Post? Share?

My experience is that quality content posted consistently over time is the key to growing a following. And, in general, I would lean toward quality rather than quantity.

That said, based on the algorithms for the main sites, I would recommend the following:

- Instagram posts: Every two to four days.
- Instagram story: Minimum once/day, but go wild if you desire.
- Facebook: One to four times/week.
- Twitter: One to five times/day.
- Myspace: However much you want – no one will see it . . .

How many hours a day do you think an actor should be dedicating to this kind of work?

The more intentional effort put forth in *any* aspect of our career, the better our results. You can spend dozens of hours per week or only a couple and still get value. The amount of time you spend ought to be matched with your goals.

> "As for social media, the more time spent the more benefit possible."

Broadly, if we're not spending at *least* 40 hours/week on our acting career, then we certainly can't expect results that are better than a full-time job would be. Further, my experience as an entrepreneur is that it often took many *more* hours than a full-time job to create a successful, profitable company.

As for social media, the more time spent the more benefit possible. [Entrepreneur and internet personality] Gary Vaynerchuk was spending 18 hours per day on Twitter and he grew his business by millions of dollars and eventually became repped by CAA. Kylie Jenner is a 20-year-old self-made *billionaire* because of her family's social media empire. (Fun fact: one million seconds is 11.5 days; one billion seconds is 31.75 *years*.)

That said, even a few hours per week can provide tremendous benefit. You can absolutely plan and curate content ahead of time, and spend even 20 minutes per day interacting with and adding value to your relationships on social media.

If you are committed to growing a sizable audience, then more time will be required. Quality content, posted consistently and strategically over time, is the foundation of doing so.

One option is to hire a person or company to manage your social media. As someone who does this for people, my best advice is to look for someone who adheres to the four keys of social media I outlined previously. You want to be in partnership with them to ensure an organic, authentic experience for your followers. It is so easy to tell when someone has purchased followers or likes, and it's never worth it.

People, companies, and brands care far more about engagement than the number of followers. And cultivating an audience that is highly engaged often takes time but will also yield the best results.

Does an actor run the risk of annoying people with their social media?
Absolutely. Sometimes it's easy to forget social norms when we're in the comfort of our own home behind a screen.

Remember, there is an actual human being on the other side of the computer. If you saw a casting director at the mall would you run up to them and ask them to give you feedback on your website? I certainly hope not. So why would you do that online?

The #1 mistake I see actors making on social media is that they approach it from the standpoint of what they can *get*, rather than what they can *give*.

Real talk: this business doesn't owe you anything. No one forced you to choose the life of an artist. Connect with what you have to *give*, the stories you want to tell, the difference you're committed to making.

Bring that generosity to everything you do – online or offline – and watch your career take flight.

I'm concerned about social media because I might mess something up or offend someone. Any advice?
The fact that you're concerned about this means you're highly unlikely to commit any serious errors. Think about it: are jerks worried about being jerks? No. That's what makes them a jerk.

Your concern says you are being mindful about what others think. So take a deep breath, and just be yourself.

Your job is *not* to please everyone. In fact, if you try to please everyone you generally please no one. Your job is to be authentic, add value, and engage. There are *billions* of people on the planet, and *hundreds* of casting directors. Do *you* jive with every single person you ever come across? It's not personal. Be yourself and share your gifts with the world.

Pro tip: if you're *really* struggling with this then pick your favorite actor. Now google their name and the word "sucks." Let me guess, *millions* of pages in the results. This is not meant to be discouraging, but rather a reminder that even that extraordinary performer you so admire is not pleasing everyone.

How important is having an agent or manager?
Extremely important. And not at all. Let me explain . . .

An effective rep working their ass for you can be the push that leads to massive career success. Good agents and managers have relationships with casting, pitch you for auditions, and negotiate better pay and billing for you. Managers especially can help guide your career, keep you sane, help you nurture relationships with decision-makers, get you meetings with agents, and so much more.

If you think actors get rejected, then try being a rep. They are generally being told no 10 times for every one audition they do get us. (Side note: I don't believe that actors actually get *rejected*. We didn't have the job in the first place, so even if we don't book the audition, we didn't actually lose anything. No one can ever prevent you from being an actor, so is that really rejection?)

Finding a good rep is like finding the perfect spouse – it often takes a long time and plenty of misfires (read: learning opportunities) before finding the right fit. So if you have an awesome agent or manager be sure to remind them how grateful you are.

On the flip side . . .

Remember that agents get 10% of your money, so how can we expect them to be doing any more than 10% of the work?

> "My experience is that our agents and managers can only help us as much as we help ourselves."

That means it's (at least) 90% on you to get auditions. The days of sitting by the phone, waiting for an audition, are long gone. I often hear actors complaining that "My agent isn't getting me out." While it may feel good to say that, it actually gives all of our power away. It implies that reps are the only ones who can move your career forward, not you.

The question, then, is what are *you* doing to give your reps more leverage? My experience is that our agents and managers can only help us as much as we help ourselves.

Actor Checklist to Support My Reps

Do I have:

- Killer headshots?
- Two minutes of *amazing* footage that demonstrates incredible acting, and looks like it came from legit film or television?
- The ability to put myself at a moment's notice on tape that's well lit, sounds good, and isn't in front of a distracting background?
- Recognizable training on my resumé?
- Professional, authentic online presence (social media profiles, etc.)?
- All of my online profiles (Actors Access, IMDb, LA Casting, etc.) up to date?
- A properly formatted resumé?
- Significant experience on set?
- A winner's mindset?
- A current place in a class, or am I otherwise exercising my actor muscle *regularly*?
- Relationships with casting?
- Relationships with decision-makers (producers, directors, show runners, etc.)?
- A clear understanding of the roles that are in my wheelhouse?
- A healthy, balanced life that allows me to be fully present and abundant in my auditions?

Everyone starts out with zero credits and experience, but if you're not working toward everything above, then there's a good chance a rep would rather sign someone else who is. It's not personal; it's a business.

How do you feel about doing small independent films? How does one get cast in those?

I'm a *huge* fan of independent films for a variety of reasons, including, of course, the opportunity to be on set and tell a great story.

In addition, they can be a wonderful way of building one's resumé (decision-makers like to see that you have experience on set), garner footage for your demo reel, build relationships with filmmakers, and, every once in a while, get into festivals and win awards.

Of the dozens of independent films I've done, some have come through the traditional audition process through my reps, some I self-submitted for on casting websites like Actors Access, and many of them came through relationships.

The relationships have started in myriad ways. Everything from social media, film festivals, networking events, and volunteer work I was doing, to referrals from friends.

Lastly, doing great work and being an awesome human matter greatly. Many of the directors I've worked for have hired me for other projects, sometimes even years later.

Do you believe in support groups for actors?
One thousand percent.

Frankly, I believe in support groups for everyone. No one achieves massive success on their own, and even if you could, what's the point? Is there some sort of gold star we get for making things harder for ourselves? If there is then I haven't seen it.

So much of my success has resulted from mentors and peers cheering me on, alerting me to my blind spots, offering advice, and keeping me accountable to my goals. Even as someone who currently runs an ongoing group mastermind class for actors, I myself have participated in mastermind groups for the last decade. And at times when I couldn't find one I liked, I reached out to other people and created my own.

Find a group where you can learn from people who are farther along than you, while always looking for how you can add value to the group. Someone may have more television credits than you, but maybe you've developed an expertise on health or personal finance.

Further, consistency is key. I have repeatedly seen that the most value from these groups comes over the course of many months and often years.

"It's not just who knows you, but who actively thinks about you at the appropriate time."

Is it important for an actor to market themselves? I don't want to be all "self-promotey."

"It's not who you know, it's who knows you," right? How can someone hire you if they don't know you exist? You might be the best actor for a role, but if the casting director doesn't know who you are, how will you get the audition?

Let's take this one step further. It's not just who knows you, but who actively thinks about you at the appropriate time. To increase our odds of success, then, we have to stay top-of-mind to the people in our network. Sounds kind of intimidating and salesy? Let me offer another way to think about this.

All we have to do is *remind people we're alive*. That's it. Simply reminding other humans that you exist.

Your first job, of course, is to be a master storyteller and an excellent human. As such, people will love meeting you and working with you, and want to hire you. After that, your job is to consistently, authentically, and coming-from-a-place-of-generosity, remind them that you exist.

Let's do an experiment.

Right now, write down every actor you know personally who you would love to work with. Go ahead, I'll wait.

Okay. Now pull up your phone and start scrolling through your address book. Come across anyone you want to add to your list? Go through all of your contacts and write down every additional person you now want on that list of people to work with.

So, what gives? How come there were all those people you didn't remember? It's not that you wouldn't want to work with them, they just weren't top-of-mind. The human brain can only *actively* remember so many people at a given time.

So when casting directors say they remember everyone, that's generally true. But that doesn't mean if their producer says, "Hey, I need five actresses in their mid-thirties who play tough as nails but have a vulnerable side for this role tomorrow" that your name will come to mind.

Your job is to be on that short list that pops up in people's minds when they're looking for actors like you.

Okay, so how do you remind people that you're alive?

Individual communication is most effective, but you also don't have enough time to contact every person you know individually. Accordingly, there are ways to stay top-of-mind to your broader network, while also focusing on more personalized communication with a smaller number of your top contacts.

From the broad to the narrow:

- Social media: IMHO, the easiest way to reach a large audience in a short amount of time. Remember: Listen, engage, and *add value*.
- Email newsletters: I use MailChimp to send updates to most all of my email contacts every 1–3 months. Again, find ways to make it personal and authentic, and add value!
- Postcards: Most of my postcards go to casting directors (use AmazingMail. com to save time). I use CastingAbout.com, IMDb Pro, and the CSA (Casting Society of America) website to verify addresses of any casting directors who have seen my work. You can update them on bookings, classes, and marketing materials, or better yet, make it about them! Send valuable information or a congratulations related to what they're casting.
- Individual emails: Who are the top 5–10 people who have mentored, guided, shaped, or otherwise supported your career in major ways? Find ways to individually reach out to express gratitude, share good news, or add value (are you getting the idea?).
- Phone calls: You know that camera in your pocket with the internet on it? It can actually also make phone calls. Give it a whirl. You can cop out and send a text, but if you're going to stretch your comfort zone in acting class, why not do it outside of class as well?
- In person: Whether it's a large networking event or a one-on-one lunch meeting, there is nothing quite as effective as face-to-face interactions. I challenge you to set up one coffee date per week for the next year with industry professionals. Do that and shoot me an email (benwhitehair-coach@gmail.com) with your results.

Notes

1 "audition". Merriam-Webster.com. 2019. www.merriam-webster.com.
2 Kristof, Nicholas D., and WuDunn, Sheryl. 2009. *Half the Sky*. New York: Knopf.
3 Thoreau, Henry David. 1854. *Walden*. Boston: Ticknor and Fields.
4 Actorsandcrew.com. n.d. "The Top Ten Best Books on Acting Ever Written." www. actorsandcrew.com/press/2011/07/the-top-ten-best-books-on-acting-ever-written/

CHAPTER 3

FINDING SUCCESS

Success! Well, sort of. Success as an actor might not mean you're banking the big bucks. Or it might! It might just mean that someone saw you in a play or a short film and brings you in to audition for one day on a television show. Or it might mean you met someone on set who thinks you are talented and will introduce you to his or her manager. This chapter will include practical advice for when you're in demand and making sure your career choices are setting you up for further success. We'll talk about the varied ways actors get agents. We'll get advice from a prolific director about what he expects from actors on set, and vice versa. We'll also address what you might need to do, once you get visible, at this point in your career, and the emotional complexities involved with success and working under pressure and high expectations. And, most important, we'll remind you not to spend all that money you are making . . . because you need to save some for those career highs and lows.

For every actor the definition of success may differ. I've never equated success with happiness though. I separate the two, so that one is not dependent on the other. And for me the ultimate goal is happiness. It's a quality of life thing for me.

No matter how you look at success, the consensus of our contributors is that it always takes dedication and hard work fueled by passion. So that seems highly attainable if you are willing to put in the work. It also seems to be tied into opportunity, but we will talk about that, or creating those opportunities, more in the next chapter.

Here's what we're going to address in this third chapter:

- Success requires hard work.
- Success goes hand in hand with respect, responsibility, and courtesy to your fellow craftspeople and creators.
- Why you must bring the best you can offer to any situation.
- While you are on set working, ask for what you need. Communication is key.
- How to figure out when is the best time is to approach the director and the wisest time to not bother the director.
- The director is there to make the scene work and to make you look good. Scene prep is completely on the actor and must be completed prior to the shoot.
- Listening, believing, and responding truthfully is essential to good work, but life experience and a unique point of view are what truly fascinating actors seem to offer.
- Striving for balance is essential.
- As far as publicity goes, quantity is necessary to get the public's attention but, in the long run, quality is what will make you stand out as an individual.
- "Buzz" follows the work. It never leads.

Take a look at our experts' advice. They all have history and experience to back them up. Then, you should define your success on your own terms. So, find your way . . .

A DIRECTOR'S PERSPECTIVE

▶ A Q&A with Andy Wolk

Andy Wolk's directing career began with the much-lauded HBO movie *Criminal Justice*, which made *Time* Magazine's "Ten Best" List. Starring Forest Whitaker, it received the Silver Prize at the International Festival of Audiovisual Programmes (FIPA) in Cannes and was named Best Cable Movie of the Year. He has been nominated for the Directors Guild Award twice and has directed episodes of shows such as *The Sopranos*, *Ugly Betty*, *Damages* (for which Glenn Close won an Emmy), and *The Practice*, including the "Final Judgement" episode for which Alfre Woodard received an Emmy and Andy the Humanitas Award. He also directed the pilot of the HBO comedy hit *Arliss*, along with *Seal Team*,

Figure 3.1 Andy Wolk

Photo by Hannah Zackson

Girlfriends' Guide to Divorce, Criminal Minds, Gossip Girl, Without a Trace, and *NYPD Blue*, among many others.

He has directed many movies for cable and network, including *Deliberate Intent, Fighting the Odds, The Defenders: Payback, Choice of Evils,* and *Taking the First,* along with *When Angels Come to Town,* starring Peter Falk and Katey Sagal; *Finding John Christmas,* starring Peter Falk and Valerie Bertinelli; *The Christmas Shoes,* starring Rob Lowe and Kimberly Williams; and *A Town Without Christmas,* starring Patricia Heaton and Peter Falk.

Andy (Figure 3.1) has been on the faculty of the American Film Institute, the University of Pennsylvania, and the Sundance Institute's Filmmaking Lab.

What homework do you expect an actor to do before showing up on set?
Be prepared! First, know your lines! Be completely off book!

But preparation is more than just knowing your lines – you should really have studied the script, so you know what happened in the scenes before the ones you are shooting and what happens in the scenes that follow. In other words, before Day One, attack the script! Know it inside out, so that you should have a good idea of what the arc of your character is for the entire episode.

> "You should really have studied the script, so you know what happened in the scenes before the ones you are shooting and what happens in the scenes that follow."

If it is a television series, watch episodes of the show to understand the style and how it's written and shot, and to get a sense of how the actors play scenes.

You should come in with a good idea of what your character wants from the other characters in the scenes you will be shooting. You want to understand your character's objective in a scene and how it plays out. To do this, you should also have a feel for what is the turning point in the scene – the key moment that is the reason the scene is in the show. Think about how things are different for your character at the end of the scene than they were at the beginning.

Other things to think about before showing up are blocking – where you might move in the scene – and some activity you may be doing. Have ideas. Even if they are ultimately not used, they show you are deeply involved in the work.

And if you have questions for the writer or director, make sure you ask them. That's what they are there for, so hearing their thoughts beforehand will be an added bonus.

Are there rookie mistakes that are avoidable for someone who is doing his/ her first job?
Not knowing your lines and asking for "sides" is a big one. *You have to know your lines.* And, along with that, you should not be constantly referring to the sides. Your attention should be on the actor you are rehearsing or shooting with. You want to be the most prepared person in the room.

> "As you work on the scene with the other actors, make sure you are listening to them and taking in what they say, not just silently waiting for your cue line."

Be on time! Actually, better than being on time, be early!

As you work on the scene with the other actors, make sure you are listening to them and taking in what they say, not just silently waiting for your cue line.

Another mistake is talking too much. You can talk a scene to death, as opposed to just doing it. There is talking about acting and then there is acting. You want to be acting.

Remember what you did in the audition. That's what got you the job. Don't come in with a totally new idea that the writer and director do not expect to see and spring it on them. If you do have something new that you think is better, discuss it briefly with them beforehand and see if they want to give it a shot.

Don't be afraid to ask the director how he or she is covering the scene – is it a master and then closer coverage? Is he or she doing it all in one-shot? You need to know these things.

What should an actor expect or hope for from a director when rehearsing?
A good director will be watching you and listening to you and responding to what you bring to the table. He or she will then be giving you notes or ideas on things to do with business and blocking.

So truly what you need is good communication going both ways. Listen carefully to what is being asked of you and then try it.

At the same time, if you are unclear about something in the scene – for example, anything from your objective, or the turning point, or on what line you should cross – ask the director. Don't fake it or wing it. It does not work. So ask for what you need. It is always better to put this in the form of a "What if . . ." question.

And don't be afraid to ask questions. If there is one thing a director is used to, it is having people ask him or her questions. So go ahead and ask. And posing your idea in the form of a question is a smart way to go. This is a very good way to get an opinion back from the director that you will be able to use in your work on the scene.

You should also ask for what you need in terms of the set – for example, is it quiet? Are there crew members moving around in your eye line? Are there props you need that have not been supplied?

Again, communication is key. If you want to try something different, let them know. If something isn't working for you – an interpretation or blocking or a line reading – let them know. Everyone – especially the director – is there to make the scene work and you look good.

What should an actor expect or hope for from a director when shooting?
That same kind of attention and communication. You want a director who communicates frequently and clearly and imaginatively with an actor, but you may not always get that, so you have to be prepared with your own thoughts and way to go. Some directors let actors do their thing and are concerned mostly with camera issues such as moves and composition. Other directors will be very performance-oriented and want to work on all aspects of what you do. No matter what kind of director you get, you need to be prepared and ready to do your work.

> "You have to know when not to bother a director – like when they're setting up a scene or a camera move."

You should remember that the director is juggling many things during the shoot – from schedule to performance to camera angles to lighting to transitions to other scenes, etc., etc. So you may not always have their full attention. Therefore, you have to know when not to bother a director – like when they're setting up a scene or a camera move. Be aware of those things and save your questions for when he or she has a moment.

And they will have a moment, because ultimately the most important thing for the director is the performance of the actor in executing the scene, so his or her attention will definitely turn to you. Be ready in terms of the shooting of the scene and anything you want to ask or try after they say, "Cut!"

In that moment, you should expect that the director is there for you and for your performance and you will get the care and thought from them at that time. Ask for what you need. This is your moment for that. If you don't need to ask something, don't. Just take the notes and do the work.

Can you talk about what gets shot, and in what order, and why those decisions are made?

A key element to making a movie or television episode is the schedule. Shooting days are built around the location where you will be shooting so that if, for example, there are three key scenes in an episode that take place around a dining room table in the beginning, middle, and ending of a show, those three scenes will almost always be shot consecutively so that you don't leave that location.

And to make it more complicated, let's say that the third dining room scene is the dramatic end of the show, but is has to be shot on Day One of the shoot because that is the only time the dining room location is available. Yikes! You are shooting the ending on the first day. But since you have studied the script and have attacked it and know it well, you will be emotionally ready to go where you have to go – even if it is Day One!

> "When shooting a scene, a typical pattern for a director is to shoot the widest shot first."

The reality is that you will be confronted with something like this because virtually every show is shot out of sequence. So be completely on top of it in terms of knowing where you are coming from at the beginning of the scene and where you are going to be at the end of it. Those scenes that have not yet been shot will inevitably influence what you are now shooting.

When shooting a scene, a typical pattern for a director is to often shoot the widest shot first. This is called the master shot. Then the order of shooting moves toward tighter shots and ultimately to the close-ups. But sometimes in heavy emotional scenes, the director will have the actor do the close-up first so that the emotion is not wasted in big wide shots where the viewer may not really be able to see the actor's face. If you have that kind of scene, it is a good idea to discuss with the director the order of shooting and when you feel you can best reveal the emotion.

In fact, it is always valuable if you can talk with the director about what shots they are going to use to cover the scene. This will give you a sense of how many times you have to do a scene and where the director's emphasis seems to be. For example, if they are planning to do the scene in just one long shot and there will be no close-up, you definitely don't want to be saving your performance for a close-up that will never come. Again, ask. Communicate.

What is the best thing to do, while shooting, if an actor forgets his line or "goes up"?
Don't panic. Just call out "line" and then go back, usually to a few moments beforehand so you can get a good run at it.

Let the other actor know that is what you want to do.

Or you can start over at the top of the scene if that is better for you. But don't get upset – it has happened to all actors, and directors and crews have seen it many times.

The key is to just take a moment and gather yourself and then go on.

What is block shooting? Why do directors do that?
Block shooting is done most often to save time.

It is done by shooting in the same direction for a number of scenes in a row, rather than turning around and doing different angles to complete the first scene.

For example, you are playing a pitcher in a baseball game. There are three big scenes in the show where you pitch. There are many other actors to be covered in the game in each scene – batters, fielders, the players on the bench, those in the stands watching. If you were to do all the coverage for all the people in Scene 1, then go back and do all the coverage for all the people in Scene 2, then do all the coverage for everyone in Scene 3, it would take a tremendous amount of time and the camera and shooting crew would be constantly turning around, which is very time-consuming.

"For the actor who is block shooting, you have to be ready and prepared to jump from scene to scene as they are shot in this fashion. Keep notes for yourself on what you have done in each scene, so you don't forget or get confused as you jump from scene to scene."

Instead, you shoot all the pitcher moments from each angle you need for all three scenes. Then you turn around and shoot all the batter moments you need for each scene, then shoot all the reactions in the stands for each scene, then on the bench, etc.

Thus, by shooting each element in blocks for the three scenes you have gotten all the coverage of the three big scenes in a timely fashion. No one will ever know when they are edited together later.

Then, for the actor who is block shooting, you have to be ready and prepared to jump from scene to scene as they are shot in this fashion. Keep notes for yourself on what you have done in each scene, so you don't forget or get confused as you jump from scene to scene. This is a good time to consult the script supervisor, who should also have very clear notes of what you have done.

How do I deal with a character, creature, or object that is not there?
Prepare the scene as if it were completely real so that you know what you will do before you get to the set. In other words, *make the movie in your head!*

How do you do that? Get drawings of the creature from the designer so you know what you will be looking at. Get storyboards if they have them so you can see how the action plays out visually. Ask for those things – don't be shy – and in virtually all cases production will get them to you because they know you will need them to make the scene work.

Also, make sure the person who reads the lines is doing it full-on, not in a perfunctory manner.

Make sure the crew gets you something to look at for your eye-contact and eye line, even if it is just a tennis ball on a C stand.

On set, talk to the visual effects supervisor so you are clear about the shot and your action in it. Make sure they tell you what they are planning to do with the creature – how it will move, etc. They normally love talking about this stuff and they will be very helpful because they want you to be great, and they are the ones who have to execute this by integrating your performance into the whole.

If the creature is moving or doing something to you or near you, make sure you have someone call out what exactly is happening so you can follow it in your mind and do the appropriate actions. Your goal is to make contact, to talk and listen as if you were doing a scene with a real person.

And then pretend!

ABOUT AN ACTOR WHO WORKS ON BOTH COASTS . . . AND LIVES ON NEITHER

▶ A Q&A with Josh Cooke

Josh Cooke has worked as an actor since 2001. He has starred in four network series as well as several pilots and films. He's had recurring and guest roles on numerous shows, including *The Marvelous Mrs. Maisel, Castle Rock, Grace and Frankie, Dexter, Longmire*, and *Hart of Dixie*. Josh (Figure 3.2) originated the role of Robert Merkin in La Jolla Playhouse's production of *Junk* by Ayad Akhtar. Other theater credits include *The Common Pursuit* for The Roundabout and *Come Back, Little Sheba* at Center Theater Group.

Figure 3.2 Josh Cooke

Photo by Eleisha Eagle

You seem to have moved back and forth between comedic roles and dramatic roles easily in your career. Is there a difference when you are approaching one over the other? Do you prefer one over the other?

Comedy is far more technical than drama. As an actor, your goal for either is to serve the story by finding your character's needs, wants, and point of view. But whereas drama can shoulder a variety of interpretations, delivery, moods, and timing, comedy is much more specific. This is especially true for multi-camera comedy, which is perhaps the most rigidly rhythmic format.

Whatever the funny is, whether it's a joke, situation, or character dynamic, the comedy will absolutely die if the timing isn't right. A lot of this can be helped in editing, of course, but having a sense of what is funny about a script and why is extremely important.

I think these days I prefer comedy, multi-camera comedy to be specific, because the day-to-day process is a lot more fun than on a single-camera show.

Where have you lived and found acting work?
My whole career up until 2015 was spent in New York or LA. With the exception of one sizable job I got from a self-tape while living in Louisiana for a few months, all of my work came from me physically being in the room with the casting director.

Why did you move from one coast to the other?
The first time I moved to the East Coast was in 2012 in an attempt to expand my career. I did a number of series and pilots, but all of them had been comedies and I couldn't get seen for anything else. So my wife and I decided to move to New York in the hopes that I would get some theater work. Fortunately, I did end up getting a play at the Roundabout within a few months, and that is still the most excited I've ever been to get a job. At the end of 2012, we found out my wife was pregnant. Simultaneously, I was offered a pilot in LA, so we moved back.

We made our second and permanent move to Philadelphia in 2015 for a variety of reasons, but primarily to be close to family and raise our daughter in a smaller, quieter town. Due to the prevalence of self-taping and our home's proximity to New York, we felt that I would still be able to be competitive in the acting world. So far, that's been true!

How does music fit into your life?
Music is the most important art form to me. I'm constantly looking for new music, reading about music, writing music . . . There's always music playing when I'm at home. I've played guitar and written songs since high school. Songs pour out of me; I write constantly. And though I've written a musical, and several scores for theatrical productions, won a small art contest with an original song, and have focused far more passion and energy into music than anything else, I never thought to pursue it as a career. It just never occurred to me. I'm trying to remedy that now.

Do you ever teach acting classes, and regardless of whether you do or don't, what would you want an actor who has never acted on screen to know about what you've learned from your extensive experience?

Cultivating a strong point of view about life and the world for you personally is perhaps the most important thing I can suggest. Of course, going to a good acting class (one with a focus on craft rather than one that focuses on television scenes and auditioning) is an excellent idea, paying attention to the technical side of filming (which lenses to achieve what shots, for instance) can be tremendously helpful. Understanding that really listening to what is being said in a scene, believing what is being said as reality, and responding truthfully, is essential.

However, having a strong sense of identity and point of view of the world is invaluable. To do this you must find who you are as a person. Who you are and what you think about the world is what will pop on screen, not to mention in the audition room. Anyone can do all the steps I wrote above – LA is teeming with aspiring actors who steep themselves in the "biz" and forget to actually have a life. I know this because I was one of them. Life experience and a unique point of view are what truly fascinating actors seem to offer.

> "Who you are and what you think about the world is what will pop on screen, not to mention in the audition room."

There's a quote about acting that I believe is attributed to James Cagney. When asked what his technique or approach to acting was, he said, "Hit your mark, look the other fella in the eye, tell the truth." To me that sentence is everything. It covers technical, technique, and life. The "truth" is what an actor has to offer, and at the core of that truth is his or her unique perspective on the world.

The other essential thing to have is *confidence*. Confidence comes when you've made strong choices, understand the need of the character, and bring a strong point of view. Confidence is probably the number-one thing a casting director wants to see when you come in a room. Not arrogance – that is different; that is bluster and often a smokescreen of fear and/or ignorance. Confidence carries a kind of weight, and it is easily felt. That's why it's imperative to make informed choices about the character and how the character views the world.

> "Confidence is probably the number-one thing a casting director wants to see when you come in a room."

I know you are highly regarded by directors who get to work with you. What do you do to earn that regard?

I think if that's true it's because I prepare. I always show up knowing the script, the scene, and the lines, and having a strong point of view. Now, some of my ideas may not work, but I know the scene well enough to make adjustments as needed.

How do you balance work . . . and family . . . and being on location?

I'm fortunate to have a phenomenal wife who completely understands my job and is wholly supportive. She is truly incredible, and I wouldn't be able to do any of this without her. Most jobs I've had in the past few years have only taken me away for a week or two. Being away is never ideal, but because the time away has been minimal and segmented, it's been okay so far.

When there is less time to rehearse when acting on the screen, what does an actor have to do to make sure he or she is bringing to life a three-dimensional character?

I think it's important to be clear here that, at least in my experience, there is pretty much zero rehearsal in television. Yes, there is the obligatory walk-through with the cast and director at the top of each new scene, but that's more of a stumble through to figure out lighting and blocking rather than figuring out the scene or character. This is mostly due to the grinding schedule – there simply isn't time to rehearse.

I make this point because I think most actors, especially if they're coming from theater, don't realize that the scene prep is completely on them and to be completed prior to the shoot. You must come to set having analyzed the scene, found the character's want/need, and made a number of choices, and know your lines. That's really the answer to your question: you must be a one-person theater production per scene. If you do all of that work, you will have some interesting choices and ideas to contribute to the nominal "rehearsal" time on set.

> "You must come to set having analyzed the scene, found the character's want/need, and made a number of choices, and know your lines."

Let's also note here that the above is *essential* for guest actors. Series regulars will have a little more freedom to ask questions, take time, try things, etc., but if you come on set as a day player and ask a bunch of questions and screw up the day, then you will not be long for that set or any other.

What happens if I disagree with a director's note or something a writer has on the page?

I see myself as part of a team that's making something together. For that reason, I try to take every note and make it work. There have been many times that I don't agree with the note that's given and instantly think I know better than the director and the writer. However, I don't often know all that's going on. In television especially, there may be a storyline they're working toward that I'm completely unaware of.

Most notes will make some kind of practical sense. In the event that I get a note I truly don't understand or can't square with the character, I simply ask for clarification. But this is the delicate part. If I get a note that seems to imply whatever I just did wasn't very good, I'm instantly ashamed/embarrassed. This is completely insane! That's the whole point – you're all making something better together! So I try to always come at it from a collaborative perspective. What is this director offering me to make the scene better, and how can I take that note and transform it into something better than the director could've imagined?

Is there a difference, besides long-term employment, between playing a recurring character or series regular and a guest star who just pops into one episode of television?

I touched on this before, but absolutely. It deals with comfortability and understanding your place on set. I've been all of the above, so I know whereof I speak.

As a series regular, you're home. The show is your home, the cast/crew/writers are your family, you're playing this character and seeing the stories develop so you have maximum context creatively. You also understand all the interpersonal relationships, gossip, etc., on a set.

As a recurring character, I've achieved that level of series-regular familiarity, but also had jobs that kept me in the day-player box. That all depends on who the regulars are, how often do you recur, and for how long. Usually as a recurring, you're seen as part of the team.

Then there are guest stars. This is the hardest because you're coming in for one episode to execute a specific job that moves the story along. How well this goes for you and how comfortable you are on set depends on how well you do your job, how friendly you are, and last but certainly not least, how friendly the regulars are. There is a staggering difference on a set where the Number One is nice and welcoming, versus a Number One who is closed off. It's often said that Number One sets the tone, and that is 100% true in my experience. That's why when I've been a regular, I try to be as welcoming as possible, because no one does their best when they don't feel comfortable.

What's the next step after you start working regularly? Have you ever had a publicist?
That'll be different for everyone, but generally the next step after working regularly is to work even more regularly and in increasingly better/bigger projects.

I did have a publicist once, but only for a few months and not much came of that. I never played the "game" well – the business side of Hollywood was rather revolting to me. But it absolutely is a business, and that business absolutely is about who you know and your relationships. I would be in a much different place career-wise had I been more social and accepting of the way the business works.

Something else I'll say that I've recently gone through: make sure that you like your representation and that they're working for you. Nearly every actor I know feels like they aren't working enough and will question their reps. That's a good thing. For years I felt that my reps weren't really getting anything done, but I ignored my gut because a manager of mine kept telling me how much work was being done behind the scenes and how much they believed in me and *blah, blah, blah*. I let it go for way too long. I got new reps, and, much to my relief, started working immediately. This is important in regard to your question because if you don't have a team around you that you [believe in], your career will be in jeopardy.

Do you feel pressure to use social media to promote yourself or the shows you are on?

Yes, and I hate it because I'm a grumpy old man. I resisted social media from the get-go because I'm fairly private and sharing a thought or picture with the world never occurs to me. However, as I mentioned before, it is a business . . . one at which I continue to fail!

I finally folded and got onto social media at the behest of my reps, but I really suck at it for the aforementioned reasons. I also don't think it actually translates to anything real. Networks will now cast someone not on talent, but on followers, though as far as I can tell, that hasn't yielded any more viewers. There was a spate of YouTube and Vine stars getting television and movie deals a few years ago, but obviously those projects all failed and you've never heard of any of them. I believe that's because social media is just that: social. The followers of a social media account want to feel like they have a dialogue with the person they're following. They can comment, like, post, reply, retweet, etc., none of which you can do with a television or film screen. The business produces great art when it hires the right people for the right reasons, and those reasons are creativity, vision, and passion . . . not a number of followers. The business continually fails when it is reactionary and pandering. That, to me, is what social media is – they view it as a marketing tool, when it's actually a social tool.

Again, grumpy old man here.

MAINTAINING AND GROWING YOUR CAREER

Finding Success

▶ By Jason George

Jason George is an established film and television actor with over nine series-regular television roles to his credit in primetime television, and 50 guest-starring roles. Jason graduated from the University of Virginia in 1994 with a double major in Rhetoric and Communication Studies and Drama. He landed his first major role on Aaron Spelling's NBC daytime drama *Sunset Beach*.

Figure 3.3 Jason George

Photo: Peter Augustin

Jason can currently be seen co-starring in Shonda Rhimes' new ABC drama series *Station 19*, after having been on *Grey's Anatomy* for several seasons as Dr. Ben Warren. Jason will return to reprise both roles in the upcoming second season of *Station 19* and the 15th season of *Grey's Anatomy*.

Other television and film credits include his fan-favorite series-regular role on ABC's drama series *Mistresses* alongside Alyssa Milano; *Eve*; *Eli Stone* with Victor Garber and Jonny Lee Miller; *Playing the Field* with Gerard Butler; *With This Rising* with Jill Scott, Eve, and Regina Hall; *Witches of East End*; *The Climb*; and *Barbershop* with Anthony Anderson and Ice Cube.

A classically trained theater actor, Jason's most recent stage work had him starring in the well-received but controversial production of *12 Angry Men* at the Pasadena Playhouse, the State Theater of California. The play, with its half-white, half-black cast, won the NAACP Theater Award for Best Production and Jason had the honor of playing Juror #8, the role made famous by Henry Fonda and Jack Lemmon in the film versions. In a prior stage outing, Jason played the lead in US poet laureate and Pulitzer Prize-winner Rita Dove's epic drama

The Darker Face of the Earth. The play relocates Sophocles' *Oedipus Rex* to the plantation South in 1820 and received high critical acclaim.

Jason (Figure 3.3) resides in LA with his wife and three children.

Congratulations!

You're a series regular in an on-air television series or you're an important character in a major motion picture. You are now officially, by any measure – including your parents' – a successful, working actor. Now the question is: what steps must you take to maintain the *successful* and *working* parts? There are many different paths to take and even more decisions that will need to be made, but every choice is to some degree informed by one central, undeniable fact of an actor's career: this gig is going to end.

In the same way that death is the one guarantee in life, it is equally true that every actor working on a project, for five days or five years, will eventually hear the words, "That's a wrap." So how do you deal with the idea of the inevitable end? Do you obsess over the unavoidable, walking on eggshells every day, afraid that it might be the last? Do you ignore the laws of nature, flying as fast and as high as you can until your engine prematurely gives out and you fall back to earth? Or do you live each day to the fullest, reaping the full rewards of the day you've been granted while planting seeds for the future, should you be blessed enough to get more days? If that last option sounds about right, then we are of like mind and I have some tips that may be of use to you.

Successful, working actors essentially do three things on every gig. In the broadest terms you must:

1. Perform the role you currently have.
2. Prepare for the role you want in the future.
3. Live a balanced personal life.

At first glance this may seem simplistic, but you'd be surprised how many actors leave out at least one of these steps. They instantly put all their energy toward booking the next, bigger role, and their work in the current role suffers. Or they are so consumed by the role they are performing that they forget to take a breather for a little self-care. Or worse yet, they pull out all the stops in their personal life, lapping up luxuries and excesses to the detriment of both their present role and future plans. Each of these three elements is essential and in some ways they overlap and each has several sub-elements, so let's break them down in order.

> "Instead of looking to your director to solve your problems, isolate potential character, script, or even props issues early, then present your director with two or three possible solutions to choose from together."

Performing the role you currently have seems straightforward enough, but you must remember that you currently perform not only the scripted role itself but also the roles of on-set leader, ambassador for your project, and high-profile performer in the acting community. Performing the scripted role is your most obvious responsibility, so let's start there. You're a professional actor. Act! Keep your chops tight. Stay in acting classes, if that helps you stay excited about the process. More to the point, develop the process of being a problem-solver. Instead of looking to your director to solve your problems, isolate potential character, script, or even props issues early, then present your director with two or three possible solutions to choose from together. Have a thoughtful work process and be mindful of how that process fits in with your collaborators. If possible, save the crew time and the director headaches by asking questions and getting answers via email before you even get into the rehearsal space. Once in rehearsal, know what (and who) each scene is about. When your character is central to a scene, ask your questions and present your solutions up front and early in rehearsal. When your character is present in a scene but not central – when the scene is not about you – it is probably best to save your questions until those initial questions about more central characters have been answered. In all likelihood, those central answers will provide you with your answers as well. Don't direct your fellow actors. Better to ask a question of the director that will push them to direct other actors.

Working with writers requires professionalism and a deft touch as well. Your job is to bring to life and protect the integrity of your character, but "my character would never do that" is a phrase too many actors use – and most writers hate. "Help me understand why my character does this" is far more productive and speaks to the unique relationship between writers and actors. It's as if the actor is the conscious mind, the writer is the subconscious, and the conversation between the two is a kind of therapy where the reason for an action is revealed. Neuroses and instinctual responses to people and events are part of being human and make for interesting characters. When the writer explains the justification of an action, it will either give the actor the information needed to play the role or force the writer to acknowledge that further consideration is needed. An extension of this concept exists, particularly in television, where actors are often unaware of the character's full backstory – because the writers aren't fully aware of it either. An actor or writer may have a working backstory but it's all theoretical until it's manifested on screen, because while decisions about backstory open up possibilities, they also close many doors. Both the actor's and writer's initial ideas of backstory may be supplanted when the writer finds better opportunities created by a different backstory. When it comes to backstories or seemingly uncharacteristic actions, you can see the lack of absolute clarity as a problem or an opportunity unique to the collaborative relationship between writer and actor.

Besides the scripted role you've been hired to play, it should be obvious that you also play a role as a leader on the set. In the past, however, some actors chose to ignore or refused to accept this leadership role, believing their only responsibility was to show up each day with lines memorized. But virtually every crew member's job interacts directly with the actor – not just the wardrobe, hair, and make-up people who make you look good but also the dolly grips, set dressers, and props people (all of whom also make you look good). Like it or not, you are a huge part of setting the tone of professionalism and respect on set. If you are late to set, throw tantrums, and take that phone call right as the director yells "Action," you will create a set full of crew members that resent you, have no respect for actors, and can't wait to move on to their next job. However, if you take the time to greet crew members warmly each day by name, treat their time and job as valuable, and try to learn a bit about the skill sets used in their jobs, you will create a warm environment full of crew that will go the extra mile to help you (like when you direct for the first time). You'll also become a better actor with an understanding of subtleties like how color schemes and camera angles inform and magnify your performance. Always remember that your crew may change slightly on any day with additional or substitute staff. You should go out of your way to welcome these folks, especially if they happen to be performing what may be the hardest job in all entertainment – the guest-star role. Guest stars and supporting players must perform powerful, emotional arcs on unfamiliar sets with no friendly faces in sight. It will help their performance, and by extension your project, if they are as comfortable as possible. In short, treat guest stars as if they are, well, your guests. When this gig ends and you're required to cry on cue while guest-starring on another cast's set, you're going to wish for a welcoming group of actors.

> "If you take the time to greet crew members warmly each day by name, treat their time and job as valuable, and try to learn a bit about the skill sets used in their jobs, you will create a warm environment full of crew that will go the extra mile to help you."

Another role you play as a major cast member is that of ambassador for the project. You are expected – and often contractually obligated – to promote that project through appearances, promo spots, photoshoots, and social media. This type of promotion is generally coordinated by publicists that work for the network or studio and will largely focus on the performers seen as the public faces of the project. Don't obsess over whether or not you're seen as one of those faces. You have little or no control over that. Focus on the work, and the work may make you one of those faces. Viola Davis, Allison Janney, and Sandra Oh didn't start out as "the faces" of *Doubt*, *The West Wing*, and *Grey's Anatomy* but their stellar work demanded that they be part of future PR campaigns. But always remember you are a creative being with agency, not a puppet. Promotion should benefit all parties involved and your time, image, and social media presence always belong to you. That said, you are still an ambassador and, as such, your actions on and off the set – especially with fans and on social media – have direct consequences for your project, positive or negative. You need to always remember the *social* part of all media. It's public. *Really* public. Blowing off a respectful fan or posting that offhanded comment about a celebrity may feel good in the moment but can quickly become entertainment news fodder if your offensive post goes viral or the fan shares video of your rude encounter. The fans don't own you and you always have freedom of speech, but remember that despite the minor, immediate cost in time and energy, reconsidering the sharing of a post or taking a selfie with a fan may pay dividends in a longer life for your current project.

There's one other role you now play that's worth mentioning. You are now a high-profile actor – a leader in the professional acting community of SAG-AFTRA members. Remember, you worked your tail off to earn your SAG-AFTRA card because it was a sign that you were a professional actor (if not a successful, working one yet). You became one of the 155,000 performers who depend on SAG-AFTRA, the performers' union, to negotiate minimum wages and working conditions. Without SAG-AFTRA, actors could literally be forced to shoot 24 hours a day, seven days a week. Without SAG-AFTRA, producers would not be required to have a qualified stunt coordinator on set when you're doing that dangerous stunt. Without SAG-AFTRA, you wouldn't have a health or pension plan to take care of you when you're sick or you're ready to retire. The power of any union is primarily in the sheer number of its members and their collective will to stand united behind the union's contracts. But without high-profile actors, the successful contracts of SAG-AFTRA would be negotiated much slower and may be more painful to achieve. In your role as a high-profile actor, SAG-AFTRA and your fellow professional actors would appreciate your paying it back or paying it forward and giving any assistance you can provide. It's usually as simple as just showing up when asked. In the process, you'll gain knowledge of industry trends and Hollywood economics that will prove invaluable as you navigate the rest of your career.

Just as there are many elements to the role you're currently performing, there are several parts to preparing for your future roles, including: networking, personal promotion, auditions and meetings, and proper representation. Networking is key to every business, and while you should be making connections at every event or festival you attend, remember that every set provides one instant opportunity for organic networking: video village. Video village is the small area of chairs set up in front of the camera monitors where the director, writers, and producers sit. Video village is also where that warm and welcoming nature that creates a great set will now plant seeds for your future. Every director, writer, and producer that works on your project will go on to work on other projects and will undoubtedly remember if you created a positive atmosphere on set, solving more problems than you caused. And those problem-solving sessions will sometimes take place in video village, one of only two places where you have real face time with the creative team. Table-reads are the other, but they happen only once, at the beginning of a film or once per episode in television, and in either case there are so many people present that it's difficult to do anything other than small talk. Video village is available every day, all day, providing a serious opportunity to forge personal relationships with directors, writers, and producers and ask them questions, like what they seek from their actors and how they've navigated their own career. You'll learn that the seeds for many actors' transition to their next role as an actor, director, writer, or producer occurred thanks to relationships that began sitting in video village.

> "It's key that you learn to subtly differentiate between publicity for your current project and promotion for you as an individual and your 'brand' as a performer."

Another essential element of preparing for future roles can easily be missed because it appears to be the same element used to perform your current role: publicity and promotion. It's key that you learn to subtly differentiate between publicity for your current project and promotion for you as an individual and your "brand" as a performer. Instead of simply doing sit-down interviews promoting her current action film, a performer may take a journalist rock-climbing to show she personally shares her character's addiction to adrenaline. Or the star of a comedy series may bring a journalist into his art studio to show he has an artistic spirit, thus broadening perception of his range. Though subtle, it's a real difference in the kind of publicity you're seeking to prepare for future roles and the studio or network publicist likely won't pursue or fund much of this kind of promotion. This is where you may need to hire your own personal publicist. They are not cheap, running anywhere from $2,500 to $5,000 a month plus expenses, and it can be difficult to tell if you're getting appropriate bang for your buck. The personal PR engine is still fueled largely by your latest project and much of that PR "gas" is sucked up by the actors seen as the faces of that project. Actors further down the call sheet may want to exercise more strategic bursts of personal PR for shorter periods of time or when they have a major story arc. Publicists often come with other perks, such as connections to stylists and photographers, which may be advantageous to actors preparing for future roles in the fashion business. However, some publicists may justify their cost by keeping you running on a hamster wheel of photoshoots and interviews for publications that don't have significant readership or audience penetration. Quantity is necessary to get the public's attention but, in the long run, quality is what will make you stand out as an individual – especially when it's on your own dime.

Also, the social media you've been doing to promote the current project will naturally be part of how you carry your fanbase over to the next project. But social media can also be the launching pad for other entrepreneurial projects. High-profile performers sometimes earn serious money doing direct advertising for products via social media or lifestyle websites. Balance is necessary because, if you do too much, you run the risk of inadvertently rebranding yourself as a marketer instead of an actor. This is definitely something to watch out for if you're only earning free merchandise for social media posts. However, you may not mind the brand of marketer if you're earning $50,000 to $75,000 for a single post to your millions of followers, or your lifestyle website just raised $15 million in venture capital.

A word of caution about social media and publicity in general: in the words of an actor and coach I worked with briefly, "You can't PR this shit." It's important to note that, as useful as it is to grow your public profile and social media following, they will never, in and of themselves, get you work – otherwise every Instagram star, YouTuber, or celebutante would have a scripted television series. However, it may be the tiebreaker if you are on a shortlist of people perceived to be equal choices creatively. In truth, the ability for wide-ranging, free promotion of a project has always been an important – but never the primary – part of casting, even for major stars. Virtually no actor today guarantees great box office. But they can guarantee you two segments on multiple late-night and morning shows, five magazine covers, and a million followers willing to at least check out the trailer. You will always know that Will Smith or Scarlett Johansson has a movie coming out. Deciding to buy a ticket is a different story. A built-in PR machine is very useful but when producers make the mistake of casting purely for the promotional benefits a performer brings, their projects usually pay the price. No amount of PR will make you or the project good. Only talent and craft accomplish that, and most producers and casting directors worth their salt know this. "Buzz" follows the work. It never leads.

The ultimate goal of all that shameless self-promotion is to get you into a higher class of audition room. That's right: auditions never really go away. However, at a certain point your body of work becomes a major part of your audition and you start occasionally having "meetings" where you don't perform – at least not scripted lines. In these meetings, directors, producers, and show runners attempt to ascertain if your personal presence is a match with the vibe they want for the character. They're also trying to decide if they want to be trapped with you for 12 hours a day, five days a week, for the next few months or years. It's important for you to remember that you are also choosing to work with them. From the very start of your career, you have the power to say "no," so don't wait until you are "successful" to examine your choices thoroughly and put thought into what you want out of a project. Actors generally take projects for one or more of four reasons: the role, the people, the billing, or the money. Playing Hamlet is its own reward, as is working with great directors or writers. Billing is an attempt to solidify status as a guest star or above-the-title, marquee performer. And, although money is always a necessary element, if it is the only reason to do a project, the experience is often diminished. Remember that directors and writers take projects for essentially the same four reasons. Consequently, your career will bounce back and forth between regular auditions and meetings based on the acclaim of your latest role and project versus the acclaim of the creative team behind the new project and the demand for the new role. The x-factor in this auditioning equation is your representation. You are now at a point where an agent or manager may make a significant difference, turning auditions into meetings or getting auditions that were previously out of reach. Of course, this is all subject to the power and connections of the individual agent or manager. This now begs the question: is your agent or manager powerful enough to keep you a successful, working actor?

Knowing if you have the proper representation and when to change agents or managers is a very difficult thing. On the one hand, loyalty can never be under-valued, and I believe in going where you're celebrated, not tolerated. Often representation at a mid-sized company that truly believes in you will serve you better than representation at one of the biggest companies that thinks you're an adequate addition to their stable of actors in your type category. That said, this is a business, and there is no agent or manager working that won't eventually drop a client that hasn't booked a job in forever. How long that takes is roughly equivalent to how much you previously booked multiplied by their faith in your ability. Your calculation for leaving must also be based on business realities. Do they have strong connections at the level of film or television you are now pursuing – direct relationships with top casting directors, producers, directors, and writers? Do they have commercial, voice-over, and literary departments that support the roles you want to pursue as a diversified actor or as a writer, director, or producer? Often, managers act as stepping stones to more powerful agents and vice versa, so perhaps you can make this decision in consultation with whichever representative you're keeping. And, on that note, remember that great communication is vital because proper representation is a marriage of sorts and, while power and connections are essential, at the end of the day it's all in support of you.

Achieving proper representation may also mean you consider adding an enter-tainment lawyer to your team. It's not typically done in the early stages of "successful, working" actors because lawyers charge an additional 5% commis-sion (on top of agent's 10% and manager's 10–15%) and they are probably most useful for the complex back-end deals reserved for writers, producers, and the biggest name actors. That said, a lawyer can be an extremely useful ally on those rare occasions when you are being seriously sought after and are negotiating from a position of strength. In this instance, it's worth noting that a lawyer's only agenda is to get as much as possible for the actor, whereas agents and managers need to maintain positive relationships with casting directors and producers to get the actor's next audition or meeting. However, that extra 5% may barely justify itself in the more likely circumstance where your negotiating strength is unclear and your lawyer is able to net only a salary in the average range for that category of work. Lawyers usually don't sign exclusively with clients so, with a little business savvy, you may be able to utilize them on a case-by-case basis, thus having your cake and eating it too.

In the midst of performing and preparing for your current and future roles, it's important to remember that all roles are fueled by the life of the actor. An actor who's never really lived has no experience to draw from. And burnout is a fast way to ruin a creative spirit. Live a balanced life. Give yourself a reward proportional to your hard work. Finish a film? Take a vacation. Wrap the first season of a series? Maybe buy yourself a sensible car. A house on season one is probably a bit much. However, if you can get a monthly mortgage roughly equivalent to what you'd pay in rent anyway, the down payment may be a smart investment. Moderation in all things (including moderation), remembering that this business is feast or famine in a way that directly affects your career. Some actors find balance by doing big-budget projects in order to afford taking the smaller more creatively fulfilling projects. Conversely, some brilliant actors' poor movie choices coincide directly with financial pitfalls like divorce or bankruptcies. The more balanced an actor's financial situation, the more stress-free their choices. Business managers can help maintain your creative freedom by keeping your spending in line with your earning. Business managers are part accountants, part financial planners, and part investment managers. They advise you about saving for the future while helping you minimize your tax burden today by creating loan-out corporations or LLCs. Business managers often cost 5% of what they manage but some are available that charge a flat rate because whether you earned $5,000 or $500,000, it's the same amount of work for the business manager to cut a commission check.

It's also important to remember that you're more than an actor playing a role on a set; you're a citizen and human being here in the real world. Your recognizable face gives you a much louder voice to raise awareness for the charities and causes that are important to you. Knowing you helped others is a great way to feed your soul and in turn feed your acting. And take the time to create and maintain lasting relationships that exist outside the business. You need people *not* on your payroll to tell you that nose job is one too many, you're taking too much too often, or you're just being a jerk. These are also the people you will believe when they tell you your work is good, you have value outside your net worth, and that you can get through the hard times. As we've discussed, every gig will come to an end and so will every life, but no actor on their deathbed reminisces about how much money they earned or the good deal they negotiated. Actors reminisce about the work that made them proudest and the great collaborators and friends they met along the way. Long careers filled with great memories. That is the ultimate definition of a successful, working actor.

HE ACTS, HE WRITES, HE DIRECTS

Four Decades of Wisdom

▶ A Q&A with Ruben Santiago-Hudson

Ruben Santiago-Hudson is a Tony Award-winning actor, an accomplished writer/director with three Obie Awards. In addition to an Emmy and Golden Globe nomination he received numerous accolades for his screenplay of HBO's *Lackawanna Blues*. Most recently he received a Drama Desk Award for Outstanding Director of a Play for his Tony Award-winning revival of August Wilson's *Jitney*, which also garnered Outer Critics Circle, Drama League, and NY Drama Critic Circle Awards, along with six Tony Award nominations. Ruben received a 2013 Lucille Lortel Award and an Obie Award for Best Direction of August Wilson's *The Piano Lesson*, and in 2016 an Obie Award for Special Citation: Collaboration of the play *Skeleton Crew* with playwright Dominique Morisseau. He co-starred for three

Figure 3.4 Ruben Santiago-Hudson

Photo by R. Radstone

seasons as NYPD Captain Roy Montgomery on the hit ABC series *Castle*, and in the BET series *The Quad*, where he also made his television directorial debut. He recurs in Showtime's hit series *Billions* opposite Damian Lewis and also in OWN's new *David Makes Man* alongside Phylicia Rashad.

On film, Ruben (Figure 3.4) starred opposite Denzel Washington and Russell Crowe in *American Gangster*, Halle Berry in *Their Eyes Were Watching God*, Samuel L. Jackson in *Shaft*, Al Pacino in *The Devil's Advocate*, and John Travolta in *Domestic Disturbance*. On television, he portrayed famed chemist Dr. Percy Julian in *Forgotten Genius* and starred opposite Gregory Hines in

The Red Sneakers. Ruben's other feature films and mini-series include *Selma*, *American Tragedy* with Christopher Plummer, *Solomon & Sheba* with Jimmy Smits and Halle Berry – the first time a biblical movie starred actors of color, and *Rear Window* opposite Christopher Reeve. Other television credits include a series-regular role on *Michael Hayes*, and TNT's *Public Morals*, plus recurring roles on *The West Wing* and *Law & Order*, and numerous guest star appearances, including ABC's political drama *Designated Survivor*.

You do it all: stage and screen, television and film, New York, Atlanta, LA, act, direct, produce, write . . . How does your craft as an actor feed the others?
One of the advantages I have in being an actor/director is communication. I am very comfortable talking to actors in a way that most directors are not. Motivating the performance and not just technical stuff.

Do you have a preference as to where you live?
I am a New Yorker through and through and although I love working in LA, Atlanta, Chicago, Toronto, etc., and they all provide wonderful experiences for me, I live in the Big Apple and I love it.

Do you prefer stage to screen?
Stage is my heart and soul.

What are the pros and cons of each?
They both have their own challenges and joys. On stage, as a person of color, I can always present the entirety of who I am. My humanity is front and center. I don't find that opportunity so much in television, where it seems as though my authority or anger is all they really need.

> "Don't limit yourself or peg yourself in a corner."

Do you need to pick one over the other when you start out?
You should start wherever the opportunity lies. It will present itself if you continue to work hard and surround yourself with the right people. Don't limit yourself or peg yourself in a corner.

Can you talk about some challenging roles you played?

On stage, Shakespeare is always challenging, and I love it. Leontes in *The Winter's Tale* really demanded a lot from me and the reward as an actor was empowering in so many ways. As a young actor, Bigger Thomas in *Native Son* really took a lot out of me emotionally and I matured tremendously because of that experience. There are many more but that would take a lot of space.

Have you ever felt stereotyped by what you got to read for?

Absolutely. Most of the people who are at the head of our business, writers/directors/executives, usually have very little knowledge of the depth and scope of the black experience in this country. That is evident in much of what we see on television and in film. That doesn't mean they are bad people; it just means they don't know what's important to me or what someone like me is sensitive to.

As a series regular do you have a relationship with the cinematographer or make-up artist or costume designer? Special hair person?

I treat everyone with kindness and respect. My mother raised me that way. I'm a people person and I love to socialize and learn about the people who I work with. I love family and community and I consider my cast and colleagues family. Outside of certain cast mates who I bond with instantly, I'm usually closest to my make-up artist and costume designer/dresser, but it varies.

> "When I walk on a set, all I am hoping for is the best environment so I can bring the best of what I have to offer each day."

Can you talk a little about the difference in being a series regular and a guest star?

As a series regular, you know you are going to get treated a certain way because you are part of "the brand." As a guest star, you never know what you are walking into. Moody stars, tense set, second-class status, conflicts, etc. When I walk on a set, all I am hoping for is the best environment so I can bring the best of what I have to offer each day.

What made you want to direct as well as act?

I have been fortunate to have a career that spans almost four decades. I've been directing theater for all of those years as well as acting. I've learned from some incredible people. I felt it was time to pass some of that knowledge on. I also want to take care of the stories that honestly reflect my experience, my ancestors, my culture, instead of leaving that in the hands of strangers, as is often the case.

Is there any job that you have now done in show business that you don't want to do again?

There are situations that I never want to be in again. Meaning with certain people; whether producer, writer, actor, or director. I have only once taken a job that I knew I shouldn't take. I will never do that again. My work means too much to me, and I give it too much of my heart and soul, to be miserable doing a project.

Is there any job you are eager to do again?

There are so many people who I absolutely loved working with and adore. My hopes and prayers are that we come together to work our art together again. Those experiences keep me humble, grateful, and ever thankful.

ACCOMPLISHING HER LIFELONG DREAM IN A BETTER WAY

Redefining Success

▶ By Tania Gunadi

Tania Gunadi is known for her roles of Private Park in Fox's *Enlisted*, Sashi in Disney XD's *Penn Zero: Part-Time Hero*, and Miko in *Transformers Prime*.

Born in Bandung, Indonesia, Tania won a Green Card lottery and relocated to LA as a teenager and began taking acting classes. She began her career with roles in short films and television commercials, eventually finding her way to Disney Channel with a recurring role in the television series *Even Stevens*, supporting roles in Disney Channel original movies *Pixel Perfect* and *Go Figure* and a series-regular role in *Aaron Stone*. From there she brought her "quirky girl next door" persona to shows such as *MyMusic, Graves, It's Always Sunny in Philadelphia, Bizaardvark,* and *AP Bio*.

Figure 3.5 Tania Gunadi

Photo: Theo & Juliet

Tania's film credits include *The Magic of Ordinary Days, Bob Funk, Such Good People,* and *Snow Bride*, along with animated feature films and the series *Zambezia, Scooby-Doo, The Jetsons, Shimmer and Shine,* and *Teenage Mutant Ninja Turtles*.

Tania (Figure 3.5) currently resides in LA and enjoys game nights with friends, talking to her Mom via Skype, going to the movies with her husband, swimming, reading thriller novels, and playing with her three cats. She speaks fluent Indonesian and Sundanese.

What Is Success?

The dictionary defines *success* as "the accomplishment of one's goals, the attainment of wealth, position, honors, or the like."[1]

And that's what I used to believe. In the beginning of my acting career, for several times each year I'd sit down and write out goal after goal after goal. And I'd do everything I possibly could to accomplish them. For example, in my first year as an actor, my goals were to book at least two co-star roles and a single guest-star role. And to accomplish that, each and every month I'd swing by my agent's office to say hello, drive around town dropping off my headshots in the hopes of *casually meeting* a casting director in their offices, venture out to various networking parties trying to get to know who's who in the industry, and mail out handwritten postcards letting over 200 production companies in town know what I was currently working on – be it a short film, commercial, or a stage play. And through it all, though I would never have admitted it at the time, it was exhausting! But on some level, I was quite proud that I engaged in lots of action-oriented things to try and forward my career. Actions that I believed I needed to do to find success. Honestly, it was a struggle most of the time. But I was also proud to call myself a *struggling artist*. It was my badge of honor for the world to see.

When I'd receive auditions, I often wanted to win the role so much that I was likely perceived as being needy. I'd put everyone in the room – the casting director, producers, director, and writers – on a pedestal because, after all, they were the decision makers. After the audition, while still in the room, I'd find myself asking them what notes they had for me, what character adjustments could I make, and if they'd like to see a different choice. But I quickly found out that *every single person in the room* had their own opinions and perspectives. Often, at the first call, the casting director would want the character to be one way, yet at the callback the director or writer would have very different and sometimes conflicting ideas. I found myself getting frustrated often, as I couldn't predict what they'd want any more than I could control their decision-making process. But one thing was sure: when I didn't get the job I'd always blame myself, feeling confused over what I did wrong. Over time, this led me into feelings of sadness and depression. I'd book a few jobs here and there, but the *journey* to booking was not satisfying in the least. And while I'd have tremendous fun working on set, the days that followed, when I had to begin the auditioning process all over again, were not always pleasant. The struggling artist who I'd become was indeed struggling in my journey to find success. And oftentimes I just wanted to give up acting altogether. I knew this all had to change. If I were to make acting my lifelong career, there simply had to be a better way to accomplish it. I knew deep down that I didn't want to put my happiness in the hands of others, and while it took me a little time, I'd realized that the first thing I needed was to redefine the meaning of *success* to me.

Redefining Success

I now redefine success as having fun all along the way: "A happy ending begins with a happy journey." It is a definition I came up with inspired by another quote in Esther and Jerry Hicks' *Sara, Book 2: Solomon's Fine Featherless Friends.*[2]

I rationalized that if I were to achieve my dream of being a lifelong actor, in the end what I would *feel* is happiness. Thus, my journey of continual struggle no longer made any logical sense to me. I convinced myself that if I could just skip to the end, being happy, and find fun all along the way, I'd be in for the ride of my life.

So what did I do? Well, I stopped doing things that weren't fun or that felt like a struggle, and instead I practiced finding fun in my everyday life. It was a little rocky at first, for old habits of believing that life is supposed to be hard would creep in every now and then, but I kept reminding myself just to *practice*. I started with easy things, like noticing that I could enjoy the beautiful weather from my little garden at home, that I could feel unconditional love when I petted my cats, that I could truly enjoy being in acting classes whether I was perform-ing comedy or dramatic scenes. I was trying new things like rap musical improv, and even though I couldn't rhyme at all, I was having fun! I'd hang out with friends and have a game night or watch action movies I loved over and over. At the same time, I stopped doing the things that feel like *must do's*, like going to industry network parties just hoping to meet someone important. Instead I was going just to enjoy the parties themselves! I stopped hanging out with friends who were negative, and I stopped writing goals and putting unneeded pressures on myself. I just began trusting that if I could find happiness along the way, I'd find success. I changed my attitude during auditions. I began treating everyone the same, putting no one on a pedestal anymore. I don't go into a room anymore asking casting directors or producers what character choices they're looking for. Instead I go in with a choice that I've created, that I've prepared. And I trust that if casting has any adjustments, they will speak up. And when they do, I now have fun executing those new choices as well. Most importantly, I made a promise to myself that I am going to enjoy the audition process and that booking the gig would be a bonus. I don't blame myself anymore if I don't get the part. I continue to hone my craft in acting classes and to softly remind myself that I have no control over the bookings. The only things I can control are my mind, my process, and my having fun along the way.

Another important thing for me was changing my relationship with my close friends and family. Even though they were well-meaning, I found it was creating stress when they'd ask, "How was the audition? Who was in the room? Did you book the gig?" And if I didn't book the gig, they'd start to worry about my well-being: "What are you doing now? Are you making money, are you okay? Is there a Plan B?" I know they love me, but I didn't want to bring worry into my acting journey. I made the decision to no longer share with them all the details about my auditions and my acting aspirations. I only share with them my bookings. And that's worked out best for all of us!

> "The only things I can control are my mind, my process, and my having fun along the way."

When I redefined what *success* meant to me, I began living a more fun life. And I began working a lot. I landed series-regular roles on *Aaron Stone, Enlisted,* and *Wiener Park.* I was booking many more national commercials and I even ventured into the voice-over world, booking series-regular roles on *Transformers Prime* and *Penn Zero.*

I now know that life is supposed to be fun. It sounds odd at first because most people believe that life's supposed to be hard, that you have to struggle to make things work, that life's full of compromises. But when I say the words "Life is supposed to be fun" out loud, it just feels good in my gut. So I continue to practice the good habit of finding fun in my everyday life. In the beginning you may find it challenging as any old habits of struggle and complaint begin to slowly dissolve away. But I believe that true happiness and success are interconnected, and as you take the time to find happiness along the way, you shall find success too.

My Tips for Finding Success

These are just my personal tips, and how I find success for me:

1. Know what you're planting!

   If you were to plant the seed of corn, you can expect to reap corn, not a rose bush. In a similar way, when you plant the seeds of happiness you can expect to reap the fruit of happiness. But you can't plant the seeds of struggle, worry, doubt, and criticism and expect to receive the fruit of happiness. This goes for both your acting career and your life.

2. Ask yourself why you love acting in the first place.

   For me, the answer is simply because acting is so fun! I just love playing different characters, co-creating with other actors, and collaborating with directors and all sorts of creative people to bring a story to life. I'm planting the seeds of fun and exploration. And that's why I'm usually matched with actors, directors, producers, and crew members who are fun and love to explore. And I love that I can make a living doing something that I enjoy. That's a win-win in my book.

3. Practice the art of letting go.

   Begin to view the entire audition process differently. Go to an audition fully prepared with your strongest choice on the character, as if that choice were a piece of your favorite chocolate cake. Bring in the cake, and know that some will love it, others may not. Either way, enjoy the creation of *your* chocolate cake. If they like it, great! If not, don't take it personally. Enjoy the audition and let go of any outcomes the moment you walk out the door. The rest of it is not in our control. The only thing you can control is your mind. So practice the art of letting it all go. Just like your acting is an art form, practicing *letting go* is also an art form, not a science. While it may not be easy in the beginning, it absolutely will get easier the more you practice it. And it won't be long before you'll recognize the benefits of letting go.

4. Don't be hard on yourself.

When we see a small child first beginning to walk and she falls down, we don't tell her that she's stupid or she should have done better. We offer words of encouragement and support with a sense of ease, because we know eventually she will learn to walk. Being hard on yourself over an audition that didn't go as planned, or not getting a callback or booking the part, doesn't serve you. Be as easy with yourself as you would the small child.

> "Be your own best friend. Don't rely on others to make you happy, to soothe you, to cheer you on."

5. Love yourself.

Be your own best friend. Don't rely on others to make you happy, to soothe you, to cheer you on. If you have those people around you now, that's awesome. But if you can love and be kind to yourself, that's something you can always count on.

6. Talk yourself into feeling good.

This may sound crazy, but I love talking to myself. Like practicing the art of letting go, this too is an art! Most of the time we're not conscious of the things we say to and about ourselves, but if you can take the time to become aware of how you perceive yourself and the things you say to yourself on a daily basis, then you can make a positive and lasting change. Talk yourself into feeling better and better. And hug yourself often. But maybe do it when no one is looking . . .

HE DOES IT ALL . . . INCLUDING AUDIOBOOK NARRATION

▶ A Q&A with Ron Butler

Ron Butler is an LA-based actor with over a hundred film, theater, and television credits, most notably as a regular on *True Jackson, VP*, and an Independent Filmmaker Project Award winner for his work in the HBO film *Everyday People.*

In 2010 he wrote, produced, directed, and starred in the musical parody *Obama! A Modern U.S. President*, which has had millions of views, and was featured by the Huffington Post, Variety, Roger Ebert, and CNN. The exposure led to an ongoing development relationship with television great Norman Lear and producer, Brent Miller, who executive-produced his short film *Photographs of Your Junk* and continues to collaborate with him.

Figure 3.6 Rob Butler

Photo: Brian Parillo Photography

Most recently, Ron has expanded into the world of audiobooks and has narrated over 100 books to date. He is a multiple Earphones Award-winner and Audie Award-nominee.

Originally from the Bahamas, he grew up singing calypso onstage with his father (the country's number-one recording artist), before touring (and recording) in Europe with a jazz band. In his spare time, you may find Ron (Figure 3.6) performing lounge-inspired covers of retro pop songs with his own trio in the LA area.

You have an extensive background as an actor on camera. Can you tell us a little about your start, your move to LA?

I started studying acting with a private coach in Washington, DC, a wonderful acting teacher named Vera Katz who taught at Howard University. Then I started doing local theater in DC, and through a series of wonderful coincidences (or synchronicity?) I ended up spending a summer studying with the Atlantic Theater Company in Burlington, Vermont. After studying for three summers with the Atlantic, I moved to New York to become a company member. I was primarily a theater actor in New York and regionally. About a decade later, I booked a theater job in LA while there vacationing, and I never went back to New York; seriously, I never left. Friends packed up my apartment and shipped my stuff out to me. After two years of doing theater in LA, I made the concerted effort to shift to film and television.

You have worked steadily for decades in television as a series regular, recurring, guest star, and co-star. Can you talk about your approach to breaking into the LA market, getting an agent, and your steady work?

As with many things in this business, my break in LA happened through relationships I already had. I was fortunate enough to work on a film in New York that later went to Sundance, and the casting directors of that film connected me with a manager in LA. That manager, in turn, helped me land my first agent. Many years later, I found myself without an agent, and a close friend was kind enough to pass my materials along to her agent, which turned into a meeting, which turned into representation. This happens in countless ways. I know people who have found representation from being in a showcase, as well as meeting an agent at a party and not knowing they were an agent.

My television career had a traditional trajectory: I started by booking co-star roles and worked my way up to larger roles. It doesn't necessarily happen like that anymore. People can walk in as social media stars and get a television series; the same is true for reality stars, athletes, and celebrities from other industries (astronauts, musicians). There are no rules anymore, except to be prepared, be your authentic self, and never take it all too seriously. Oh yeah, and always have your own creative project going so that you are fulfilled regardless. That way you aren't desperate . . .

I was fortunate enough to work regularly for many years. I credit that mostly to persistence and passion. Everyone's career is different. I have friends who have gone from show to show as a series regular their entire careers. I have friends who are astonishingly talented who can't get an agent. I have friends who worked sporadically for decades and then in their fifties and sixties suddenly became full-time, working, recognizable actors. There is a certain amount of luck and timing in this industry, so once again, being prepared, authentic, and persistent is all you can (and must) do.

> "Figure out where you're getting in your own way (if you are), and do whatever training (class, coaching, meditation, etc.) you need to do so that you can bring your full, authentic, prepared, and uninhibited self to your work."

During my time in LA I continued to study. On the advice of a career coach, I branched out from dramatic training and started studying improv: I was putting so much pressure on myself to book jobs that I was tight and "locked up" while in the audition room. (This is when I was mostly going out for dramas.) The improv training freed me up and taught me that I had great instincts and that I could trust them; that I had the skills to go anywhere the room might take me. That's when I really started booking jobs regularly. So, the takeaway isn't "Go take an improv class." The takeaway is figure out where you're getting in your own way (if you are), and do whatever training (class, coaching, meditation, etc.) you need to do so that you can bring your full, authentic, prepared, and uninhibited self to your work.

Do you have relationships with casting directors? Are there casting people who have hired you multiple times? Besides your obvious wonderful work, to what do you attribute these successful relationships?

Relationships with casting directors are important because, of course, they're oftentimes the gatekeepers. I have varied relationships with casting directors: some call me in for every show they cast and have hired me many times over the years, and [there are] others for whom I've only auditioned once, or only sporadically. And then there are others who I've never met – offices that I have never been able to get into for whatever reason. Casting directors are creatives who have their own tastes and preferences. They're also charged with finding talent to fit the tone of the show and the essence of a particular character. Sometimes they just may not like you for whatever reason. Others will fall in love with you and will not be able to get enough of you. My approach with casting is always to "go where the door is open." By that I mean those people who respond to my talent, who respond to my gifts, are my "tribe." I celebrate them, maintain regular communication with them, and nurture those relationships. After banging my head against the door of that CD's [casting director's] office, I could never get into, I let it go.

Relationships with casting directors are business relationships, but they are still relationships. Over the years, I learned to stop treating them simply as people who could help me get a job, and to start treating them like, well, people. Being interested enough to know their names and, if they ever mentioned them, the names of their kids, dogs, partners, favorite vacation spots . . . basically, I started listening. And then, when I'd run into them randomly at Trader Joe's, or Runyon Canyon, or the Hollywood Bowl, I'd talk to them about anything other than "the business." I do my best to take my ego out of it, my ambition, and simply be interested in who they are and what they're doing. I have found that that is the best way to be remembered. And being remembered is the best way to get into an office. Kicking ass every time you audition in that office is the way to get invited back.

At this point in my career, I have close friends who are CDs, and I have CDs who I run into at the gym every other day who have never hired me but will call me in the office for an audition. These relationships are personal and business at the same time, and I seek to strike that delicate balance.

You are an award-winning audiobook narrator, vocalist, and media producer. Can you talk about each of these jobs, and then reflect on the skill sets for these separate jobs and how they enhance each other? Please also include your success as an actor and your skill set as an actor and how they impact those other jobs too.

I have worked in a lot of different entertainment media over the years. I grew up in the Bahamas, where my father was the number-one recording artist for most of his life, so I grew up singing. But I also grew up watching tons of television, especially the comedy variety shows of the 1970s – *The Carol Burnett Show*, *The Sonny and Cher Show*, etc. – and I remember wanting to do what they were doing: singing songs and acting in comedy sketches. When I finally started pursuing an acting career, I ended up doing a lot of musical theater, which made sense since I was a singer and a natural comedian. But there was another side to my personality too: intellectual, studious, precise. So when I began working in television in LA, I was hired for characters on two ends of the spectrum: doctors and lawyers on the one side, and goofy, very physical characters on the other. Eventually, the physical got me the most action, which led to my first series-regular job.

When that job ended, I had a strong desire to produce and direct a project. I'd learned a lot watching really talented people produce 60 episodes of a television show, and I had a desire to make my own project. I started producing, directing, and starring in projects for my own YouTube channel: pieces that reflected my own comedic and musical sensibility and satirical outlook on politics and culture: stuff that was really me. And I brought the full weight of my television experience in terms of production levels and cinematography (not necessary for new media then or now, but once again I was honoring my own aesthetic). Some of those sketches went viral, got national attention, and because of that attention, I met producers Brent Miller and Norman Lear (yes, *the* Norman Lear). That led to a long-term collaboration (short films, new media directing jobs) and development (television shows) that continues today. In short, I parlayed my skill sets and experiences into my own vehicle, which ended up creating more work.

Most recently, my career has expanded to include voice-over work; specifically, audiobook narration. I literally fell into this work: I was looking to make some extra money between gigs and a friend who had been narrating suggested I try it. I thought, "Well, I love to talk, and I like to read – dream job!" I recorded my first book, and took to it naturally. I'd say it was a wonderful coincidence, but in retrospect my skill set and experience were essential to this work. Sitting in a booth and reading a novel requires being an actor and a director: as an actor, giving voice and life (emotional, honest, and grounded life) to a host of characters; as a singer, having the vocal stamina to record for six-hour sessions; as a director, understanding story and the emotional arc of not just each character but the story as a whole. It's like making a movie script come alive, without the visuals. I find it incredibly challenging and fulfilling. I recorded my first book over three years ago, and, to date, have completed over 100 titles and won numerous awards.

How have you balanced your pursuit of work with personal and family life? Did you ever feel as if you had to sacrifice one for the other? Or if your success enhanced the other?

I'm ambitious, driven, and highly disciplined, and in the past I tended to work too much at the expense of everything. I've learned over the years that, for me, and I mean specifically for me, it's vital that I carve out time to play, relax, and have a life in order to feed my creativity and success. In turn, when I'm thriving, it enhances my desire to enjoy my life, and to make sure that I'm sharing that joy with those closest to me. I spent much of my life out of balance with regard to these things, and so now, balance is a priority. It does not come naturally for me, so it is something on which I meditate, and that I cultivate. Daily.

How have you handled, and how do you handle, being recognized when you are a television star? What are the pros and cons?

My stardom and recognizability was limited to kids between the ages of 6 and 16 at the time and they were the best, most considerate, and, surprisingly, shyest fans one could have. Most of the time, their parents would approach, apologetically, asking for photos and autographs. It was never intrusive or overwhelming. It was nothing but a crazy, wonderful ego boost all the time, so it was easy and fun to be gracious. That being said, I've seen friends and colleagues deal with fans who thought they were entitled to something from them. It can get ugly. It is, as they say, one of the many prices of fame. I think that increased exposure demands increased vigilance of one's boundaries.

Notes

1 "success". Dictionary.com. 2019. www.dictionary.com.
2 "You cannot get to a happy ending on an unhappy journey." Hicks, Esther and Jerry. 2007. *Sara, Book 2: Solomon's Fine Featherless Friends*. Carlsbad: Hay House, 214.

CHAPTER 4

GETTING AHEAD

How do you navigate moving yourself into a more visible arena? Is this the point in a career where you need to be brave and try something new? How will you rebrand yourself? Is it time to self-produce? Has your relationship with your reps gone stale? This chapter will offer real-world examples of what it takes to jump off a plateau and get your career moving to the next level. There are lots of obstacles at this point in your career – you just need tangible tactics for overcoming them.

No matter how you do this, there is room for everyone no matter your shape, size, ethnicity, and sexual orientation.

Anyone who gets ahead has his or her own path. That is what the stories and shared experiences you will read illustrate. Some are very practical, others more philosophical. All require you to make some fundamental decisions and move forward, not stand still. They also require you to open your eyes to opportunities that present themselves, even if those opportunities are not what you expect. Seriously, open your eyes! You may be delightfully surprised at what you see!

Also, while you are looking, see beyond limitations that others might have for you. Remember that you are an artist. Think outside the box and create! And tailor that creativity to that unique thing you have to offer!

Here's what we're going to address in this fourth chapter:

- When auditioning for commercials, take responsibility for how prepared you are.
- How knowing the fundamentals of improv will be a great thing to have in your toolbox.
- Why bringing yourself to the material will make your work stand out.
- What you should specifically self-produce, and how self-producing can be your answer to moving forward.
- Why you must always be mindful to save for the famine periods of your career.
- The myriad ways an actor can make a living in smaller markets, and how accessibility may be easier than in larger markets.
- How one actor found and keeps internet followers in the millions.
- Why getting ahead will be meaningless if you don't also have a quality of life.
- An example of how many little things over many years can add up to make one big explosive career jump.
- How "playing back" your auditions or obsessing at what "could have happened in the room" is a huge waste of energy.

You can make the choice to move forward or stand still. You can take control of your career. If you want to get ahead, allow these experts to inspire and instruct you. Choose to move forward . . .

ALL ABOUT COMMERCIALS

▶ A Conversation with Aaron Takahashi and Isabella Way

Aaron Takahashi is a former instructor and core performing member of Cold Tofu, the nation's first Asian American improv and sketch comedy troupe. He also was a Main Company member at ACME Comedy Theatre in Hollywood for sketch and improv.

Figure 4.1 Aaron Takahashi

Photo: © Ming Lo

Along with his multiple appearances on Conan O'Brien's late night shows as a featured player in both pre-taped and live sketch segments, Aaron has amassed numerous co-starring, guest-starring, and recurring roles on popular shows for CBS, NBC, ABC, Fox, Comedy Central, Netflix, TBS, IFC, and Disney Channel, with perhaps his most notable credit being a recurring role on the critically acclaimed USA Network series *Mr. Robot*.

Aaron has been featured as a supporting lead actor in comedy blockbusters such as *Yes Man* (2008) opposite Jim Carrey, *Welcome to the Jungle* (2013) opposite Jean-Claude Van Damme, and *The Wedding Ringer* (2015) opposite Kevin Hart.

However, Aaron (Figure 4.1) has arguably enjoyed the most success as a commercial actor, appearing in nearly 100 commercials, including multiple spots for Toyota, Dunkin' Donuts, Wendy's, McDonald's, Snapple, State Farm, Esurance, and Ebates. He occasionally teaches a commercial audition techniques workshop in the LA area.

Isabella Way, born and raised in Laramie, Wyoming, started her career by writing and recording a short, winning rap song for the Drug Abuse Resistance Education (DARE) program poetry contest. Though her rap career started and ended there, her performing and writing career is far from over.

Figure 4.2 Isabella Way

Photo: Rob Mainord Photography

Isabella has appeared in numerous television shows/films, including *Criminal Minds*, *The Blacklist*, *Days of Our Lives*, *Entourage*, and *Ricki and the Flash* with Meryl Streep (directed by Jonathan Demme), and many commercials and industrials. She played Sophie in *Master Class* at East West Players. She's danced live on the BET Awards and with the cast of *Frozen* for *The Making of Frozen*.

She's studied improv at Upright Citizens Brigade (UCB) and C3 Theatre, and musical improv and sketch at the Magnet Theater. She created and performs with Staged, where they take an audience suggestion and create a Broadway-style musical. They've performed at Magnet Theater and Peoples Improv Theater and took part in the UCB Del Close Marathon in New York in 2018. She hosts a monthly musical improv show with her all-female group, the B-Side.

Isabella (Figure 4.2) created and stars in the web series *thirtydumpling*, and co-wrote the feature *Operation Cherry Pop*. She continues to perform, write, and create in both New York and LA.

Isabella Way: Some people make a living doing commercials and some only do theatrical (television and film) work, but most actors do a mixture of both. Both Aaron Takahashi and I are examples of that. We're both long time SAG-AFTRA members, and eight years after we met on a commercial shoot, I sat down with him to revisit our careers with respect to improv and commercials. Aaron, how long have you been in LA?

Aaron Takahashi: I was born and raised here.

Isabella: You don't meet a lot of people in LA who are from LA. I'm from Wyoming, of all places, and after college I moved out here actually to pursue dance and then got into acting. Did you always want to be an actor?

Aaron: I didn't start getting into acting until after I graduated from college. I was majoring in English with an emphasis on Creative Writing. I wanted to write children's books. There's still time. I figure there will be a time when I'm done with acting, or casting will not know how to cast me . . . there's gonna be that weird age . . . that's when I'll turn to writing.

Isabella: What's your background in improv?

Aaron: I don't have a huge background. Most of my training came through a group I was a part of for years called Cold Tofu, the nation's first Asian American improv and sketch comedy group. They would bring in outside instructors and they were really good. I would go weekly to their workshops and do musical theater, work on developing characters, finding comedic beats, recognizing the game (the funny or unique pattern that recurs and is heightened throughout a scene), and so on.

Isabella: I grew up dancing and actually went to college for opera. Then I got into acting classes like scene study and comedy and then found improv and musical improv. And classes, especially improv for me, have provided a community of friends and support there . . . which I think is also important, having a community. How do you think improv has helped your acting and art?

Aaron: The ability to take direction, listen, and really be present.

Isabella: I think being present is the most important for me. There are so many other factors involved, and you're already nervous, so being present can lose out to being stiff and stale. Even in spots where you're not speaking, you probably had to improv at some point in the audition process. Commercials are different from television: you're paid as a principal actor if you're recognizably seen with the product, whether you speak or not, and you still need to make strong choices. In television, you are considered background unless you speak lines. I've sat in on theatrical castings, and some people cannot take direction. They've learned their sides one way and can only do it that one way.

Aaron: For theatrical auditions, you prepare one way, or maybe two or three ways. And if you get a re-direct, I know for me, elements of my original preparation are still in it.

Isabella: And you only have several seconds to internalize the direction.

Aaron: And the improv training helps you hear what they say, absorb that, and then try it.

Isabella: It helps build that muscle to imagine that character a different way and to make different choices quickly.

Aaron: In commercial auditions, you typically don't know what you are doing until you get there and sign in. You could be reading for a spokesperson role, you might be doing your lines with the session runner reading as the other role(s), you might be paired up or put into a group, it might be your reaction to a situation that is presented to you, or it might be a personality slate where they ask you a question about your life and you just talk for a minute.

> "You get the sides or see a storyboard when you get there, and if there are sides, you don't have to memorize it as the dialogue is printed in large letters next to the camera or on a big screen."

Isabella: Sometimes they tell you what you're going to do before you go in, and sometimes you just go in the audition room and then they do the explanation. They may have some mock-up of a location or setting and they have specific directions to go with it. So you gotta go in ready to do anything they ask of you and do it well. If there's a script, you usually get a hard copy when you arrive and sign in. You get the sides or see a storyboard when you get there, and if there are sides, you don't have to memorize it as the dialogue is printed in large letters next to the camera or on a big screen.

Aaron: Even if there's a board I try not to read it because when they watch play-back they can tell when someone is reading.

Isabella: Do you have any tips on being able to memorize quickly, or do you just pull a line and then say it? Or is it a skill you learn from just doing it?

Aaron: It's repetition basically. For commercials especially, you're not going to get five pages of sides. It's repetition and actually doing it out loud. If you get partnered up, rehearse as many times as you need.

Isabella: Taking control of your audition.

> "If you are partnered with someone who only likes to rehearse once, don't hesitate to ask to do it as many times as you need until you feel confident with the material."

Aaron: I've heard this several times and it's so weird to me. I'll get paired up and we'll rehearse it once, and then I'll ask, "Can we do it again?" and my partner will say, "No, I just wanna keep it fresh." What does that mean? They're probably going to stumble. I tell my students to rehearse as much as they need to. If you are partnered with someone who only likes to rehearse once, don't hesitate to ask to do it as many times as you need until you feel confident with the material.

Isabella: I find as actors, because we have so little control over many parts of our careers, we don't speak up. We say, "OK, fine," instead of saying, "Actually, I would like to do it one more time." Maybe that's our Asian upbringing in a way too.

Aaron: That is one thing you can take control over. You're right. There are so many outside factors that you can't control. But what you can take control of is how prepared you are when you go in. That's the thing: any element that you can control, be the most prepared for those things, and the rest you shouldn't worry about.

Isabella: And in any sort of acting, but especially in commercials, lots of people have to say yes to you. First, casting picks you for the audition, and then you get a callback because either the director and/or the agency liked your audition. Then to book it, it's not just the director who decides but also the agency and the clients. That's why "avails" exist, or in New York City they call them "First refusals." They pick their top choice and back-ups to present for approval. And then one lucky person gets booked per role. And you can't control any of that. It could be that you remind them of their ex-girlfriend and they hate their ex-girlfriend . . . I've been an actor for a while and learning to take control of what I can control. I'm really owning that.

Aaron: After the audition, whatever happens, that's out of my hands. I used to obsess about that. "I could have made a different choice," or "He didn't look up once from his laptop." That's a lot of wasted energy.

Isabella: One thing I have learned is that you can't play to the back of the house. You have to play to the person right in front of you, and at this point, to someone watching an ad on his or her phone.

Aaron: Oh yeah, that's too big. Sometimes in my classes I have people who do a lot of theater and they're fantastic – they know how to project – but it's way too big for commercials.

Isabella: Commercials want "real" reactions and they want you to be who you are. I'm not and have never played the hot, skinny girl. And as much as people talk about Hollywood and looking a certain way, I'm a curvy woman, but I've worked, especially in commercials. I've made a living as an actor, at my weight. It's going into the room exactly who you are.

Aaron: That's the good thing about commercials. They are looking for people of all shapes, sizes, ethnicities, and backgrounds. Also, in a lot of breakdowns, you'll see the casting directors ask agents to "send only your very best improvisers." This misleads actors into thinking that they need a level of skill that would basically get them an audition for *Saturday Night Live*. You don't need the ability to do characters or impressions, or be on a good Harold [long-form improvisation] team, or be great at creating a story out of nothing. I've seen actors do that and it's like, "What the hell are you doing? Where did that horse come from?" Weird stuff that they think is going to be hilarious but has nothing to do with anything that is already established in the audition. What you need is a solid knowledge of and handle on the foundations of improv.

Isabella: It's making choices that are believable. Now how do you deal with – because I've been in this situation where they have you improv – where your scene partner just steamrolls you?

Aaron: You let them. You let them because more often than not they will crash and burn, and it basically shows how bad they are. And by how terrible they look, you're gonna look that much better. Just go with it. Not "*yes, and-ing*" it but like, "I'm on this train ride, here we go," and not try to stop it. Casting directors recognize when things are going wrong and who the culprit is.

Isabella: They are also freelancers and they're trying to do a good job to get their next job.

Aaron: And if you try and fix it, it's like, "Now, they're just arguing." Also, listen and follow directions. For example, the session director will say, "On 'Action,' you're going to go to the table, sit down, and pull out your phone." This is easy enough, but people don't listen, and they do it out of order or they forget. Then you just have to go with what they're presenting or it kind of kills the momentum of the scene when you try and correct it.

Isabella: And then the energy shifts too. Because, then, it's about you trying to correct the scene . . . not be in it. At the end of the day, they want to hire someone they want to work with, spend the day with, eat lunch with, be on set at 5 a.m. with.

Aaron: Right. You might not be the best actor, but if you listen, and you're friendly and approachable, then you'll always have a shot. The director, producers, and client are going to be on set for 8 to 10 hours with this person. Of course, you still need to deliver a great audition, but don't try to predict what you think casting wants from your performance. If it's a role of a pharmacist, don't try to portray what you think a pharmacist is supposed to act like. Or, don't do your best impression of a pharmacist who you know. It won't be a genuine performance, and the casting director or director or client will be able to see the "acting." Just be the best version of yourself.

Isabella: Things have also changed in the ad business in the last few years. I know I'm going out on fewer commercial auditions than I used to. Streaming services and apps have changed things. There's more non-union commercials and runaway production than before. They have to turn around more content and now they'll use influencers to advertise their product. Or they'll cast an actual architect to play the architect in the commercial, and not an actor.

Aaron: But the key is to never appear desperate.

Isabella: It's important to have a full life. Go on vacation, do hobbies, and have friends who are not in the business. Because if acting is all you have, it's too hard with all the rejection and having life things to pull from. I used to be like that and when I didn't get a big job I was so, so close to, I would get really bummed out and dwell on it. The last job I did, we had to pretend to be software developers at the auditions and I recently worked at a start-up, so I brought that knowledge to my audition. And those booking calls from your agents are the best.

Aaron: I used to hear "Commercial acting is easy. Anyone can do it." We know that not to be true. You really need to be a good actor. Good actors make it look easy. You have to know what you are doing. Sometimes you have 15 or 30 seconds to convincingly get across what you have to get across.

Isabella: I want to touch on social media. I never post anything until that spot has aired because you may be giving away information about the campaign. My friend in production says, "They don't like information leaked without them controlling it." My rule is to never share until it's publicly released with or without a non-disclosure agreement. Any last words of advice?

Aaron: You have to be here for the long term. You can't give yourself a set number of years, however long that is. You have to be ready to basically live your life because you never know when your break is going to come. I have many friends who go back to wherever they're from and it's sad to see that defeat, but it's like, "You didn't give that your all." If that's your passion, you have to trust that it's going to happen in its own time. It's not a destination, it's a journey, if that makes sense.

Isabella: It's not just about booking. Auditioning, classes, being on time, having reliable transportation, hustling, and all that, is your job. Also, know the business of your business. I go to the SAG-AFTRA site all the time to look up rates, usage rules, on-set rules, etc. Or I talk to other actors. I'm always learning about the business. That's your life as an actor, not just being on set.

Aaron: SAG-AFTRA, our union, is so important. Because they're protecting you. And yes, shooting is the fun part. You're in the trenches when you're auditioning. And you have to be thankful for auditioning. If you dread auditioning, you're in the wrong business.

Isabella: Totally. I think I want to wrap up by saying, even as a human being out in the world, be okay with who you are at this very moment. I once asked my commercial agent if I should cut my hair or lose weight and she said, "Do whatever, as long as you're comfortable with yourself." Change things you can and want to change about yourself and the stuff you can't change, that's what makes you uniquely you and that's a good thing. And I'm all for therapy and working on yourself if that's what you need. I mean, I still have days where I struggle with all of it, but overall, I beat myself up less and I like myself more.

Aaron: I think it translates to an unspoken confidence. It's like, "I'm comfortable in my own skin and this is who I am and this is what I do, and I hope you guys like it," and if they don't, that's fine, because next week there's going to be someone who does.

Isabella: I see many young actors get caught up in minute details like, "Should I button this top button? Should I put my hair behind my ears or in front?"

> "When I slate, my mantra in my mind is 'I'm happy to be here. I'm happy to be here.'"

Aaron: Yeah, minute details like that don't make a difference. And no matter what kind of day you're having, you should always go into the audition room happy and excited to be there. And thankful. The casting director is not going to care that you had to fight traffic or whatever. Once I get there and when I slate, my mantra in my mind is "I'm happy to be here. I'm happy to be here." Be as prepared as you can, and if you leave knowing you gave the best audition in that moment, then it was a good audition and that's all you can do.

Isabella: Yeah. Do that and then go live your life.

TAKING CHARGE AND CREATING YOUR OWN WORK

Self-Producing

▶ By Phil Kaufmann

Figure 4.3 Phil Kaufmann

Photo: Greg Crowder

Phil Kaufmann has been an actor, director, casting professional, and teacher working in New York and LA for more than 20 years.

His directing credits include the pilot presentation *Intelligence* and the Emmy-nominated short-form drama *Send Me*. His short films include *Living in Walter's World*, which was honored at the Filmmakers Alliance's Directors Guild of America Gala. In theater, he directed several shows while at the Yale School of Drama, including the second production (after the New York premiere) of John Patrick Shanley's seminal play *The Dreamer Examines His Pillow*. In New York he directed workshop productions with the award-winning Barrow Group Theatre Company and in LA he has directed and produced with the Echo Theater Company and Boston Court Pasadena.

His casting experience includes work as a commercial session runner, and session assistant work for several major television and film casting offices.

Phil (Figure 4.3) is a senior instructor in Acting for Film at the New York Film Academy, Los Angeles Campus.

Why Should I Self-Produce?

Rather than waiting for opportunities to come to you, you can create your own opportunities, for relatively little money, and with higher production values than ever before.

Acting is a collaborative art. Unlike a painter who can put brush to canvas in a room alone, as actors we usually need to work with others to create our work. Then our goal is to have the results be seen by an audience. Not long ago, this only happened through a fairly small list of venues: primarily film, television, and theater. An actor would wait for someone to create a show (whether a studio, a network, or an independent production company) and then audition for it. This can be a recipe for a lot of "not doing" and waiting for lighting to strike. While one could self-produce a low-budget project, it was often prohibitively expensive.

Now, in the new millennium, we have digital technology, which has made quality film production unbelievably inexpensive, truly within the reach of anyone! As a result, you can "Greenlight Yourself."[1]

The past few years have also seen an explosion of outlets through which actors can showcase their work: most significantly in "new media" (a catch-all term, but which the SAG-AFTRA contract describes as "the internet, mobile devices or any other exhibition platform now known or . . . hereafter may be devised" – that's pretty all-encompassing, right?). Right now, it includes YouTube, Instagram, Facebook, and others, but most of these new exhibition platforms didn't exist even 10 years ago, and companies come and go with such speed that who knows what will be popular 10 years from the time you read this? (Remember Myspace? Vine?) Suffice to say, there will continue to be more opportunities and outlets to show your work with each passing year.

How Do I Create My Own Material?

There's an old Chinese proverb that says, "The journey of a thousand miles begins with a single step." You start by starting! Begin by noticing what kind of material you enjoy watching. Are you a sci-fi fan? Horror? Do you watch only funny short videos online? What are you drawn to? Any self-produced project you initiate is going to take a lot of your time and energy, so be sure it is in a genre you are passionate about (ideally) or at least an area that interests you. Don't fall into the trap of choosing something because others are doing similar projects (and perhaps having success with them) and you think you should go along with the trend. Chart your own course. Once you have an idea of what kind of project you'd like to do, start jotting down ideas whenever you think of them. Brainstorm with friends and collect lots of ideas, then sit down and sort through them to see if they start to come together around a single story or group of ideas. Don't worry about everything being fully formed or perfect at first; it's okay if it's a little messy. It takes time for stories to evolve. Also, remember that while most stories have been told, they have not been told by you. Try for originality, but don't let the paralysis of perfectionism hold you back. I've seen well-worn story ideas be cleverly re-imagined into great short films by adding just a little twist. For example, I know of someone who created a series of funny short videos based on characters from one of her favorite television shows, but she re-imagined them in a group therapy setting. The videos got lots of views, and the project developed into a live action "fan-fiction" theater production as well as a successful parody musical. Note that she did not have the rights to the characters, and might have run into trouble from the television network, except that when the network and the show runners became aware of the production, they liked it and let it be! For them, it all worked out, but be careful.

So, Should I Write It Myself? Or Find Someone Else to Work With?

That depends on you. If you are a writer, or want to become one as part of this process, then go for it! Just recognize that writing has a separate skill set from acting, and requires practice and technique. You might want to find a writing coach – there are lots of them. With new technology, you can easily work with a coach who lives in a different city. If you are in a larger city such as New York or LA, you could join a writers' group, meeting on a regular basis to exchange ideas, feedback, and resources.

> "If you are not a writer, find one! You don't have to go it alone."

Choose carefully who you share your drafts and ideas with. Like bad acting teachers who focus on beating up aspiring actors (and in so doing keep them coming back for more lessons), there are bad writing coaches who will criticize your work without offering much in the way of constructive suggestions. Seek out mentors and advisors who are not only skilled in their craft, but also supportive and helpful in their feedback.

If you are not a writer, find one! You don't have to go it alone. If the goal of the project is to create something for yourself as an actor, why not find a talented collaborator who loves to write, and let them do their thing while you do yours. Ask friends or go online to find writers, especially those who are interested in the same kind of material as you (see above).

Once you decide to collaborate, it is a good idea to discuss in advance how each person will be credited, and who the resulting work will ultimately belong to. If the idea is originally yours, and you bring it to a writer to flesh it out, there are basic "work-for-hire" legal documents you can find online, and you could do a deal for "one dollar" and a shared "story by" credit. If an idea is truly developed together, maybe everything will be credited and owned 50–50. If it gets more complicated, don't hesitate to talk to an attorney specializing in entertainment or intellectual property law. Many of them have very reasonable rates for a single consultation. In any case, have these conversations even if you are good friends with your collaborators, and trust each other completely! Friendships have been lost because of self-produced projects that became successful, when some contributors felt they were cut out or left behind.

Should It Be a Short? A Feature? A Web Series? Funny Scenes for YouTube? Scenes for My Reel? How Long Should It Be?

Again, ask yourself what really excites you and makes you wake up in the morning wanting to get to work. Then, think about where it would show best. If you write a script for a film, and it starts to get to 20 or 30 pages, you are well on your way to feature length – and maybe your story wants to be that. Keep writing.

For short films, shorter is better. Your chances of getting into festivals (if you go that route) are much better with a film that runs under 10 minutes. For festivals, these are easier to schedule in a block with other shorts, or as an accompanying film to a feature. If your "short" film is 25 minutes long, it will be harder to program, and might get into far fewer festivals.

If your story feels like it can best be told as a series of short films (say five to eight minutes each) all on a common theme, or building a story episode-by-episode, then it sounds like you have a good candidate for a web series.

Any of the above can be good for your actor reel, but if you are only looking to create material for that purpose, then perhaps you want to just focus on doing just that. There are companies in LA (and probably in other major cities) that will help you produce "shoot to suit" scenes, providing writers, directors, and crew (for a price). A short scene (under two minutes) can be shot in an after-noon, with excellent production values. These can be useful whether you are at the beginning of your career and creating your first reel or you are farther along but looking to fill in a gap in your existing reel, showing a different side of your acting abilities.

How Much Should I Spend?

The gambler's rule of "only bet what you can afford to lose" is a good one. Don't spend beyond what you can comfortably part with. That said, you don't have to spend a lot to get a good result. Good writing and acting is far more important than whether you rent the latest expensive camera. You do need to spend *something*, however. Even if your crew is only a few people, they still need to eat and drink good coffee. There are consumables on any shoot: gaffer tape, colored gel for the lights, an external hard drive to store footage, etc. *Very important: you will need to pay your sound person.* This is not optional. Beware of the sound person who will do your project for free. They probably don't have the skills and equipment to do it right, and if your production sound is no good, it is nearly impossible to fix later. You are in big trouble and all your other work may be wasted. Beyond that, you might need to rent some lighting equipment, depending on your specific project, and post-production has some expenses. Just as you may have collaborated with a writer, you might consider finding an aspiring low-budget producer to work with. Many film schools have producing programs that turn out graduates each year, who might be looking for a fun, low-budget project to work on as they build their resumés. Producers are skilled at making things happen on a budget, finding great deals, and taking care of paperwork. If you are not good at (or not interested in) these things, find a collaborator who is.

Should I Do This through SAG-AFTRA?

SAG-AFTRA is the guild of professional actors in the US. If you are a SAG-AFTRA member, you can't work on any non-union project. (You knew that one, right? It's called Global Rule 1.) If you want to use any SAG-AFTRA members in your cast (even if you are not in the union) you need to register your project and produce it through one of the appropriate low-budget contracts. This may not cost you much, if anything, or there might be a moderate expense. As of this writing, you might choose a Short Film contract or New Media contract, and defer pay (meaning you promise to pay later, if your project ever makes money). These contracts change from time to time, so do your research as to the current possibilities and the requirements and benefits of each. SAG-AFTRA can be very helpful in making this easy for you, and there is a lot of information on its website. It has representatives whose job is to make the process as easy as possible for a first-time filmmaker.

By going SAG-AFTRA, you will open up your casting to a huge talent pool of skilled professionals. You may not need to do this, and your project might be fine with non-union talent, but if you want to work with SAG-AFTRA actors, or to become one yourself, I encourage you to investigate and consider doing the paperwork and working with the guild.

Do I Need a Director? Where Do I Find One?

Yes, you need a director. Sure, you can find successful examples of actors directing themselves, but why give yourself an extra handicap? You are already the producer and the lead actor (you did cast yourself as the lead, right?). You will benefit from an outside eye to watch your work and give you feedback.

> "In a director, you are looking for someone you trust and work well with."

Also, a film set needs a director to captain the ship. How would the USS *Enterprise* run without James T. Kirk? Beyond saying "Action" and "Cut," the director serves as the person at the top of the hierarchy who makes final decisions. Regardless of the size of the production, a film set needs this command structure to be efficient. Filmmaking is a collaborative art, sure, but there's an old saying that you don't want "too many cooks in the kitchen." If every creative decision has to be made by committee, your shoot will be long and frustrating.

In a director, you are looking for someone you trust and work well with. They might be a fellow actor, or a trained, experienced director. If you don't have someone in mind, ask your circle of friends – get their recommendations. Perhaps look at some web series or shorts you like (and have the tone you want), then google them or see if IMDbPro.com has more info on who produced and directed.

You can also check out film schools in your area. If you are near a major city there might be several. Current students will probably be busy with their own projects, but how about recent graduates? Ask the alumni office for referrals, or for guidance where you might post a notice online or at the school. If there are no film schools in your area, a local college might have a Film Studies department.

And, of course, there are large online resources for all crew and creative positions. Mandy.com and Stage32.com are two current examples.

Where Do I Get a Crew?

From the same resources for finding a director described above. In addition, if you find an experienced director, they will likely come with a list of referrals for other crew: a director of photography they have worked with, assistant directors, lighting technicians, editors, sound people, etc.

What's in It for Them?

As you assemble your production team, think about what you can offer other than money (since you are on a budget). Specifically, can you give someone a job on your production that will be a promotion for them? Someone who has only been a make-up assistant on other short films could be your "make-up department head." Someone who has been a set decorator (an assistant-level position) could be your "production designer" (the department head). This helps your crew build their resumés. This principle works wonders. By making sure that everyone has "something in it for them," you create a team that will work harder, be more cheerful, and put up with long hours.

One other piece of advice about crew: if someone is openly unhappy, or a major complainer, they can be toxic to an entire crew. If possible, gently but firmly get rid of them as soon as you can. It doesn't have to be a big drama to say to someone, "Thanks, but we're all set in your department, and won't be needing you tomorrow." If they are in an essential position, you may have to make sure you have a replacement before you do this.

> "Toxic people can spread their bad attitude to a whole crew. Be on the lookout."

This sometimes happens if you bring on people you don't know (referred by a friend, or the like) and they don't have a sense of "something in it for them" (or possibly how modest your budget is). Once they arrive on set, they act out as a way of expressing that the project is "beneath" them. Don't put up with it. Toxic people can spread their bad attitude to a whole crew. Be on the lookout.

Are There Any Pitfalls to Avoid?

I've mentioned some things along the way (remember: always pay your sound person!) but the main piece of advice I have is: go for it. You will learn by doing, and you will make mistakes, as we all do. Don't let it stop you, and don't wait for others to give you permission to express yourself. Keep creating stories and sharing your work and your unique voice. As Dr. Seuss says, "Today you are You, that is truer than true. There is no one alive who is Youer than You."[2]

Useful Websites

- Filmmakers Alliance (LA-based filmmaking collective): www.filmmakersalliance.org.
- No Budget Film School (website with resources and excellent weekend workshops on how to produce on a micro-budget): www.nobudgetfilmschool.com.
- SAG-AFTRA (the guild of professional actors in the US; look for the "Production Center" area of the website for Short Film, New Media and Student Film contracts): www.sagaftra.org.
- SAGINDIE (the SAG-AFTRA website specifically aimed at independent filmmakers): www.sagindie.org.
- The Streamy Awards (the Awards for New Media – see what others have done and be inspired!): www.streamys.org.

REALITY! FROM HER LITTLE HARRY POTTER STUDIO BELOW HER BASEMENT STAIRS

Get a Life!

▶ By Marsha Mercant

Marsha Mercant is a multi-award-winning actor/singer/voice-over artist who has performed internationally on stage as well as in film and television. Her many stage credits include the first national companies of *Cats*, *Les Misérables*, and *Lady in the* Dark, in which she starred in both San Francisco and Beijing, China. She can be heard on the original cast recordings of *Mountain Days* (Craig Bohmler/ Mary Bracken Phillips) and *Dawgs* (Sherman Brothers).

Figure 4.4 Marsha Mercant
Photo: Stockwell Photography

Marsha is currently the voice guiding customers through the voicemail maze for such companies as Spectrum, Aetna Health, HSBC Bank, PSEG New Jersey and Long Island, Hertz, Thrifty, and Citibank International, and is the official voice of New York City's information line, 311.

Turning her creative passion to writing, Marsha (Figure 4.4) was co-editor of and contributor to the Amazon #1 bestseller *Fearless Women: Visions of a New World* (Fearless Women, 2012), and co-writer of *The Gift of Cancer: A Miraculous Journey to Healing* (Skyhorse, 2014). Marsha's play *When You Get There* has had workshops in New York and LA and is currently considering various production options. Her play *Exit Plan* was produced last year in New York and has been optioned as an operetta and a short film.

A funny thing happened to me on the way to being a movie star. Reality. Yeah, I'm not crazy about it either, but it seems to be an inevitable component of living. So what's an up-and-coming mega-celebrity supposed to do? How do you survive in this business until you can actually survive in this business?

The reality of trying to make a living in show business can be daunting. We've become a celebrity-obsessed society. And too often a young, or even not so young, actor's focus is on the brass ring without an understanding of how to maintain a place on the merry-go-round. I'm not talking about settling for less than your goals. I'm talking about getting real about what it takes to have a financially viable career in the arts.

As you embark on this vocation, you'll undoubtedly hear much unsolicited input about having a fallback position, a Plan B, a soft place to land should your lofty ambitions not be rewarded. You know what I say to that? Phooey! A big ol' *phooey*!

Now, that's not to encourage pie-in-the-sky unrealistic goals.

If your business plan is, (a) move to Hollywood (or New York), (b) get an agent, (c) book a pilot that (d) goes to series and that (e) lasts for 10 years and (f) morphs into a directing career, resulting in (g) being honored with a lifetime achievement award from SAG-AFTRA, and (h) moving to your own private island in the Pacific, that's great. But is it real? Is it viable? Do you have the tools to execute this plan?

There is nothing wrong with getting an education at an institute of higher learning, and if that works for you, it's a fantastic choice. But it's not the only choice. Success in show business is not a one-size-fits-all affair. There are as many career paths as there are actors. I was always careful to explain to my students that if they were embarking on an acting career because of the prize at the end, they should consider some other line of work. This path is not linear and, make no mistake, the path *is* the prize. Being open to where that path may take you is one of the great gifts of a career in the arts.

Unlike studying to be an accountant, a scientist, or a lawyer, where a fairly clear-cut map to success has been forged for you, a life in the arts comes with not only no guarantees but also no assured plan of action for getting you there, wherever your *there* happens to be.

My own path has been and continues to be circuitous, at best. Looking up synonyms for *circuitous* I find *roundabout, indirect, twisty, meandering, winding, tortuous, oblique*. I'd say that covers it! When I look back on the winding road that is my career, what I see is that I could not possibly have known where it would take me.

My first move from my Northern California home was to Southern California. Now, being that I was a musical theater actor trained in all the requisite disciplines – acting, singing, and dancing, the logical place for me to go would have been New York. But what I knew about myself at the tender age of 19 was that I did not have the emotional fortitude to go that far from home. I'm sure that a mentor, if I'd had one, would have recommended my going east but even if she had, and I had gone, I don't believe the results would have been productive.

So, after having saved $1,200, figuring it would last me a year, I moved to LA. Yes, my financial planning was a bit askew, but armed with abundant amounts of excitement and naiveté I forged ahead.

I share this with you not to lose all credibility, but to illustrate that while we are working to have a career in the arts, we are simultaneously having a life. And that life and who you are, the very essence of why you were put on this earth, all conspire to create your unique footprint as a teller of tales, an illustrator of stories, a conduit to feelings and experiences that only your unique perspective can convey.

Once I decided to make my living in the arts, I pretty much made my living in the arts. I did have a few temp jobs, but I never got roped into anything that would take my focus away from my dream of performing. If the arts are really what you want, don't get embroiled in a job that takes all your time and energy and has no flexibility to go on auditions. No auditions = no work!

Focus your time and energy on developing your unique skill set. When I moved to LA, I didn't know anyone. I had no idea what I was doing. I did not have a plan. Mind you, I am not recommending that. It's called show *business*; your career is a business. And to succeed in business you need to be organized, focused, aware of opportunities, and honest about developing and expanding your abilities to make yourself as marketable as possible. In addition, you are the product, and as such, you must also serve as your own advertising agency and your own public relations firm.

What I knew about myself when I first hit LA was that I could sing. It was the skill I felt most confident about so I did it wherever I could. There were abundant opportunities in the form of showcases around LA and I sang at them all! None of the showcases paid, but they did offer exposure and that is the new actor's Holy Grail!

Doing one of those showcases led to my getting a job with a band. Not my ultimate goal, but that band, playing in a little club in Big Bear Mountain, led to my meeting a manager who was just getting his business off the ground. Signing with him led me to my first television role, a guest star on *Hawaii Five-0*.

Now, here's where I didn't mind my business.

My next step was to get an agent. I was feeling pretty cocky, having scored a guest star on my first television outing, and I didn't make the best decision considering where I was in my career. I went with an agency that was too large for me. They were pretty and sparkly but what I needed was a small boutique agency that would nurture and develop my relationships. I don't believe there are any mistakes so I have no regrets, but had I been clear on my business plan, things might have turned out very different.

Fast forward one failed marriage and a half-dozen co-star roles later and I returned to my roots: musical theater. I truly loved singing and dancing and what better place to entertain than a place that is in the business of entertaining: Disney World. I booked a new Broadway review and moved east . . . well, southeast . . . for a six-month contract. Two years later, I returned to LA.

One piece of business I was always careful to mind was my finances. This business can often be a feast-or-famine affair and I was always mindful to save for the famine periods. It's one of the strategies that kept me out of having to take on jobs I didn't want to do. I also fell into three pensions. I say *fell into* because when you're in your twenties you rarely think about retirement. But I can't tell you how grateful I am now to know that I will have a steady stream of income from Actors Equity, SAG, and AFTRA. Something you might want to put in your business plan.

Upon returning home, I worked a lot of gigs performing at corporate events all over the US. They were great gigs that paid well and were a lot of fun to do. Plus, any time you spend on stage helps keep your instruments in shape. Like any discipline, if you're not using it, you're losing it. And the more skills you have, the greater possibility to be employed in your chosen field.

Not long after returning from Disney, I went on an open call for *Cats*, which was going to be playing at the Shubert Theatre in Century City. A beautiful venue that sadly is no longer. Seven callbacks later, I was cast as Jennyanydots, the Gumbie Cat.

After a two-year run, more live shows followed, and not too long after *Cats* closed, *Les Misérables* came to town. Having been cast by the same New York casting office for *Cats*, I was invited to callbacks for *Les Miz* and did not have to go through the audition process. That presented a real good news/bad news scenario.

The good news: no endless auditions. The bad news: no endless auditions. I had one shot to get this job; one five- to 10-minute slot to convince the creative staff I was their gal. To make the most of it, I hired a director and a musical arranger to help me pick just the right song and coach me on creating the character I would be auditioning for.

It was the best money I ever spent! In an ironic twist, they didn't want to hear the song I had prepared, but because I had spent so much time creating the character, it didn't really matter which song I sang. I brought that character to the songs I did sing. That is an example of minding your *business* so you can do the *show*!

After a year in *Les Miz*, I left the show to work on another production at LATC [the Los Angeles Theatre Center]. After that, there was a shift happening in my life. You know, the life thing we talked about earlier?

My then boyfriend, now husband, and I decided to leave LA and move up the California coast, certain we were both done with show business. We came to find out show business was not done with us. After a couple years kicking back trying to decide what was next, we decided to move to San Francisco and were immediately sucked back into *the biz*. Thus began a new exploration of the myriad ways an actor can make a living in smaller markets.

The business in the Bay Area is a totally different animal than in the other markets we'd each lived in, and though my husband had tremendous success, immediately booking a movie and a national commercial, he didn't care for the type of work that was predominant in the area, which was a lot of industrial film, theater, live spokesperson, and voice-over.

For me, it was nirvana! I loved the hosting aspect of training films and live convention shows. And the Bay Area is where I was able to break into voice-over, which is a huge part of what I do now. Breaking into a field that can be difficult to get into in a large market was much more accessible in a smaller one. I did a lot of national work as well as training/informational videos and local news promos. It was a fantastic entrée into the world of voice-over that served me tremendously going forward. It was a great skill to add to my arsenal that continues to keep me from having to work at McDonald's!

I also did some of the most rewarding theater work of my career; one original piece even resulted in a cast recording. While my husband was not interested in the work available there, what he had been dreaming of was building an acting school whose emphasis would be on film and television. I'm proud to say we built the premier studio in the Bay Area for film and television training and ran that school for 11 years.

Also, between *Cats* and *Les Miz*, I started teaching acting with a focus on cold reading and auditions. I loved teaching, and again, it kept my skills in shape while providing some income that was still related to my field. Running our school in San Francisco was a very special period of our lives, a time I hold very dear.

> ## "I got everything I was seeking and nothing I expected."

After 13 years in the Bay Area another shift was rumbling. We had loved the school but were ready for a new challenge. I finally felt I had the emotional fortitude to move to New York, so we grabbed our dog, our clothes, and our dreams and went east.

What I like to say about this latest chapter in my show business life is that I got everything I was seeking and nothing I expected. I came to New York to realize my dream of being on Broadway. I've worked in venues worldwide but hadn't broken through to a Broadway stage. I saw it as the ultimate realization of my childhood dreams.

When we got to New York I hit the ground running. The creative energy that permeates the city was my catnip. I loved everything about it. I did workshops of several original shows, had a 14-month gig in an Off-Broadway show, and lots of positive feedback and callbacks on my auditions for Broadway.

But dreams change and life happens in mysterious ways that can take us down unexpected roads. Mine came in the form of losing my best friend to cancer.

Her loss changed my trajectory, as performing lost its luster. What got my creative juices flowing was writing. I wrote originally to ease my pain; to have somewhere to put my profound grief. But soon I realized that this was a calling my soul was reaching out for.

I now have two books published and a play produced in New York with several others in the works, and know that this is my next creative expression. In the meantime, while I build up to actually producing income from my writing, I do voice-over from my little Harry Potter studio below my basement stairs.

It's that living-a-life thing we talked about earlier. It happens. You can't stop it. But you can listen to the still small voice that leads you to your best life. Even if that life is nothing you expected.

This business is not easy. It's not supposed to be. If it were, everybody would be doing it. So, while there'll always be the fable of the starlet discovered at the soda fountain or today's equivalent, the YouTube sensation gone viral, the rest of us have to work for it. Just remember that while you're out there trying to build a career, you don't forget to have a life.

DEAF ACTORS NEED TO BE HEARD

▶ A Conversation with Suanne Spoke and Shoshannah Stern

Figure 4.5 Suanne Spoke

Photo: K. C. Marsh

Suanne Spoke has an extensive career in theater, television, and film, appearing in the critically acclaimed film *Whiplash* and starring in the feature film *Wild Prairie Rose*, winning multiple awards on the festival circuit. On television, Suanne recurred on *Switched at Birth* and *Famous in Love* and has guest-starred on many others. She can currently be seen recurring on *General Hospital*.

She has performed at numerous theaters and has won every major acting and producing award in LA, including being a three-time recipient of the Ovation Award/Lead Performance by an Actress. She was most recently seen in the Workshop World premiere of Wendy Graf's *Exit Wounds*, at the Grove Theatre. For her performance, Suanne won Best Actress 2019 from TicketholdersLA; the play was the Gold Medallion Winner of the Moss Hart/Kitty Carlisle New Play Initiative.

Suanne (Figure 4.5) serves on the faculty at the California Institute of the Arts, teaching acting in the Graduate Film Directing program.

Shoshannah Stern represents the fourth generation of a deaf family. She started off in the theater, winning numerous awards for her work onstage at Gallaudet University. She appeared as the leads in *Open Window* and *Children of a Lesser God* with Deaf West Theatre. Shoshannah was the female lead in both *Adventures of Power* opposite Adrian Grenier and Jane Lynch and the festival favorite indie *The Hammer.* However, Shoshannah (Figure 4.6) is probably best known for her recurring and regular work on television, including *Weeds, Jericho, Lie to Me, Another Period,* and *Supernatural.* She is also the creator, writer, executive producer, and star of *This Close* on Sundance TV and AMC's premiere streaming service Sundance Now. It happens to be the very first show written and created by deaf people, and is based on *The Chances,* the web series she created with her

Figure 4.6 Shoshannah Stern

writing partner Josh Feldman that premiered at the Sundance Film Festival. She lives in LA with her husband and daughter.

Suanne Spoke: I don't remember exactly where we first met, but it was most certainly at Deaf West Theatre. And my most heartfelt congratulations on *This Close.* I got to see two of the episodes up at Sundance, watched the rest upon my return home . . . and thought it was just wonderful.

Shoshannah Stern: Well, I remember where we met! I was maybe 19, if that. I had applied for, and somehow gotten into, the pilot program of Deaf West's first ever professional summer school session. Apart from doing as much theater as I possibly could in school and at Gallaudet University (I think I was in my second year at the time), this was the first "real" experience with acting I'd ever had. The way they did it was they had half of the class be actors from LA and half of the class be young babies like me who didn't know what they were doing. They would pair us up for the month with a more experienced actor and so we'd work together on pieces we were assigned. I'm ashamed to say that I don't remember who my partner was. But I do remember that Suanne was one of our teachers there. I remember her talking about a monologue from *Streetcar* [*A Streetcar Named Desire*] and me just hanging on her every word and move. And then years later when we made *This Close,* Andrew, our director, and I were talking and we found out Suanne had taught him too!

Suanne: I first had an opportunity to do a production of *Talking With* years ago and the woman who was directing was an interpreter. She asked me if I would be willing to "sim com" [simultaneous communication – speaking and signing] one of the monologues and I jumped at the chance. I had always loved the beauty of the language and wanted to know more about it. I then served on the board of directors with Deaf West to help with fundraisers. Artistic Director Ed Waterstreet asked me to do Blanche in *A Streetcar Named Desire* and that production opened their new permanent theater in 2000. My involvement and advocacy has lasted ever since, up to and including teaching acting at Deaf West Summer School, guest-starring on *Switched at Birth*, and most recently working with Troy Kotsur (Stanley in *Streetcar*) in *Wild Prairie Rose*.

Shoshannah: Troy was one of my very first role models growing up. I remember me begging my mom to take me to see him onstage in a play in Sacramento. It was quite a drive, but I'm blessed to have my mom. She was always committed to doing incredible things like that for me. And so she drove me to Sacramento to see the play, and I met Troy afterward and he talked with a little 15-year-old me about wanting to be an actor. He doesn't remember, of course, but it was like a dream come true for me. She also drove me to LA regularly so I could see Deaf West plays, and she picked me up and dropped me off for summer school. Without her, it's not even about where I am today, but who I am. I wouldn't be who I am without my mom. She was an actor herself. She played the first role onstage that was written by, and for the deaf: Alice in *Sign Me Alice*. So she's in all the history books and that still makes me proud to this day.

Suanne: Now, Shoshannah, having just co-written a short and producing theater for myself, my first question is what was the precipitating idea that led you (and Josh) to create *This Close*? When was that moment when you trusted yourself to tell your own story?

Shoshannah: There wasn't one moment. It was more a series of, maybe not moments, but events, which led up to that. I had always been interested in writing, and I've written all my life, but I always felt like it would be presumptuous of me to try to call myself a writer, especially in this town when there's so much talent out there already. So I was writing screenplays, but I was very much in the closet as a writer and I didn't really talk about it. Then I met Josh Feldman, who's my writing partner now, through mutual friends. He's deaf too, and he was out here trying to get in the door as a screenwriter. We very quickly became friends and I just opened up to him, also very quickly. I always say I came out as a writer to him. We started talking regularly about our respective work, reading each other's stuff and giving each other notes. He'd say, "Hey, let's meet up at a coffee shop and just write separately together." So he really forced me to make time to write. That was always a hard thing for me to do, so I really have him to thank for making me do that. Then one day I had this audition from hell, just really soul-crushing stuff. I met him after for a hike and I was venting about it and he just said, "Well, why don't we write something together for you?" The idea had never occurred to me, but it was so simple and, of course, he was right. What was I supposed to do for the rest of my life? Wait for someone to some-how read my mind and write something that I felt was right for me? Or maybe I could just write something that I felt was right and quit bitching about it. The first thing we wrote wasn't *This Close*; that was maybe the second or the third thing we did together. Then, when we did come up with it, it went through sev-eral iterations. The first version was called *Fridays*, and we had originally pitched that, and written it, as a story about a friendship between a deaf woman and her hearing best friend who was gay. Looking back, I think Michael was writ-ten that way because we were just so conditioned to seeing deaf people paired with hearing people. But anyway, we came very close (*this* close!) to getting that version off the ground, but ultimately they came back to us and said, "Hey, we love the idea, but we just don't understand why the character of Kate is deaf, so we're going to pass." Well, thank goodness they passed, because when that didn't happen we were devastated of course, but because of that we went to "happy hour" to drown our sorrows and got to talking. We realized we didn't know how to answer that question. Why was Kate deaf? I don't know. Why is anyone deaf? Why am I a woman? Why are you a man? Why do I have brown hair and brown eyes? And then we quickly realized that instead of trying to tell people why, we had to show them why. And to show them, we needed to just do the thing ourselves and put it on YouTube. Then, that led to me thinking, "*Well, if we're really going to do it ourselves then why don't we just go balls to the wall and make both characters deaf?*" I knew I'd never seen that before – two deaf leads together – and I knew that if we didn't do it, who would? I remember Josh staring at me like, "Wow, that's a great idea." Then he went, "But who's gonna play Michael?" And I just looked at him. So in the end, he forced me to be a writer and I forced him to act.

Suanne: What obstacles have you faced and what have you done to overcome or bypass them, or simply break them down?

Shoshannah: There's a scene in *This Close* where there's a disability panel, and that scene to me is really about perception. In this scene, we cast different disabled actors to play, basically, versions of themselves, and one of them was a Push Girl from the show *Push Girls*, Angela Rockwood. She got into a car accident in her twenties and became paralyzed as a result. Her experience is far different than the one I'm living, because this thing happened to her. Her life changed overnight. She can and does compare what it was like for her, before this defining event and after, and she answers questions like this beautifully. She actually does in that scene. Her dialogue was written for her and with her, based on her experience.

> "There are stages in my life and they have their own colors. Some of them are brighter, some of them are darker, but in the end they blend together and become a part of the finished portrait."

But for me, questions like that are always so difficult to answer. It's one that I get a lot. I never know how to respond. I'll tell you why. I was born this way. Everything that I am now, I've been my whole life. Being deaf is a part of me. And when I think of obstacles, I always see a literal obstacle course in my mind, like hay bales and hurdles and mud pits. The narrative that requires is like, "Okay, you're going to struggle to get over them for a little bit and then, *boom*, you're up and over and through. You've overcome it and you're done, you leave it all behind and you run in slow motion to the finish line and everybody is cheering." But in reality, what's the obstacle? Not having the sense of hearing, at least in the way that other people do? That's always going to be there. And where's the finish line in life? When you die? Or maybe there just really isn't one, or there hasn't been one in my experience. My experience is more that there are stages in my life and they have their own colors. Some of them are brighter, some of them are darker, but in the end they blend together and become a part of the finished portrait. And when that one picture is done, then you hopefully move on to the next thing you're doing. That's my biggest challenge maybe, always hoping that there will be something to move on to.

Suanne: Do you have any suggestions to help show runners and casting people widen their casting concepts to include *all* actors? And do you find yourself thinking outside the casting box when you are creating work, as you are writing the new season of *This Close*?

Shoshannah: I know that casting is a creative process, and it's one that is underappreciated and not recognized enough. Most of the jobs I've been lucky enough to book in my life have come from casting directors who have taken a chance on me and said, "Hey, why don't we try and see what she can do with this?" It's the most exhilarating thing reading for characters who aren't written as deaf. And while it's obviously been rewarding and exciting for me on my end, I also get to talk about that through things like this. The casting directors don't always get that chance. But I know in my conversations with them that it's been really fun and satisfying for them too (or so they've said!). But it can't be easy for them.

For me, getting in the room is already a challenge, but then I leave, and if they like what I've done, they have to convince so many people above them to try to take a chance on me too. There's always pushback at first. And so for everyone who has taken a chance and gotten me in the room and then, on the few occasions an actual role has materialized out of that, I know that's been hours and hours of conversation and really pushing hard on their end, and I'm just so unbelievably grateful for that.

> **"I believe that thinking outside the box is good for everyone and anyone."**

I believe that thinking outside the box is good for everyone and anyone. When you think about what a box is, it's four walls holding something in a restrictive space. It's placing limitations on what the thing inside can be. I think restrictions make your job, any job, harder. When we write for *This Close* we're really inspired by people we know in our lives and then we write around them because we know it's incredibly difficult to cast actors based on an idea and not in reality. Sometimes it feels as if I'm being put in a box already, and then sometimes characters who are written for the box that I'm in force me in an even smaller box, and I feel like I'm flattened up against the glass with my face all smooshed. Sometimes specific is good, but sometimes to specify a character past a certain degree makes it almost impossible for everyone involved. Like with the disability panel, we reached out to real people and then we wrote characters for everyone around that specific actor because we were inspired by their realities. With all the other characters we asked, apart from one character I'll get into later, we also didn't ask for specific ethnicities for any character; we just were drawn to their work. The role of Paul and Courtney #1 and #2 in Episode 4, *The Way We Were*, are instances of that. We had a loose vision of what that character was going to look like, but then we fell in love with the essence that one of the actors in that mix had. We wanted to work with that actor so much that they changed everyone's perception of that dynamic. In the end they made that specific bit better than what we had on the page. But at the same time, representation is important to us. We are learning about the specific experience that deaf people of color have and recognizing the lack of representation they have. Because of that, we specifically required that the fan in the first episode was a person of color. We're still learning, and we're still growing and changing. We're understanding that the process is a lot more difficult than people may realize, but then it always is. If there's one suggestion I have, it's just: use your imagination. Being creative is really exciting. I want to encourage show runners and casting people and directors to just say to the box, "You know what box? Fuck off. Just leave. Go away. We don't need you."

Suanne: Explain what needs to happen in a rehearsal, or on set, that is any different when casting a person who signs. Having spoken with my friend/former student Andrew Ahn, who was your director on the first season of *This Close*, it was clearly an awakening for him and such a creative opportunity to work with deaf, hard-of-hearing, and hearing actors combined. It forced him to expand his visual language.

Shoshannah: I honestly don't know. I've never not been a deaf actor or not been a person who doesn't sign. I don't think it's that different. Andrew and I connected right away because his family also speaks a minority language, and so he understood immediately what that experience was like. I remember me trying to explain to an executive that it was going to be harder than they thought finding actors who really sign as opposed to seeming like they sign. They weren't really getting it, and then Andrew stepped in and said, "You know what? She's right. I remember trying to cast actors who spoke Korean for my film, and casting directors said, 'Hey, we have this great person and they speak Korean fluently,' and then when I saw them they could barely speak any of it authentically." And I was just like, "Yes, yes, that's exactly it." Beyond that, as a person, he was just really open and we were able to create our own rhythm. We talked about a lot of things, not even professionally, but just about everyday things. We asked each other a lot of questions and listened to each other, and so I feel like the rapport and level of mutual respect we were able to develop was really just incredible. I think that's an incredibly important dynamic for any director to have with their actor. There has to be a level of trust so it feels like a collaboration and not a preconceived thing they think they need to have. I've worked with some directors who have just dictated how the process needs to be, and I've thought, "Wow, they really don't like deaf people." And then later in time, I find out that other actors on the same set who weren't deaf and didn't sign had the same experience. So I'd like to think, and I think Andrew would agree, that it really doesn't have a whole lot to do with working with actors who use sign language or if they hear or not. If you're a good director, you're going to hopefully understand how to give an actor what they need because all actors have different processes and needs, whether they're deaf or not. And if you think you can dictate things and things have to be a specific way, that probably won't work out well for anyone.

Suanne: Are there any television shows, films, that have gotten it right? Working on *Switched at Birth*, I found their storylines reflecting the issues faced by the deaf community and yet encompassing what all families face.

Shoshannah: As with all things, there have been some great characters and storylines, which is great. There have been some not-so-good ones, and that's okay too. I've always said that just one narrative isn't enough to encompass an entire minority. In any minority, there's a spectrum, and that spectrum is widely varied. Even with the best television shows and films of all time, you're going to have people who love it and you're going to have people who don't. Liking something isn't necessarily the same thing as wrong or right. Just because you don't like a movie doesn't mean it's bad. I think my issues with the stories I personally don't connect with have everything to do with the lens that story is told through. I think, as women, there are some female characters who we see on the page or on screen and we sense immediately that they've been written by a male. It's the same for stories about my community. They're often told for an audience of people that isn't deaf and by a person who isn't deaf themselves, and so their lens is wildly different from mine. It can be disorienting trying to audition for characters written as deaf and then trying to figure out exactly how the person who wrote it thinks being deaf is like as opposed to how it really is for me.

Suanne: And lastly, Shoshannah, Guillermo Del Toro recently said, "What Latin artists need to make their creative mark in the world: roots and a passport." What do you think deaf artists need?

Shoshannah: They need to be heard. Pun intended. There seems to be a really great burst of interest in deaf characters on screen and on stage, but having deaf people behind the screen as creative partners and collaborators is so important too. Listen to what they say, and trust them.

ACTOR. ENTERTAINER. CROSSDRESSER. AUTHOR. SOCIAL MEDIA SENSATION

▶ A Q&A with Willam Belli

Figure 4.7 Willam Belli

Photo: Mathu Anderson

After being disqualified from a cross-dresser game show (*RuPaul's Drag Race*), Willam found success as a whorespondent anchoring shows for MTV, Logo, and AOL while appearing as an American Apparel Ad girl, Sephora model for OCC Makeup, and Magnum Ice Cream lady in a Cannes Golden Lion-winning commercial. He's performed shits and hits like "Boy Is A Bottom" from his #1 Billboard charting comedy album on six continents, spent a few nights in jail, and enjoys writing in the third person while rewatching old episodes of *Nip/Tuck* he was on. His first book, *Suck Less: Where There's a Willam, There's a Way* (Grand Central, 2016), missed the *New York Times* list by less than 100 copies, so just go shoplift it or something. IDGAF. You might have also seen Willam on YouTube because, who knows, maybe you're one of the 200,000,000 views? Willam can be found on Twitter, Instagram, and Facebook (@willam), and more recently in *The Kominsky Method*, *Difficult People*, and *A Star Is Born* opposite Lady Gaga.

You wear so many hats: a social media star, entertainer, author, actor . . . How do you have time for all of them and how do your prioritize which hat you are wearing, and when?

I make a lots of lists and have two wipe boards and keep a physical calendar on my wall. I've been doing it long enough to know that if I'm gonna be on the road for a while, I better have a backlog of videos ready to go beforehand because I won't have time to film them while touring. Writing, for me, was too laborious a task to sit down and actually focus, so I did a lot of voice notes and transcription to keep my voice. It's hard to prioritize any of them because I feel like everything I do kinda builds toward one greater goal of having a career in entertainment in general.

Can you talk about your book Suck Less ? Did you approach your publishers, or they you?
An editor found me amusing on Tumblr, when I would answer random people's asks in a public forum. She pitched me to the Grand Central Publishing people and I came into a boardroom for a meeting in a Versace fur and a vintage Moschino big-business type of lady suit and I killed it in the room. It was helpful that there were straight men in the room and it forced me to explain drag slang, which led me to talking about the dictionary in the book and a lot of other things that just about anyone can learn from a drag queen. They loved my "how to get out of a DUI" and "covering a cold sore" make-up tutorial. I guess some of the public did too because the original print was 15,000 copies and the current print count is now 31,000. For a first-time author, I'm told those numbers are bonkers good, so I'm happy.

> "I make sure to tweet and Facebook each day at least once a day for whatever I'm working on or about to release."

How much time a day do you spend on social media?
The first thing I do most mornings is get on the elliptical machine for a solid 30 minutes, so I do most of the work part then. I make video clips that fit on Instagram that will serve as little commercials for people to click the link in the bio of my profile (#marytoddlinkinbio) and go see my YouTubes, which translates to actual dollars with the views. I make sure to tweet and Facebook each day at least once a day for whatever I'm working on or about to release. I'd say I don't spend more than an hour on it. I tried replying to every message but there got to be too many platforms, so now I just stay in touch with my ride-or-die fans on a site called Patreon, where fans actually pay for direct access to me and my videos one day earlier than the public. I don't read the comments any more.

How did you build your millions of followers?

Continually releasing a steady stream of content helped me build a fan base. I don't have a million yet on Instagram or Twitter but even if I did, that would just mean I take a good picture and people like to look at it. I do, however, have the highest YouTube subscriber base and view count of any of the *RuPaul's Drag Race* girls and I'm proud of that. My high numbers on YouTube make me feel way better because I know I'm engaged with the fans and they're actually responding and watching and laughing at the same stuff I am. It's more than just a heart button on a pic. It's making someone laugh and creating that butterfly effect of happiness in someone's day, even if it's for a moment. I went from one video a month to one video a week to two videos a week in the span of four years.

Who books your international appearances? Do you write your own shows?

My touring schedule is booked by my agent Michael Benedetti and my manager at my multi-channel network for YouTube, Mahzad Babyan. I write all my own stuff but I do collaborate on music often.

You came to Hollywood after working in New York. Why did you switch markets?

Well, when I was 16, I was graduating high school a year early. I asked this smart lady I know named Mary Lou Belli [MLB] what I should do since I was emancipated and ready to become famous. It basically came down to me realizing going to LA without a SAG card would be useless. So I went to Philly and bridge-and-tunneled for a few months and got my SAG card on my first audition/job for MTV when I was 17. Then I did a small but memorable bit on *Sex and the City* and was doing *Tony n Tina's Wedding* in Philly on weekends while doing extra work and learning about being on sets and going to auditions and open calls in New York. Did this for almost two years and then an arrest warrant was issued for me because of unpaid Lincoln Tunnel tolls. I was struggling with money going back and forth waiting for my big break. Then I wasn't cast in what I thought would be the biggest parts of my life. I had enough callbacks and a work session with Michael Greif for *Rent* but didn't get that, and then lost a saxophone-playing chorus role in *Cabaret* that I really wanted, too. So I decided to go to LA by January 2002.

But then September 11 happened, and I hightailed it off the east coast so fast that I was in LA by September 14.

Being the person I was, I wanted to do it on my own, so I signed up for Central Casting and by chance, the next week, an episode of *The Hughleys* was being directed by none other than my Aunt MLB and she saw my picture in the packet that Central sent over for her to picture-pick some 18-to-look-younger mall teen extras for a scene. She called me first to yell at me for not telling her I was out there already, and then I saw her on set later that week. She's been my best acting coach, just from running lines with her for jobs I asked her to pre-read with me for, and I learned how to break down a scene from her and use it *every* time I get sides to audition for.

Do you have a staff that helps manage the work of your career?
I have a trusted assistant and producer and best friend all in one. He tells me when my outfits are ugly and helps foster a creative output for me that I didn't have before. He's like a muse.

Are there any projects that you wish had gone another way? (Rock of Ages? RuPaul?)
Y'know, I tend to think that everything happens for a reason, especially now that I've hit the highest height of my career being in a movie with Lady Gaga and all (*A Star Is Born*). No one's gonna be able to tell me nothing. I'm playing Gaga's friend in a movie. That's like the highest role any drag queen could ever aspire to, and I did it. *Rock of Ages* really helped me find my voice musically and I found lots of friends that I work with still. One of the dancers from that tour has choreographed videos and tours for me and it made me a better all-round performer. *RuPaul's Drag Race* was a great experience for me all in all because it gave me a quick 15 minutes that I was able to parlay into an actual career with a lot of hard work and some luck.

> **"'No one's gonna work harder for you than you' is my motto. Ya gotta do at least one thing a day for your career."**

Can you talk about your resilience and entrepreneurial spirit?
"No one's gonna work harder for you than you" is my motto. Ya gotta do at least one thing a day for your career. It sucks to know that plenty of people come to the big city with aspirations and many don't come true. Having blind faith and just hoping you'll achieve them without putting in hours and hours of leg work is a pipe dream. I never said no and I tried it all: workshops,

classes, networking things, sleeping around, extra work. That's why I like to call myself an entrepewhore.

Is there another book in the pipeline?
Yes! My working title is *Tranifest Destiny*.

People talk about how funny you are . . . When and how did you develop this singularly funny unique voice?
I turned off the seven-second delay in my brain and I just say the first thing that comes to my mind, usually. Most drag queens play a character, and me just being me (albeit in a wig and heels) is an easier reach across the aisle to people that may not find drag funny. If you took Bluto from *Animal House*, a bit of Divine, and some Lady Bunny, you'd have a pretty good description for who I am comedically.

How do you feel about the internet?
The internet is a fickle mistress. It can grant careers and ruin them. The vastness and foreverness are so scary to me so I just try to respect it the way a sailor would the ocean. Knowing it can get me wherever I need to go but remembering to always be careful of the variables that can't be controlled. My dad says a lot of quotable things and I've adapted his "Think twice/speak once" into "Think twice/post once" as my internet protocol.

If you're reading this, say hi to me, @willam, wherever and check out my YouTube at www.youtube.com/noextrai.

SKETCH COMEDY TO SERIES REGULAR

My Biggest Leap

▶ By Kirstin Eggers

Kirstin Eggers has been a working actor and writer for over 15 years, with extensive commercial, guest, and recurring television appearances, including as a series regular on the ABC sitcom *Work It*, for which *Entertainment Weekly* called her "phenomenal." With a focus on comedy off-camera, she has performed sketch and improv at the Groundlings, UCB, and Comedy Central Stage, and accepted invitations to appear at comedy festivals nationwide, including SketchfestNYC, Chicago Sketchfest, and the storied HBO US Comedy Arts Festival in Aspen (winning the Best Sketch Comedy award with the troupe Summer of Tears). Kirstin (Figure 4.8) is a faculty member at the University of Southern California (USC) School of Dramatic Arts, and also holds a BFA in Acting from USC, where she

Figure 4.8 Kirstin Eggers

Photo: Dana Patrick

won both the Jack Nicholson Award and Ava Greenwald Award for Outstanding Actor while an undergraduate and was a member of USC's premier comedy troupe, Commedus.

Let me tell you my somewhat interesting story of my biggest leap of "getting ahead." I had been "working" with minimal results for at least seven years (more, really, although the math gets complicated). I did work commercially some, and was able to sustain myself a little thanks to Pepto Bismol, Swiffer, and Van de Kamp's Fish Sticks, in addition to my many jobs of substitute teaching, cater waitering, running teleprompter for industrials, running a cooking class for an after-school program, planning Shabbat food for a synagogue, etc., etc., etc. I got an agent through a friend, and it worked out okay for a while. I was also consistently doing improv, sketch comedy, plays, taking classes and casting workshops, making, meeting, going to festivals. I watched my comedy friends from college (the men) get big-time agents and start their careers. I had meetings all the time with people who were interested but not quite enough. I had what felt like so many "close calls."

And I cried. Oh, I *criiiiied.* In my car, my bedroom, on the treadmill. Why not me? Why them? Why not me? Will someone please just represent me? I know I can do something if you help me, fancy-officed Hollywood People!

And I don't really know why not me. Maybe it's my look. Maybe I suck. Maybe I didn't try hard enough.

And then one day I had an audition for a pilot. I'd never had an audition for a pilot. I'd heard people compare their pilot seasons for years. With nothing to contribute but a smile and a nod while catching tears in my throat. The pilot casting directors knew me from a random co-star call-in that I think I self-submitted on years before. They called me in via my commercial agent because I had no legit representation. And I got a flip-floppy stomach walking on the Warner Bros. lot and I did the audition. And then later that afternoon they called and said I was going to Testing: Studio, then Network. And if they chose me, then I was on an ABC pilot.

They said I needed 25 copies of my headshot and resumé right now. I didn't have 25 copies of my headshot and resumé. You don't need them for commercial auditions, and I didn't have a "real" agent so why would I need copies. I think I had them at some point and I ran out, sending them blindly in big manila envelopes to random agent addresses I found.

So I ran to the Kinko's and was color-copying the one headshot I had and doing all this weird cutting and stapling and crafting, trying to make 25 copies so a friend could pretend to be a courier and drop them off at Warner Bros. They looked terrible. But it's all I had.

So the Studio test came. I was a strange combo of scared and intimidated out of my mind but also . . . calm and confident. I knew how to act and do comedy. I had been doing it constantly in slimy little rental theaters and in mildewed classrooms for over a decade. I did it. I chatted with the actress I was up against. She was more famous than I, of course. Everyone was more famous than I. I had no agent.

Then I got the call that I was going to Network Test. Same deal. I did it. I felt like I didn't deserve to be there, but also felt fine and good. I went to my kosher grocery-buying job that afternoon as usual.

And then: the call. From my commercial agent. Who didn't know how any of this worked and asked a friend to help. I didn't know anything either. I was cast. On an ABC sitcom. As a series regular.

> "The writers wrote for me because I was ready to work, as I always had been. Soaking it up, taking what they gave me and running with it."

A couple months later, we got picked up to shoot 13 episodes. I finally got an agent and a manager, although I still didn't even have one when I shot the pilot.

My part throughout grew and grew because I was just . . . there. The writers wrote for me because I was ready to work, as I always had been. Soaking it up, taking what they gave me and running with it.

They ended up airing two episodes before cancelling it. But. That's Hollywood. I'm still so proud of every moment, from start to finish.

It seems like all that happened out of nowhere. But it was really so many little things over many years adding up to make one big explosive career jump for me.

That was a few years ago. Now I teach acting and comedy and improv and love it and feel like know what I'm talking about most of the time. And I have a spouse and a toddler child. And a house. And chores. But I also have a 3:30 a.m. call time this very night for a night shoot of a film I was offered without auditioning! For me now, this is "getting ahead," even though it might have been different from what I thought it might be.

Notes

1   "Greenlight Yourself" is the motto of the Filmmakers Alliance, an excellent filmmaking collective in LA.
2   Seuss, Dr. 1959. *Happy Birthday To You!* New York: Random House.

CHAPTER 5

STARTING AGAIN

This happens more times than you might imagine over the course of a career. You've enjoyed some success, perhaps been a series regular on a show and been identified as a certain character, and maybe you've just gotten bored being cast over and over as the same "type." In every profession, there's a point at which we need to begin again. In this chapter, we'll look at ways to refurbish a tired acting career or consider rebranding an existing one. We'll hear from actors who took on new genres or reshaped their career by tackling something the industry has never seen before. In Hollywood, perhaps more than in any other industry, we can count on the old adage: it ain't over 'til it's over.

The overwhelming consensus is that your acting experience and intimate knowledge of the process of acting can be the basis for so much more. That so many actors morph their acting careers into different or expanded adventures. Your adventures might even take you to new cities. Or give you the opportunity to give back. Your love affair with acting may be eclipsed by a whole new love affair!

Here's what we're going to address in this fifth chapter:

- How a smaller market may have a smaller pool of actors, and that may give you an opportunity to stretch.
- That the intimacy of a smaller market may lead to a more generous, kind, and supportive environment for auditions.

- Your personality is intrinsically tied to you getting the job.
- The study of acting is an education in how to deal with people.
- Why being well-versed in one area helps you to navigate others; thus, hyphenates thrive.
- How diversifying your skill set keeps things interesting, and gives you a much better chance at career longevity.
- Why fame and money have virtually nothing to do with being a person of worth, of character.
- Advocacy can enrich your life in countless ways and give back to your acting career.
- Actors do an enormous amount of passive learning, absorbing so much about the business by being on sets.
- Your love of acting can fuel the love of another career or a tangential one.

New beginnings can be so much fun. Where you will go might be directly related to where you have been. If you are starting again, let that new passion be the fuel on which you soar. So don't stop, keep going . . .

SAN FRANCISCO: A SMALLER, KINDER MARKET
Bay Area Bound
▶ By Catherine MacNeal

Figure 5.1 Catherine MacNeal

Photo: LisaKeatingPhotography.com

Born in Manhattan, Catherine began her acting training at the Neighborhood Playhouse at age 11. After a move to suburban Philadelphia, she apprenticed at Hedgerow Theatre for three years, then joined the People's Light and Theatre Company after graduating with a degree in theater from Carnegie Mellon University.

Catherine spent 22 years in LA, with many acting credits, including *Star Trek*, *Cheers*, *CSI*, *Judging Amy*, *Night Court*, *Days of Our Lives*, *The Young and the Restless*, and Nickelodeon's *100 Deeds for Eddie McDowd*. Her films include *The Muse*, *Clear and Present Danger*, and *Under Siege 2*. Catherine produced as well as acted in theater productions at Theatre West, the Zephyr, and the Matrix, and in tours to the Dublin Theatre Festival.

In 2003, Catherine relocated to Berkeley to raise her two daughters. She has also appeared in the Hulu series *Chance*, Woody Allen's *Blue Jasmine*, and plays at San Jose Rep and the B Street Theatre, and as the voice of San Francisco Ballet.

Catherine (Figure 5.1) has served on the board of Cambodia Tomorrow, a non-profit she helped found that provided education to Cambodian children. She is the owner of Lavender Hill Farm in Vashon, Washington.

In 1999 I made a decision to move from LA to the Bay Area, knowing that my acting work would dwindle or disappear. Immediately after I made that decision – you guessed it – I was cast as a regular in a series *in LA*, so I stayed. Part of the reason I got the job was being completely relaxed in the callbacks because *I knew* I was moving away. It helps when the pressure is off and you can have fun doing your best work.

So I stayed in LA for four more years – working on the series for two years, and doing episodic work and becoming a mother twice through adoption. Life is funny that way.

While I was still in LA, I signed up for the Theatre Bay Area (TBA) general auditions three years in a row. TBA provides this service – a chance to do one or two monologues (or a monologue and song) in front of an invited audience of producers, directors, and casting directors for all the theaters in the greater San Francisco Bay area. You provide a stack of headshots and resumés, do your best three minutes, and see if it brings any work.

I am still getting calls *years later* because of the TBAs. My resumé was in their file and has resulted in auditions and work. It really is the best way for actors new to the Bay to be seen. Making the rounds of annual general auditions at specific theaters is also a chance to get to know casting directors, refresh your monologues, and be seen.

When I did move to Berkeley, I did not look for acting work for several years – I had a 2-year-old and an 8-year-old and was focused on being a mom and running a nonprofit for children in Cambodia. I thought I would be able to hang on to some of my LA career, but the first time my LA agent called me to read for three lines as a doctor, I knew I wasn't able to run back to LA for those roles. It didn't fit into my life. Television casting is so fast that even casting directors, directors, and producers who used me frequently didn't call, because I wasn't in town.

A phone call on a rainy Saturday kickstarted Career 2.0. It was the B Street Theatre in Sacramento, needing a last-minute replacement for Sister Aloysius in *Doubt*. And yes, my resumé from the TBA auditions was in their file! I drove up the next day and was in rehearsal later that week. After two productions at the B Street, I thought maybe it was time to find a San Francisco agent. I sent my photo, resumé, and cover letter to the two talent agencies fellow actors recommended.

Three weeks later Dee Dee Shaughnessy called from JE Talent and apologized for taking so long to respond. I laughed and told her that in LA, three weeks was a nanosecond. I still haven't heard from the other agency – it's been nine years. Not holding my breath.

There were some challenges to starting over in the Bay Area. When I went back to doing theater, I was in a different age range. I was now auditioning for older; filling those 60-and-up roles. Who doesn't remember being in high school and playing an old lady of 55 (!) and putting baby powder in our hair, drawing wrinkles all over our faces and walking stooped over with a cane? My 86-year-old mother doesn't look as elderly as my early character work as the mother in John Millington Synge's *Riders to the Sea*, which I played in 9th grade – bad Irish accent to boot.

I have referred to my Bay Area acting work as Career 2.0. It's not what I spend most of my time doing, but auditioning and working is a pleasure. My LA credits get me in the door in San Francisco. When I met with the agents at JE Talent, it was clear they wanted me to join them. We hugged. Really.

Since starting over, I have worked with Woody Allen and Cate Blanchett in *Blue Jasmine* and with Hugh Laurie in the Hulu series *Chance*. I have shot commercials, industrials, recorded voice-overs for San Francisco Ballet radio and television ads, narration for documentaries, and print work for pharmaceutical companies – you know, those healthy older couples hiking with their dogs while there is a 60-second disclaimer about a certain drug. That's a niche market here and an opportunity when you get old enough to look like your husband could be on Medicare.

> "Casting people in San Francisco aren't afraid to tell you when you've done a good reading. They are generous, kind, and supportive."

I have truly enjoyed the opportunity to do voice-over work. This was an area I found hard to break into in LA. Because San Francisco has a small pool of actors, there is more opportunity to stretch.

Casting people in San Francisco aren't afraid to tell you when you've done a good reading. They are generous, kind, and supportive. With the smaller pool of talent, casting directors remember me and call me in for anything remotely right.

Agents here understand that people have lives – families, other jobs, and commitments. They know that most actors are not making their living solely from acting (and they aren't in LA either, but in LA there is more of a stigma about having a "day" job). I haven't felt bad here for turning down an audition for a family event or work commitment.

> "I found that I was more comfortable in auditions – the environment felt safer and I had fun reading for roles that sometimes were a real stretch."

My resumé was presentable in LA – solid training; decent theater; guest-star, recurring, and regular roles in television; small parts in big films and big parts in small films. In San Francisco, the number of television and film credits on my resumé put me in a category where I was called in on any film or television project with a role in my age range – from a wealthy overbearing mother to a mentally ill shut-in. I didn't face the kind of resistance I found in LA, where the producers would want a name or stunt casting, or my lack of network series-regular credits eliminated me from opportunities. I find casting directors, directors, and producers here eager to praise good work. I found that I was more comfortable in auditions – the environment felt safer and I had fun reading for roles that sometimes were a real stretch.

There is less work here, although some actors are making a living, but the odds of booking jobs are better and there is a kindness here that wasn't always present in LA. Maybe I approach it differently also. There isn't so much on the line and I work more collaboratively in the room. I'm looser. I'm comfortable.

Some of that could be age. Now in my sixties, I'm not walking into an audition wondering if I am pretty or sexy enough. If I don't like the vibe, I can walk out. I don't need it and I wish I had stood up to some of the Hollywood treatment when I was younger. I remember an audition at CBS Radford where the casting director was on the phone the whole time, signaling me with her hand to just keep going. I should have kept going out the door. I remember sitting in a casting office waiting to read for a role and listening to an assistant making an offer for the same role on the phone with an agent. In 1981, when I first arrived in LA, a theater actor with five years of rep behind me, the beauty standard was Heather Locklear and Donna Mills. I had three different agents tell me I wouldn't work without a nose job.

I stay in contact with my friends in the business – actors, directors, writers, and producers – but I haven't marketed myself in years, except by doing general auditions at theaters and checking in with my agents. After so many years doing that in LA, before the days of websites, email, and YouTube, I have some resistance to doing it again. I have thought about a voice-over reel, a website, a new compilation reel, but I haven't done it. I think I needed a long break from it, and I'm afraid that might take the fun out of my Career 2.0.

I recently took Marie Forleo's B-School, a six-week online course for entrepreneurs and small business owners with an emphasis on online presence and marketing. That got me thinking about the marketing component of an acting career and how much the technology has changed. Gone are the days of driving from Hollywood to Culver City at 5:30 p.m. to pick up sides for a reading at 10 a.m. the following day, or mailing out VHS copies of your reel. Gone are the faxed sides, or driving to your agents to record a voice-over audition in their studio. Marketing is easier and less expensive. I can now receive sides and a script and never leave my house. I can record a voice-over audition in my car on my iPhone.

In my 22 years in LA I had many outside jobs. I worked in retail. I was the office manager at Theatre West. I produced plays and worked as a celebrity personal assistant. When I arrived in Berkeley, I volunteered at my daughters' school, helping to fundraise and teaching acting in the after-school program. When they got older, I took a job as administrative partner to a family here, drawing on my personal assistant skills; I have held this job for eight years. I also moonlight as a lavender farmer. Since 2006, I have owned a house on Vashon Island with half an acre of lavender. We open every summer for six weeks for people to come and U-Cut and shop in the little farm store. The farmhouse is a vacation rental through Airbnb and VRBO and I run that business as well.

After 22 years in LA, I have now spent 15 years in Berkeley. My time here may be drawing to an end. My youngest daughter has one more year of high school and the relationship that brought me to Berkeley is now over. I am now part of a family with four children, who will always be a big part of my life.

So soon I will be starting again. I am contemplating the next chapter – will it be Career 2.1 or Career 3.0 (big upgrade), or a complete change like Farmer 1.0 or Caregiver 3.0 – as the daughter caring for aging parents on the East Coast and showing up for my sister in Texas who has ALS? Playing caregiver and provider may be my most important role for the next few years. And do I return to LA (and would anyone remember me?), move on to the lavender farm, go east? Do an *Eat, Pray, Love* world tour?

Stay tuned.

TEACHING FILM SCHOOL . . . EVERYTHING HE KNOWS FROM ACTING, EDITING, AND CINEMATOGRAPHY

Branching Out (Not Standing Still)

▶ By Charles Dougherty

Charles Dougherty's career as a professional actor, film acting instructor, and cinematographer has spanned over 40 years. As an actor, Charles has appeared in reoccurring and guest-star roles on such television shows as *Happy Days*, *Equal Justice*, *Quantum Leap*, *Diagnosis Murder*, *Wings*, *The Drew Carey Show*, *Monk*, *Bones*, *The Middle*, *Rosewood*, and the Disney comedy *Bizaardvark*, to name a few. He had a major role in the feature film *Beautiful*, starring Minnie Driver and directed by Sally Field. He starred in the cultish Roger Corman film *Ultra Warrior*. He also appeared with the late Martin Landau in the film *An Existential Affair*.

Figure 5.2 Charles Dougherty
Photo: Michael Helms Photography

Charles is currently on the faculty of Academy of Arts University in San Francisco. He has taught filmmaking for US Performing Arts and been a guest lecturer at California State University Long Beach and Hofstra University, as well as the director/cinematographer for the BFA major's senior digital showcase at the University of California, Irvine.

As a director of photography and producer, Charles shot the short film *America*, for which he won the Best Cinematography award at the Freedom Shorts Fest in Philadelphia. He was director of photography and producer of the short film *Straight Eye for the Gay Guy*, which won best short at the California Indie Film Festival as well as playing at Woods Hole Film Fest, Ojai Film Fest, and Northeast Film Festival. He also was the cinematographer on all episodes of the web series *The Drunk Lonely Wives Book Club*, which was an official selection of the Paris Play Film Festival. He was the cinematographer and producer on the first season of the web series *The Naked Truth*. In addition to teaching, Charles (Figure 5.2) has served as a mentor to college filmmakers through the American Pavilion internship program at the Cannes Film Festival.

I don't like to think I ever started over . . . I just branched out. I got my first acting job in LA in 1975. At that time, I was hellbent on being an actor at all costs. The only thing I wanted to do was act. To that end, I made it a point to train myself for nothing else. Before my commercial career took off, the only survival job I had was as a helper to my agent's husband . . . who was a tree cutter. When you are 5 ft 7 in, 135 pounds, and afraid of heights, tree cutting is not a job with a future. As I alluded to, my commercial career intervened and saved me for many years. It continued to save me financially when I moved to New York. I did have a few survival jobs between commercials (the most notable was walking around the New York Toy Show in a Garfield the Cat costume . . . a rather humbling experience). Next to tree cutting, walking around a trade show in a rubber suit being pummeled by 12-year-olds is something that does not feed the spirit or give one optimism for the future. The money was good but the bruises from the fists of 12-year-olds was real.

Jump cut to LA, Take 2. Married to the woman who has become my lifelong partner. Working as an actor, but with the starting of a family, it was clear to me that I had to find something that I could count on for income when acting jobs were not coming in.

As it turns out, we had just bought a small house and there was no money left over to hire anyone to fix it up. I had a few friends in the acting world who were working on the side as painters and carpenters. I had actually worked with them as an extra hand on some painting and carpentry jobs. Armed with this minute amount of experience and boundless 35-year-old energy, I embarked on my first house remodel . . . doing what needed to be done to improve the quality of our living space that we would be welcoming a family into. By trial and error and some help from others, I was able to successfully create a beautiful environment for my family which also now had an additional bathroom.

"Running a business taught me about people."

The most important part was that the bug had hit . . . I enjoyed what I was doing with a hammer (or, more accurately, a nail gun) and I felt an artistic connection to my new skills.

Of course, the thought hit me: why not do this and get paid for it while still controlling my time (to some extent)? I ended up starting a carpentry business and excelling in finish carpentry and cabinetry.

So this is where this first story begins. It is not about how I was able to provide for my family between acting jobs . . . though that was certainly a happy fact. It is more about what being a carpenter taught me about acting. More specifically, it is what running a business taught me about people. I ran my small carpentry business for 20 years. I controlled the time I spent doing it and had numerous periods when my acting career came calling to the extent that I put cabinetry and finish carpentry on hold. Working as an actor, not working as an actor, auditioning, not auditioning . . . my business kept me connected to the world around me. You see an intimate side of people when you talk with them about fixing or remodeling their homes. I say "homes" as opposed to "houses" because I ended up dealing with people in regard to how they were going to live. I did a lot of cabinetry, bookcases, kitchen spaces, and entertainment spaces . . . which are all very personal. I got to know how people view the world and think about themselves. I also had to deal with their frustrations and insecurities . . . and then I had to negotiate a fair price for them and myself. Talk about the use of transferable skills!

Whether you want to think so or not, when you hire someone to do a job, you are hiring them on their personality. More specifically, you are hiring them on a feeling of confidence which you pick up through the way they animate themselves. The trick here is (if you are an actor doing a straight job) to "act as if." This is something that all good actors learn how to do in an early acting class. "I'm not a lawyer, but I've played one on television," has helped me have many legal discussions with law and non-law people. Same for "I'm not a doctor, but I've played one on television." Obviously, I do not know enough about the medical profession to talk as an expert, but on a good day I know enough about the medical profession to ask the right questions. If anything, actors learn how (and why) to ask questions.

> "Most actors have heard the phrase 'You have to be a sponge.' Well, I am always wet, and I have applied this trait to life as much as I have to my acting work."

Actors also learn how to give answers – at least I have, and I credit that talent to my training and experience as an actor. It is my world view that most people are looking for answers and that I am being of service by providing those answers. Now I don't just pull these answers out of thin air (not much, anyway). They are created by the use of a composite of information and personal observation that I have soaked up over the years and I am constantly adding to. Most actors have heard the phrase "You have to be a sponge." Well, I am always wet, and I have applied this trait to life as much as I have to my acting work.

The study of acting is an education in how to deal with people.

As I was luxuriating in the 42nd year of my professional acting career, an extraordinary thing happened: a university teaching job fell out of the sky and hit me on the head. It was not just a university teaching job, but a film school teaching job. I was offered the job of teaching young filmmakers how to make films.

So why was I the one being offered the film school job? Because I got skills!

I have been working on the craft of cinematography for a little over eight years. For the past four years I have had the opportunity to work as a cinematographer in the low-budget/ultra-low-budget independent film world.

How did the craft of cinematography find me? Again, something fell out of the sky and hit me on the head. I was working for a national company that offered professional-level summer training programs for high school students in performing arts that were run on different college and university campuses across the country. At that time I was happily running an improvisational theater program for this company. The boss of the company called me one afternoon and offered me a proposition: would I be interested in being the "videographer" for a couple of Acting for the Camera programs she was going to run? At that point the only experience I had was making home movies with my camcorder. Somewhere along the way I had heard the term "crossing the line" but wasn't really sure what it meant. I had taken still photos all my life and had a good sense of image composition – hell, I was overqualified. I immediately said yes.

I was extremely fortunate that the boss was not expecting miracles my first few times out and was able to overlook some really bad edits in favor of giving me the chance to grow.

After the first Acting for the Camera program or two, I teamed with a working television director who was teaching in the summer to give back and because she wanted to be with her husband . . . me. Together, we shot countless scenes as though we were doing very fast (very cheap) television. I honed my shooting and editing skills; learned many, many things about directing from my talented wife; and gained confidence in my ability to put it all together. During this time, I did many acting jobs and found myself sitting on set with a new appreciation for the different crew positions. This 10-year summer gig was our laboratory to shoot and experiment. I was the director of photography (and sound engineer) and she was the director. This is what gave me skills.

When I was offered the film school job, these skills, combined with my 40-year acting career, gave me the confidence to know I could do the job. And as it turned out, when I stood in front of a class of 20-something film students and opened my mouth, out came 10, 20, 30, 40 years of experience and observation about the film industry coupled with a fair amount of "as if." From my perspective in the trenches, both in front of and behind the camera, I instinctively knew what I needed to teach that would help in the real world.

FROM ACTING TO WRITING AND BEYOND

▶ A Q&A with Liz Vassey

Figure 5.3 Liz Vassey

Photo: Florian Schneider

Liz Vassey began acting at the age of nine, performing in over 50 plays in the Tampa Bay area. At 16, Liz moved to New York to join the cast of *All My Children*. For her work on that show, she received the first of her two Daytime Emmy Award nominations.

Since *All My Children*, Liz has appeared as a regular or recurring character on 11 television shows, including *ER*, *Maximum Bob*, *Necessary Roughness*, *Brotherly Love*, *Push Nevada*, *Two and a Half Men*, and Fox's live-action version of *The Tick* and the Amazon reboot. But she is probably best known for her five-year run on *CSI* as DNA technician Wendy Simms.

Liz has also guest-starred on many television shows (including *Castle* with Nathan Fillion), starred in many pilots (including *Dragons of New York*, written by and starring Hugh Laurie), and appeared in several films (including *Man of the House* with Tommy Lee Jones).

In addition to acting, Liz is an accomplished writer. She co-wrote an episode of *CSI*, and has sold seven television pilots and a television movie, developing for such networks and studios as NBC, Freeform, Universal, Imagine, Sony, and Netflix. An avid runner, Liz (Figure 5.3) is also the director and producer of the recently released documentary feature *The Human Race*, which focuses on runners over the age of 50.

Can you talk a little about the difference in being a series regular as well a guest star?

In one word: mortgage.

I'm kidding. But not really. Being a series regular means a much bigger paycheck for a while. So, if you're fortunate enough to be one: *save your money.*

That said, there are many other differences, too. In two words: job security.

> "I've always thought of this business as sort of a circus. We're all here to perform, and many times casts turn into surrogate families."

As a series regular, you may not know how long your series will run, but you *do* know that you won't be out there auditioning for the next television job right away. I fondly remember being on *CSI* and being so grateful to get to sit and breathe for a while. For me, the job is the easiest part. It's the auditioning process that starts to grind away at me a bit. It's not digging ditches, and I'm acutely aware how lucky anyone is to even get to audition here in LA, but from my perspective, being able to work consistently and *not* have to audition is heaven.

But there's more to it than that. I've always thought of this business as sort of a circus. We're all here to perform, and many times casts turn into surrogate families. So, in my experience, being a series regular means I get more "family" time. I'm still dear friends with many people from several shows I've worked on for long periods, and I'm grateful for the large tribe of people I've got in my life.

As far as being a guest star, it's a great gig but it also feels a little like the cafeteria in Junior High. It helps considerably if the series regulars are nice. And it's a funny thing: when I'm a guest star, I can always see which series regulars have done a lot of guest roles in their lives, because they're *always* the ones who are the most welcoming. I have also learned to emulate that behavior when the shoe is on the other foot. It costs nothing to be kind, it's tough for someone to come spend time with another "family," and a little nice goes a long way.

What made you want to write as well as act?
Naren Shankar, the executive producer while I was on *CSI*, asked if I wanted to co-write an episode with my co-star Wally Langham. I said yes before I took the time to think about it, because I knew I'd always regret saying no.

From the very first page, I had an epiphany. I loved it. I also sat with the writers to learn how to break a story, how to structure the acts in series television, and anything else I could glean. After I was finished with the episode, I realized I wanted to focus on writing more than acting. I have been acting since I was 9, and it was a welcome shift. I also found that the feeling of creating something – something that hadn't been there before I wrote it – was intoxicating in the best ways. I'd always loved to write since I was a kid, and it was gratifying to pick it up again that much later and find out I still enjoyed it. I truly believe this is what I'm supposed to be doing at this point in my life.

Did being known as an actress help with being taken seriously as a writer?
Yes and no. It definitely helped to have contacts. I've been acting since I was a fetus (okay, 9 years old) and it was incredibly fortuitous for me to be a known commodity in Hollywood. Getting meetings wasn't as hard for me as a brand new writer because, in many cases, I'd worked with the producers or studio or network as an actor in the past, so they were already aware of my work ethic.

I don't know that being known as an actor helped me be taken more seriously, though, because (and make no mistake: I'm happy about this) the proof is on the page. I was taken seriously when people saw I could do the work.

In many ways, I think people kind of roll their eyes when they hear that some-one wants to become a hyphenate, but I truly believe that being well-versed in one area helps considerably in navigating the others. Having acted on television for 30 years, I was already very familiar with the structure of scripts and the nature of how scenes move. I think it would be beneficial for any writer to take an acting class, and vice versa. If nothing else, it certainly gives you the ability to empathize with others while they're doing their jobs.

Do you have a set time that you work on your written projects?
I know the "right" answer is: "I spend eight hours a day writing, no matter what!" But I don't. The truth is, I usually have quite a few things on my plate at once, because I like it that way – and I can't spend eight hours a day every day on one thing. What I do is have certain ideas on the back burner of my brain all the time, and write down notes constantly. (My husband especially appreciates it when it's 4 a.m.)

However, when I *do* sit down to actually write the outline or script, I can go for 12 to 14 hours straight. I work like that for days. Then I give it a rest for a few days while I get notes from other people, and then dive back in. I'm not suggest-ing this method for anyone else, but it works for me!

Can you talk about "pitching" a series idea?

It's a lot more work than I ever used to think it would be. Somehow, I thought people just went into rooms and talked about their series ideas. Nope. You are truly trying to sell a product. And not just a product, but *seasons* of a product. As my friend says, "You have to show 'em it's got legs!" And that's a huge part of it.

My pitches usually go for about 15 minutes, plus Q&A. I talk about the characters (their quirks, their relationships, their pasts, etc.), the theme, the world, the pilot cold open, the pilot story, the tone, and arcs that we'll see during the series itself.

And I also spend a lot of time talking about why I'm the person to write whatever the project is. We all have personal connections to our work and many reasons why we need to do it. Don't be afraid to talk about that. I've found that executives love hearing (and are relieved to hear) that you're drawing from a well of personal experience. And yes, even if it's a sci-fi show set on Mars in 2305. What do I mean by that? I mean, is said sci-fi show ultimately about family?! If it is: talk about your own family triumphs and challenges. Is it about survival? Cool. Talk about the time you felt *you* had to work to get through something.

Ultimately, you are truly putting on a little show in those rooms, and I go in very prepared. "Winging it" is not really my thing. I like to walk in knowing that no matter what, I am going to say everything I want to say. Because remember: they're also watching you to see if you have the wherewithal to run a television show, which is not a small job.

> "A network is considering spending a lot of money to make your show, so you need to prove to them that it's worth it and will make them money for a long time."

What do you need to do before pitching a series?

Prepare. Take the time to write out what it is you want to convey. Take the time to figure out how to talk about each of the bullet points I mentioned above. And keep in mind, you will be hearing a lot of opinions and getting a lot of help during this process. Most things are pitched with a "pod." Meaning: a production company. Each company I've worked with has had their own special way they like to pitch. It's a group effort. It's all doable, and even fun, but my best piece of advice is: *do the work*. And make sure you're able to talk about *why* this show can go on for years and years. I can't stress that enough. A network is considering spending a lot of money to make your show, so you need to prove to them that it's worth it and will make them money for a long time.

Does acting come into pitching?
Absolutely! I've definitely benefited from having an acting background because those network rooms can be intimidating if you're not used to them. Or hell, even if you are! But after all the years of experience I've had "tap dancing" in front of these people, I have a whole set of mental gymnastics I know how to do before I go in. I'm comfortable in those rooms, but it took a while. The other thing is that writing is often a solitary profession, so asking some writers to go in and *talk* about their projects is, understandably, like pulling teeth. After every pitch, I'm grateful that I've had experience talking in front of groups as much as I have.

You have directed and produced an amazing documentary, The Human Race. What was the genesis of that project?
Thank you! I'm very proud of it. In a nutshell, it's a film about six runners, all over the age of 50 and all of vastly different levels of expertise (a transcontinental runner, an ultra-marathon runner, a newbie runner) as they each tackle a different race. I'm an avid runner myself. I've always felt it helped keep me centered in the midst of some crazy times. My mother unfortunately passed away in 2012 and I always credit running with keeping me vertical. I wanted to know if there was an age at which I'd have to hang up my shoes and do something more "sensible" (like mall walking or pinochle) and I found out there are people out there running in their nineties! Even past 100.

I'm not a fan of any of your basic "-isms": sexism, racism, ageism. I realized that by making a documentary like this, I could fight the latter in a loud and hopefully impactful way. And by being a female director and putting it out there, I could also battle the former. Also, our country has taken a dark and divisive turn. I wanted to put something joyful out into the world. This is not a documentary only about running. It's mostly about the human race and the unsinkable nature of the human spirit.

What did you learn?
Everything. I'm only half kidding. I now know about shooting 2K versus 4K and the benefits and drawbacks of both. I know about editing. I know about

sound mixing. I know about color correction. I know about distribution. I know about legal clearances. And shooting permits. And music cues. It was a very steep learning curve, but I had wonderful teammates to help me through. I also learned that *anyone* who makes a movie deserves a lot of credit for finishing. She or he also deserves cookies.

> "I think diversifying your skill set keeps things interesting, and gives you a much better chance at career longevity."

Is there any job that you have now done in show business that you don't want to do again? Or are eager to do again?
I'm eager to do almost any of them again. I say "almost any" because after my debut as a boom operator for my documentary, I would definitely want to hire a professional from now on!

But I think diversifying your skill set keeps things interesting, and gives you a much better chance at career longevity. Plus, I can't stand being bored. I am haunted by the idea of wasting any talent or ability I might have. I'd hate for anyone to waste his or her talents. I think I'd enjoy trying motion capture sometime, now that I'm thinking about it. My husband worked as a cameraman on *Avatar* and I thought it looked like big fun. Plus, no make-up and hair!

As a series regular, will you please talk about the evolution of your relationship with the cinematographer and make-up and or hair artist and costume designer?
I talked before about how people in a series-regular position become a sort of family, and I didn't mean only the actors. The relationships you develop with the crew can be very intense and very strong. Remember, you're working 14- to 16-hour days sometimes, so you're basically spending more time with the crew than you are at home. The evolution of the relationships you mentioned above all follow the same arc, in my experience, and it all has to do with intimacy. And, although I did marry a camera operator I met on a movie, I do *not* mean that kind of intimacy! What I mean is this: these people see you at your most vulnerable. They see you after three hours of sleep, after you've been slammed by a reviewer, when you're fighting the flu, when you're fighting your own demons . . . all of it. I had a make-up artist who could tell just by looking at me

if I'd had salt the night before. I had a cinematographer who was able to tell me how much sleep I'd been able to get. I had a costume designer who could tell when I wasn't getting enough water. I'm talking crazy voodoo stuff here! The point is, they know you. I've always loved my crews (again: I married a member of one of them!), so as these relationships become more intimate, I've found that these people have taken care of me. My director of photography could make it look like I'd slept like a baby. My make-up artist could remove the excess baggage under my eyes. My costume designer knew exactly which parts of my body I wanted to show off and which made me feel a little too exposed. My biggest piece of advice here is: be *kind* to your crew. First of all, because we should be good humans. That's second and third, too. But fourth of all, because if you're kind to them, they will be kind to you. And when it's your face, body, and hair up there, you will appreciate all the help you can get.

ACTING CAN LEAD TO ADVOCACY

▶ A Q&A with Nanci Christopher

Nanci Christopher has been an actress for over 30 years. Her theater credits include the LA premiere of Lee Blessing's *Down the Road* and Diane Samuels' *Kindertransport*, both at the Tiffany Theatre; *Home Fire* and *Letters Home* at Theatre West; *The Transmogrification* and *Open Your Golden Gate* at Playwrights Horizons with Bob Moss. Her film credits include HBO's *Crime of the Century*, directed by Mark Rydell, and *The Check Is in the Mail*, directed by Joan Darling, and television credits include *Two and a Half Men*, *ER*, *USA High*, *Ryan's Hope*, and *All My Children*, among others, plus numerous commercials.

Figure 5.4 Nanci Christopher

Photo: David Carlson

Nanci became a first-time writer with her autobiographical solo show, *And Baby Bakes Two: An Adoption Tale* (*ABMT*). This ran for almost three months at the Santa Monica Playhouse in the fall of 2007. It was nominated for the prestigious 2009 Susan Smith Blackburn Prize.

In addition, Nanci (Figure 5.4) is currently an associate member of Pacific Resident Theater in Venice, CA; was a long-time member of Theatre West in LA; and was a co-founder of the Joint Theatre Company/CBS Radford. She was an invited guest at the Actors Theatre of Louisville Humana Festival and the O'Neill National Playwrights Conference in Connecticut. She is also a member of the Dramatists Guild of America and the proud Founder/President of the Sugar & Stilettos (S&S) Charitable Foundation (www.sugarandstilettos.com).

Nanci, you have used your skill and love of acting and combined it with creating content and advocacy. How does one feed the other?

They are both fueled by passion. I am passionate about acting; the power of it to move people to tears, laughter, thought-provoking change. It is the same with content and advocacy. I am inspired to connect with people because person-to-person dialogues are so important, so essential, and so vital to being a thoughtful, participating human being on this planet. For me, advocacy easily intersects with acting and content. The three combine passion and the power of the heart. In my experience, if you reach out to people with your heart and your passion, they are going to listen to you. If you make them laugh and cry, they are going to listen to you. And then once they are listening, their hearts will open, their passions will be ignited . . . together you will create change . . . and magic. That belief makes my soul sing . . . literally sing.

> "I was surrounded by famous, rich people my entire childhood. I was able to see early on that one's fame and money had virtually nothing to do with being a person of worth, of character."

You clearly have a knack for raising money, and have been around show business all your life. Why do you focus your energy on advocacy?

I was raised by the most compassionate, kind, loving, and philanthropic father imaginable. I learned from a master what is important in life. It's not being famous and having lots of money, though there is nothing wrong with either one of those things. I was surrounded by famous, rich people my entire childhood. I was able to see early on that one's fame and money had virtually nothing to do with being a person of worth, of character. My father came from nothing . . . a poor, skinny Jewish boy from Brooklyn. He never forgot where he came from; what it felt like to have nothing, what it felt like to feel less than, what it felt like to be discriminated against. Love of family, integrity, dignity, honesty, and compassion ruled his life. It came to rule mine too. Since my father ended up with a life he *never* could have imagined in his wildest dreams, and though he didn't start making real money until I was well into my young adulthood, I saw first-hand how much he always gave back, how much he always helped others . . . not just with money, but with kind, compassionate deeds that changed people's lives. So advocacy came naturally to me. I can't imagine for a second being in the position of privilege that I'm now in and not giving back, not trying to make a difference in the world. In Judaism, there is a tenet called *tikkun olam*. It states that it is the moral responsibility of every Jew to help heal the world while they are alive. I am not a religious person – nor was my dad – but we both took that tenet very seriously. I must also admit that it is a completely selfish joy to advocate for others, for causes I am passionate about. I'd be crazy not to do it!

Have you visited the rape crisis centers or food kitchens that you have raised money for?

I have visited the food kitchens and many of the centers/facilities that help women cope with rape, domestic violence, homelessness, mental illness, and substance abuse. The people who dedicate their lives to this work are beyond amazing. They all work 24/7 in the nonprofit world in ways that you can't even imagine. I am constantly blown away and humbled by their compassion, empathy, and devotion. Special shout out to everyone at the Westside Food Bank and the People Concern . . . you inspire me to be my best self.

What was the genesis of your plays *And Baby Makes Two: An Adoption Tale* and *One Minute of Happiness: A Tale of Sisterhood and Baking (OMOH)* ?

Both are autobiographical solo shows based on two very important stories in my life: the adoption of my son Joshua as a single mom and the relationship I had with my sister Gloria, who suffered from severe bi-polar/borderline personality disorder that deeply affected the dynamics of our relationship and our entire family. In an unconscious effort to heal myself, I felt compelled to share these stories. With *ABMT* I began really using my acting skills to advocate. We raised over $10,000 during the run of the play, most of it going to the American Liver Foundation in memory of Joshua's birth mother, Elizabeth, who died of liver disease at 30 years old. Without Elizabeth's selfless decision to give her baby a better life, I would not have my son. I was so happy to be able to honor her. With *OMOH* I have become my sister's lost voice. The Neuropsychiatric Institute at UCLA invited me to do a reading of the play in their Open Mind Series. After the reading there was a Q&A where audience members revealed their stories and how the play helped them better understand mental illness; either their own or a family member's struggle. It was incredibly empowering to use my voice as an actor for something bigger and more important than myself. It also made me more aware that *everyone* has a story. It has increased the depth of my empathy for others a thousandfold. People constantly approach me after a show, either in the theater or by following me out to my car to speak more privately . . . always wanting to tell me their life story and how I/the show has impacted them. It is a beautiful gift that they unwittingly give me.

How did you get your play published in two languages?

For the English-speaking publication, the play was submitted to Samuel French. We were told that the process could take a year and that, in general, they did not publish solo shows as standalone plays. They sometimes would publish them in anthologies . . . say of women's plays, or monologues in my case. They were trying to be honest and therefore were not encouraging in the least. Then lo and behold, a year later I received a call and email that, in fact, they were going to publish *ABMT* as a standalone play! I couldn't believe it. Samuel French, the oldest and biggest theatrical publishing house in the world, was going to publish my play . . . my first play. It was mind-blowing. After that, I made arrangements to do a reading of the play in Paris, where I had lived for almost a year (1991–1992). I learned to speak French when I lived there, allowing me to develop a lot of friendships in Paris which exist to this day. It was a dream come true to be in Théâtre d'Aire Falguière with a full house reading *ABMT*. From that reading I got a French literary agent (who also has offices in New York) and the translation came from that and other French connections that I already had in the artistic community there. A French translation of *OMOH* is already being worked on.

Your first play was very personal. Was that loss something that inspired you to tell your story?

Yes, I definitely think so. I had been so devastated by the loss of my first baby, who I named Austen Beckett. There were two baby showers, custom furniture ordered, a house bought, and a change of car to accommodate a new baby. I had totally transformed my life in anticipation of Austen's arrival. Then the worst happened. His was not an adoption story gone wrong, but a pregnancy story gone wrong, terribly wrong. Austen was never able to leave the hospital. When he died two weeks after his birth, I could not function for a full year. Even after Joshua came into my life, it took me several years to be able to confront the pain of that loss and write *ABMT*. My story, and ultimately our story – mine and Joshua's – needed to be told because it was/is a story of survival, of love, of hope.

Your newest play also has its genesis in a personal story. May I ask you to share that?

OMOH is the story of my sister Gloria and me: how her mental illness defined, destroyed, and created our relationship. GoGo, [as she was known] to me and other family members, went undiagnosed for over 10 years. Her behavior looked typical of teenage rebellion and in those days (the 1970s) no one even thought about mental illness. When she was finally diagnosed at 22 with bi-polar disorder (then called manic depression) after cutting her wrists in a suicide attempt, her life really spun out of control. There were more medications and psych ward hospital stays than I could possibly count. No matter how much money my parents threw at the best doctors in LA, they were never able to stabilize her (borderline personality disorder further complicated her issues). She was tormented without relief and disintegrated to the point where she was unrecognizable. Gloria succeeded in committing suicide in 1989 when she was just 31 years old. It forever changed my life. Again, it took me years to confront the pain and write about it.

Every person I feed through S&S, every homeless person I see on the streets, reminds me of my sister . . . how she could have been one of those people had it not been for the financial resources my family had. I am not afraid to look someone on the street in the eye and talk to them . . . hear their story. *OMOH* is my way of using my acting/people skills and the empathy I learned from having Gloria as my sister to advocate for the mentally ill, to change the dialogue and stigma still associated with mental illness, to give my sister back the voice she lost. I speak for her now and will until the day I die . . . hopefully giving her the dignity she so rightfully deserves.

You've been active at UCLA in advocating around mental health issues. What was the genesis of that involvement?

My family has deep ties to UCLA. My parents both went there (my dad for his MBA, my mom undergrad). My dad also taught in the Anderson Graduate School of Business for 17 years as he built his accounting/business management firm. My sister and I were born there and raised on John Wooden basketball at Pauley Pavilion. I could go on and on. My dad was just the biggest Bruin ever. He loved everything about UCLA and was an extremely generous donor in terms of medical research, academics, and athletics. UCLA has some of the most respected and esteemed doctors and programs in the world for mental health/illness issues, so it was a natural fit for us as a family, and me personally representing my sister, who had often been treated there, to get involved with their various programs. I really couldn't be happier than to be aligned with the Neuropsychiatric Institute, the Open Mind Series at the Friends of the Semel Institute, and the absolutely phenomenal work of Dr. Michael Gitlin . . . and, may she rest in peace, Dr. Lori Altshuler.

This is a remarkable time for women. Can you talk about feeling the power and support of women in all you do?

My girlfriends have always meant the world to me. I didn't have a lot of close friends when I was younger . . . I was *never* the "it" girl but I always managed to have one "best" friend. That grew to more friends, strangely enough, once I was involved in the competitive figure skating world, and then really grew when I became a sorority girl at UC Berkeley. I truly thought I had died and gone to heaven in that sorority house! As I moved through my young adulthood, I craved and sought to recreate the female camaraderie that I had had at my sorority. The S&S Baking Club, which was the precursor to the S&S Executive Committee, was born of that desire. I feel in the depth of my soul that female empowerment is pure nirvana and it was my beloved Aunt Irene who set me on that path of belief. On the S&S Executive Committee we have women ranging in age from 25 to 75 . . . multi-generational wisdom, talent, beauty, humor, and intelligence. In addition to the support I have at S&S, I have incredible support in my professional/personal life from my many women friends, including you, Mary Lou, and of course my BFF Penny. These friends have lifted me up and believed in my work and me even when I wasn't able to. What is happening in the world right now with women is beyond remarkable. It is our time to speak out and own our power . . . and it is exciting to see these young millennial women taking control of their lives, knowing their worth, and demanding acknowledgment long before my generation was able to do so. I take strength in this. In the middle of the insanity that exists right now, it gives me hope that they will change the world. Their power is my power, my power is theirs . . . and together we are unstoppable!

FALLING IN LOVE WITH DIRECTING

Backstory

▶ By Toni Kalem

Toni Kalem has an extensive background as an actress in film, television, and theater. She played Angie Bonpensiero, (Big Pussy's wife) on the HBO hit series *The Sopranos*. Audiences also know her as the Bronx teen queen Despie in Philip Kaufman's cult classic *The Wanderers*, and as the tough Private Gianelli in *Private Benjamin*.

Toni's life underwent a dramatic change when she read Anne Tyler's novel *A Slipping-Down Life*. She optioned the novel and wrote the screenplay, her first, which she also directed. The film stars Guy Pearce, Lili Taylor, and John Hawkes and was accepted into Dramatic Competition at the Sundance Film Festival, where it was nominated for the Grand Jury Prize. It also screened at numerous festivals throughout the world, where it received multiple awards and was distributed theatrically by Lionsgate Films.

Figure 5.5 Toni Kalem

Photo: © Peter Sterling, all rights reserved, 2018

Since that time, Toni has been working continuously as a screenwriter. Her background as an actress and her awareness of the dearth of strong roles for women has informed her love of literary adaptations. A voracious reader, her passion is for inhabiting the psyches of complex, contradictory, and flawed women who take control of their lives and discover their own voices.

She has adapted the best-selling novel *Patty Jane's House of Curl*, by Lorna Lanvik, which she will also direct, and *Two Lives*, the Katharine Graham story, among others. Toni (Figure 5.5) is thrilled that Anne Tyler has entrusted her to adapt her most recent novel, *A Spool of Blue Thread*, which she recently optioned.

She has also worked extensively in television. Following the release of *A Slipping-Down Life*, Toni was hired to write for *The Sopranos*. She also was on staff for Showtime's *The Big C*, with Laura Linney, as well as being the creator/executive producer on pilots for HBO, CBS, and Lifetime. She is currently developing a pilot, loosely based on her time on *The Sopranos*, about acting on a hit television series while having to move back in with her dysfunctional family.

Her next film, *Layover*, which she adapted from Lisa Zeidner's award-winning novel, deals with a traveling saleswoman who goes on the lam from her life. It is set to star Penelope Cruz and Guy Pearce.

I didn't realize that I had a passion for anything besides acting until I began the process of directing my first film. It was like falling in love slowly, and then all at once.

I originally optioned Anne Tyler's novel *A Slipping-Down Life* with an intention to act in it. The protagonist, Evie Decker, a role which Lili Taylor embodied brilliantly, was the kind of role in which I never would have been cast. I had unwittingly built a career playing tough Italians. Yet Evie was the role I felt was closest to my true self. She reminded me of Laura in *The Glass Menagerie*, which I had done on stage. Laura and Evie broke my heart, and that was the kind of role I yearned for. So when I read Ms. Tyler's novel and became obsessed with it, I optioned the book, taking money I had earned as an actress and investing in myself.

It took a long time for it to dawn on me that I could (a) write, (b) direct, and (c) have someone else play the role. And when I say a long time, I mean a very long time. I continued to act, all the while pouring my acting salary into my very expensive *A Slipping-Down Life* habit.

I went through many phases, hiring a "real writer" to write the script. After an excruciatingly long time, what was delivered to me was nothing more than a cut-and-paste of the book. My hopes were devastated. I continued to meet with other writers, and I began to see that though they gave great "meeting," their voice on the page didn't match up to their voice at the restaurants in which we met. Beyond discouraged, I met with Robert McKee, the notorious script doctor, when you could still meet with Robert McKee in a coffee shop and talk for two hours. I taped everything he said. I never listened to the tape, however, because the one thing that rang in my head was this: *write this yourself. No one but you knows the story like you do. This is your story to tell.*

As usual, it took me a while to accept (or absorb) what he had said. After all, I had a plan and it didn't include acknowledging I could write. I made a compromise decision with myself. I would "outline" what I wanted for the adaptation, and then I would give the outline to one of those "real" writers. I began to spend my days in the Santa Monica Public Library working on my outline. When I had completed my task, I shared what I had written with an actor friend. He read it and his reaction was: "You've written the script. You are the writer." Like I said, things come to me slowly.

Once the script was finished, I began the process of sending it to directors. Okay . . . maybe I could write some sort of script, but there was no way I even dreamed of directing it. At this point, of course, I was still thinking that I would play Evie. Through various connections and sheer first-timer chutzpah, I managed to get the script to some of my favorite filmmakers. None of them Americans, as it turned out, despite the fact that Anne Tyler had written a very American story. I wanted an outsider's point of view on small-town America, especially since the character of Evie was an outsider and saw the world through her own particular lens. I wanted a vision of small-town life that was more fable-like, that could be any small town anywhere. That was about someone who was invisible becoming visible: a metaphor for how I felt.

I got surprisingly positive responses to my script and built relationships with brilliant filmmakers. But their reaction to it was somewhat unanimous: *this is your story. No one will know how to tell it like you. You should direct it.* Now, having been an actress most of my life, I took their positive feedback as another form of rejection. However they were couching their compliments, in my actor mind they were still saying no to me.

Around that time, I took an acting role in a film, a misogynistic and violent one, where I played the proverbial "wife." I had taken the job to subsidize my *A Slipping-Down Life* habit. The writer/director, 6 ft 2 in, monosyllabic, and macho, had also been an actor. It was during this shoot that I started to wake up to a new possibility: if this guy, who had acted way less than I had, could write and direct his first movie, why couldn't I?

I came back from location and told my then producer about my epiphany. Her response was downright discouraging. Not only would it be a battle for me to play the lead in my own film, but it was a pipe dream for me to think I could direct it having had no directing experience. Looking back, her negativity became an unintended gift. I made the decision to get some directing experience, and I parted ways with her as my producing partner. I decided that if I was going to go into a room to try and get financing to make my movie, I needed to know how to "play the part of director." And to do that, I had to do the same extensive research I did for any other role. Since I had been the kind of method actress who was only laser focused on my role, I had never paid attention on set to the multifarious aspects of making a film. I knew I needed to take myself through every part of production: I needed to know lenses, what telecine was, and color correcting. I needed to prepare to "play the part" of director.

> "Directing actors from my own script was what changed everything for me. The realization that there was no magic wand to directing. It was a learning process like everything else. And I had everything to learn."

So I produced (myself) a short based on my script. I hustled and scrambled to pitch my project in order to get film stock donated, camera equipment donated, dollies and lights donated, free locations (Santa Monica Hospital gave me a wing for three days). A filmmaker friend leant me her house to shoot. Another friend did the catering. One thing I did know was that good craft service is crucial to actors. I met with department heads. I cast actors I had known and loved. And I did something radical. I cast another actress to play the lead.

Directing actors from my own script was what changed everything for me. The realization that there was no magic wand to directing. It was a learning process like everything else. And I had everything to learn. But I loved the experience of being in control, of making decisions, of nurturing actors' performances, and creating an artistic collaboration. And most important, I had taken the first step toward giving up my long-held dream of playing Evie. I was surprised by how freeing it felt.

As it turned out, I didn't need to go into a room to pitch my film. Except for the cast and crew, no one saw my short. What mattered was that I had done it, and it gave me the confidence to speak up and to say without apology and with full conviction, "I will direct my film." I began to meet with producers who believed in my script and wanted to support me in my journey. Luckily, this time I found the right producer. He knew an equity financier. She responded to the script and to the fact that it was a "cachet" project, since it was based on a Pulitzer Prize-winner's novel. She invested in the film, and after years of working and waiting and being told no, the actual casting and pre-production happened in a flash. I met with Lili Taylor. I sat across the table from her and I fell in love. She was Evie, pure and simple. In casting her, I wasn't giving anything up. I was gaining everything. It was a feeling I recognized from first becoming a mother. Unconditional love and finding my purpose.

Once on my own set, I realized how all my years on other people's sets were feeding me. Yes, I had anxieties about my lack of knowledge on lenses and lighting, but I had carefully hired a cinematographer, who, besides being talented, had a gentle demeanor and, most importantly, respected women. I had learned from the mere three times I had worked with a woman director that if a director of photography doesn't respect a woman at the helm, that woman is in trouble. I "cast" my crew as carefully as I cast my actors. I was looking for a collaboration. If they were allowed to be creative, then I knew that they would bring so much more to the film. I realized how much I had actually absorbed being on sets. I might not have been looking through the eyepiece to check lens size, but I was feeling the energy each set engenders. If nothing else, the one thing a director gets to do is to set the tone. Not just of how he or she tells her story, but the tone of their set. It's like inviting people to your home for a dinner party. No matter how good the food and how perfectly the table is set, one asshole can ruin the whole evening. So no assholes would be in my "home." We would have a loving and supportive atmosphere in which a community of talented people could bring their best and most creative selves.

For me, the most joyous part was directing the actors. After all, we spoke the same language. And I knew first-hand how scary acting is and how important it was for them to feel safe with me and to trust me. I knew that you can't direct every actor the same way. Each one has developed their own process that works best for them, and you, as director, have to respect that process and adjust to that, while still getting what you want.

I write for actors, I direct for actors. I took the best from the best directors I worked with . . . and I consciously worked to avoid the pitfalls of the worst

I had been with. Same with what I learned from my mother. She was the best mother in certain ways, and I am forever grateful to her for that. But the ways in which she fell short, I was consciously going to avoid repeating when I got my turn at bat. So I discovered motherhood fed me as much as anything else.

There's no getting around it. Acting, writing, and directing are each difficult in their own ways. Only after I had directed did I realize why the pressures on an actor are so intense. You are asked to show up on a set with a filmmaker and crew who have worked on their project for months, or years, or decades. You are the last to be invited to the party. And yet, at the moment "Action" is called, everything is resting on you. The clock is ticking, you spend hours waiting and waiting to be called to perform, every time you hear "Let's go again" you feel it's your fault. To say nothing of the rejection you endure over the years to land you on that set. (Rejection, that always felt personal no matter how I tried to rationalize why I was not cast.) With writing and directing jobs, it always feels less about me. Maybe my voice as a filmmaker isn't right for the project, but it isn't about my hair color or my body type or the 1,000 other things an actor cannot control.

Writing is the loneliest and most difficult job in terms of self-discipline. Most days I want to do anything but write. My house is never cleaner than when I have a blank page to fill. I sweep the floor, I empty the dishwasher, I decide I need to tone up my arms and lift some weights. Getting my ass in that chair is a challenge I can't begin to describe. I'm a master procrastinator and do best under a deadline. But, and don't tell the writing god this, I'm never more relieved than when I have a good writing day. It's like my spirit is lifted. My heart has come out of my body and I feel free. At least until the next morning, when I have to begin the battle with myself all over again.

> "Directing is the most fulfilling job I've ever had. I write in order to direct."

Directing is the most exhausting, sleep-deprived work I've ever done. Unlike an actor, you are in every scene. There is never a moment you are not being called on to make a decision and make it quickly. You are supposed to act as if you know what you want and what you are doing, even when you don't, which is an intimidating role to play. That said, directing is the most fulfilling job I've ever had. I write in order to direct. I love collaborating with other artists. I love surrounding myself with a team of creative, passionate people who form a family to build the same "house" together. I love that as a filmmaker one has the opportunity to express one's world view, to use one's total voice as a human being, and to bring some hope and heart to this world.

For me, I find living in New York much more fulfilling in terms of leading a balanced life, but much more difficult in terms of getting writing done. Unlike Santa Monica, where I lived for many years, there are so many distractions waiting to grab my attention right outside my door. Endless cultural events and invitations, people-watching, walking in the park, or just plain walking. Nothing feeds a writer's imagination like those things. And nothing keeps you from writing like they do. It takes such discipline in New York to stay in and sit in that chair. Needless to say, LA offers more work opportunities and more meetings and networking. But I had enough of my life being centered on "the business." Coming back here was a life choice for me. I still go to LA for rounds of meetings. I cram them all into a couple of weeks' stretch. I experience the solipsism of thinking about career and not much else. And knowing I can come home to the world in New York allows me to enjoy it so much more.

I am a bookaholic, so I am always reading with an eye to adapt. For me, adaptation is a natural extension of being an actress. The book is the blueprint for the story I want to tell, the way the script is the blueprint for the actor's excavation. So I always have several books under option or several books that I want to option that I pursue until either the option becomes available or I am able to forge a partnership with the producers who control it. That is what happened with my current film, *Layover*. I had pursued that book for years. It was never available. Finally, I was able to wrangle the producers' names from the agent who repped it, and from that our partnership began. After all, we were in love with the same material.

In deciding on material, I first and foremost look for material that is character-based, whatever the genre. And within that, I am passionate about finding female-driven material. Especially for older women. And when I say *older*, I'm talking over 40. Actresses, with very few exceptions, are not allowed to age. What I want to be able to do is create these opportunities and to tell stories that are driven not just by plot, but more importantly by character, by emotion, and how that drives story.

I have to say, when my daughter was young, juggling motherhood and directing was the hardest. It's one of the reasons I didn't direct more for many years. It was wrenching to be torn apart from her for such a long time when I was on location. It wasn't just the distance; it was the 24-hours-a-day utter focus directing demands. There were so many people other than her to whom I was responsible. She was used to me coming home from my office or from a set and giving all that focus to her. Not being available to her the same way was very tough.

I think it's truly one of the reasons there are so few women directors. Most women don't have wives. We don't have someone at home taking up the mothering baton while we are off making our movies. I had waited too long to be a mother, and I didn't want to miss anything.

Writing and acting were much more manageable. When wrap is called, you are done for the day. With writing, you can decide to close your computer and wait till the next morning to open it again. And once I made my film, writing jobs were steady. The kind of stories I wanted to direct and the time it takes to develop an independent film is an expensive, poorly paid habit. And I had a family to support. Writing allowed me to do that.

Writing for *The Sopranos* came out of left field. I had been acting on the show for several years when I got a call from [show runner] David Chase. Though I had already directed and I had a burgeoning writing career, I never had talked with him about that part of my life. My commitment was to doing the very best work I could playing the role of Angie Bonpensiero. I happened at that time, however, to be writing a pilot for HBO (on motherhood, as it turns out) that was being produced by the producers of *The Sopranos*. David, unbeknownst to me, was looking for a woman to come on staff to focus more on Carmela and motherhood. He asked his producers (and mine) for suggestions and they said, "What about Toni?" They sent him my film, he watched it and called me on a Friday to ask if I'd be interested. That weekend I moved to New York to start work on Monday as a story editor.

I was one of two women in the writers' room, and I was the only mother. The work was beyond challenging. I had never been in a writers' room before. And here I was in the writers' room of all writers' rooms. With a master who was changing television. I had been thrown into the deep end of the pool. Combine the three-hour time difference to my home in LA, an adolescent daughter I had left, planning her bat mitzvah and having two weeks to write a script, and that's a lot of stress and a lot of heartache. I hired a research assistant, cried a lot, worked my ass off, and had the greatest and most rewarding crash course in writing for television than anyone could dream of.

I was expanding my repertoire, so to speak, for writing in different mediums. It was akin to expanding one's range as an actor, honing your craft to play all kinds of characters: to play comedy as well as drama. Shakespeare and sitcoms. For me, it always comes back to acting. Acting will always be my home base: my training, where I was raised, my school, my family. I will always empathize with actors, look at material with the eyes I imagine they see it from. When I sit in a room and hear producers mindlessly toss comments around about actors, their ages, their ranges, their looks (all my fears realized) . . . I silently and sometimes not so silently remind them that I am one of those "too fat, too old, too not funny, not worth enough" . . . I'm an actress and they best be sensitive to that fact. It informs everything I do as a writer and, of course, as a director.

Yesterday, I had a meeting with an actress, a very bankable movie star, who had just read my script and seems interested in starring in my movie. Of course, I was nervous to meet with her. I had blow-dried my hair, picked out the perfect outfit/costume a director should wear (that's the actress in me), and reapplied my mascara too many times to count. Then a calming thought hit me: it's *so* not about that for me anymore. She and I will be talking about material and how she likes to work and connecting on a creative level. It has nothing to do with how straight my hair is in the New York humidity, thankfully, anymore. Old habits die hard.

> "Acting is where I live in my heart, and it's what drives every other passion of mine creatively."

But the most wonderful thing happened when we sat down, ordered our lattes, and prepared to dive in. She told me that before she could talk, she had to tell me something. She proceeded to share with me an event that had happened just moments before our meeting that had greatly upset her. As she told me and began to cry, as I did also, I realized what is so liberating talking actress-to-actress. She was so concerned about bringing her emotions into our meeting, but I thought this is exactly what actors must also deal with in going into a scene. What are the previous circumstances? What happened to you right before you walked in the door? How does that affect how you will play the scene? I reassured her with this. And suddenly all the tension of meeting someone new, and the insecurities we all face, melted away. I was on my home turf and she was with someone who got it.

From there, we could go on to talk about the script and character and how we like to work. But acting is where I live in my heart, and it's what drives every other passion of mine creatively. It's what gives me the confidence to sit and talk with a wonderful actor and have her know that I know. It's like we grew up in the same town, went to the same high school, and know all the same people. And yet with each new job we are in a way always starting again, with the anxiety that engenders. But, hopefully, our mutual background, our actor DNA, gives the ability to trust and open up . . . the place, for me, where all great work begins.

SHE WANTS TO DIRECT COMMERCIALS

▶ A Q&A with Katie Enright

Figure 5.6 Katie Enright

Photo: Joanna DeGeneres

Growing up the sixth of seven children, Katie Enright's goal has always been to make everyone at the dinner table laugh; these dinner-time diversions were the start of Katie's lifelong love of storytelling.

Katie began her career as a performer in Chicago, attending the Second City Conservatory, Improv Olympic, and Act One Studios. Upon moving to LA, she realized her true passions: directing and creating. Her first film, *Dog Park*, went on to win Best First-Time Filmmaker at the Action on Film Festival in Las Vegas, Best Comedy Short at the Nice International Film Festival, and numerous other nominations and awards in festivals worldwide. Katie participated in the Warner Bros. Television Directors' Workshop, an initiative that introduces up-and-coming directors to primetime television.

Katie (Figure 5.6) resides in LA. In addition to pursuing her career as a director, she has also produced several projects, including *The Drunk Lonely Wives Book Club*, a web series directed by Emmy-winner Mary Lou Belli. In her spare time, Katie says, she is a very avid, very terrible golfer.

> "I immediately downloaded the syllabus from AFI's MFA program and bought every book and started devouring them on my own."

How did your work as an actor lead to an interest in directing?

As an actor, you are constantly working closely with directors, but rarely get the opportunity of a window into their mind of what calls them to their part of the creative process. It wasn't until my mentors (ahem, you, and Bethany Rooney) wrote a delightful book called *Directors Tell the Story* [Focal Press, 2011] that I really got a glimpse at the inner workings of directors and their creative process. As soon as I got a peek behind that curtain, I was hooked – I immediately downloaded the syllabus from the American Film Institute's MFA program and bought every book and started devouring them on my own. I watched videos; I attended Q&As; I read and saw everything related to directing that I could get my hands on. After that process, I decided to put what I learned into practice and made a short film and two spec commercials.

> "Some actors need a director to be really hands on; others prefer a few takes before they're given any notes. I just try to listen and be present."

Do you think that knowing about the acting process helps you as a director, and if so, in what ways?

Everyone comes to directing with a different perspective, with a different set of natural strengths and weaknesses. Because my background is acting, I'm very comfortable working with actors. So much truly great storytelling is knowing how to be the proper midwife for a truly great take. I also understand the vulnerability that is associated with performing, and have taken thousands of hours of acting classes. Every actor's process is a bit different; I try to focus on what each individual actor needs. Some actors need a director to be really hands on; others prefer a few takes before they're given any notes. I just try to listen and be present.

Can you talk about the journey of producing your first web series, and directing your first short?

The common denominator is always finding other friends who are as excited about pursuing their art as you are about pursuing yours, and making things together. Living in LA, I'm so lucky to have so many talented friends in front of and behind the camera, and as part of the joy of creating you help them out in their creative projects, and they help out in yours. One day, we all got together and decided to make something completely for ourselves (a web series called *The Drunk Lonely Wives Book Club*). Like all first-time producing experiences, there was a significant learning curve: we raised money via Kickstarter (which is its own full-time job and its own skill set separate from content creation), we faced production restraints that impacted story and character (we shot around a single location, which was graciously donated to us), we traded favors and called in past favors to pull a skeleton crew together to be able to shoot. I think I was most overwhelmed by the generosity of my network, of how many people donated either time or money.

When I decided to transition my career from acting to directing, my first short film was called *Dog Park*. This time, I had learned from working on *Drunk Lonely Wives Book Club*: I picked a story that could be told on a shoestring, so I was able to fund that project myself, with friends donating their time and support. I greatly expanded time in pre-production because it was my first solo directing gig, and simultaneously was extremely candid the day of the shoot with my producer, assistant director, and editor that it was my first time directing. Because we are all a close-knit group of friends, they were all extremely supportive. I can't emphasize enough how important it is to have a group of creative collaborators you trust.

Is your ultimate aim to be a film, television, or commercial director? What appeals to you about each?

Ultimately, my goal is to tell a great story. I enjoy the challenge of telling a complete story with a beginning, middle, and end in 15 or 30 seconds. I also enjoy the challenge of sustaining attention for a feature-length film. At the end of the day, it's about matching the right creative to the right opportunity.

Is there any part of your hyphenate jobs – producing/writing/directing – that you don't like?

Writing! If I'm being honest, mainly because I'm not very good at it, and I don't enjoy doing it . . . It actually bothered me so much that I spoke to my mentor about it. She reminded me that (a) true humility is acknowledging our strengths and weaknesses, and (b) true stories begin with true humility. This is why we collaborate as storytellers, and that is why so many of my creative partners are writers.

> "I'm constantly inspired by the people I meet – intimate secrets told by people who know they will never see you again, wild nights, first dates,

important conversations in relationships…it's a wealth of experience in human interaction that absolutely helps as a filmmaker."

Finally, you have a survival job that helps support this transaction you are making. What do you do, and why did you choose that job?

I moonlight as a bartender. I love it! It is the "right type" of job in that it allows flexible hours so my art can be first priority, and pays enough in concentrated work-hours so that I can dedicate a significant portion of my day hours to advancing my projects. It also helps that it's at a fancy-schmancy hotel, so it also exposes me to people I probably wouldn't have the ability to meet otherwise. I met a princess and it was an incredible character study: the way she sat, how she sipped her wine, the way she addressed other individuals in the room, was fascinating. I'm constantly inspired by the people I meet – intimate secrets told by people who know they will never see you again, wild nights, first dates, important conversations in relationships . . . it's a wealth of experience in human interaction that absolutely helps as a filmmaker.

THE VIEW FROM AN EXECUTIVE'S CHAIR

▶ A Q&A with Alet Taylor

Figure 5.7 Alet Taylor

Photo: Dana Patrick

Alet Taylor (Figure 5.7) is a bi-coastal actress and writer, currently playing Laurie Farnham in Season 2 of *The Sinner*. She is also Chief Creative Officer for Stage Network, which launched in the fall of 2018 (*watchstage.com*). Her television credits include *Untitled Chaiken Pilot* opposite Katie Holmes, *The Sinner*, *The Path*, *Law & Order: SVU*, *Gotham*, and *The First Family*, and her film credits include *San Andreas Quake* and *Celeste* (Bushwick Beats series). Her theater credits include *Freaky Friday* (national tour, Katherine understudy), *God of Carnage* (Annette), *A Sign of the Times* (Goodspeed), and *The Producers* (national tour/ Vegas). Visit alettaylor.com.

In addition to your acting career, you have now embarked on another, simultaneous venture. Can you tell me a little about Stage Network?

Great question, because it gives me the opportunity to push back (with love). Stage Network is the first streaming network for premium content devoted to the world of theater. It features original scripted, variety, and reality series; live theater; documentaries; talk shows; concerts and Broadway shows; films; international theater; and more. Offering free and subscription-based premium content, Stage is dedicated to providing accessibility to this world for both theater lovers and those just getting to know the magic of the stage. I am the Chief Creative Officer for Stage, responsible for transforming rough ideas and general concepts. I direct my diverse creative team to project completion, formulating long- and short-term goals to further Stage's brand identity. Here's my push back: I suppose working for Stage is "in addition to" my acting career, but it's more "a result of." Every actor I know has been encouraged, at one time or another, to create their own content. The reasons behind it differ, but the task is the same. Actors, if they want to work as much as their heart and mind and ego tell them they should be working, have to create their own content if they want the world to see all they can do. I was resentful of this at first: "I have an agent and a manager – isn't it their job to create opportunities for me to work?" And while this is an accurate expectation of theatrical representation, it puts me in a position of relying on them. And the waiting doesn't feel very powerful. Relying on someone else to fulfill your passion is tricky. Some days you're grateful (a series of fantastic auditions), some days you're frustrated and perplexed (a dry spell), but most of the time you simply *don't know what the hell is going on*: "I just spoke with a friend who's going in for this great thing and we're the same type. Why didn't I get an appointment? Was I submitted? Should I call my rep? Am I bugging her/him by doing so? Everyone on social media is posting about booking work except me," etc. Resentment is then born and grows. Resentment affects your psyche, mood, your soul. Acting and being good at auditions come from deep within. If there's turmoil within you, it's difficult to audition. I accepted a position at Stage Network because I saw opportunities to both create my own work and help others create work. I just did it on a large scale. But I'm a hyper maniac, so . . .

How did you get this job? And does your knowledge and experience as an actor serve you in this position?

I got this job because my friends, Stage Network's creators Rich Affannato, Bobby Traversa, and Jesse Kearney, had questions regarding original content and brand specificity and I had the answers. And if I didn't have the answers, I educated myself. Quickly. It was not lost on me that I was about to lead a creative department of a new streaming network with no previous experience. But feeling like a fraud didn't feel very powerful (see answer #1), so I sought to gain the experience I needed. I sped up my own learning curve. I not only do not feel like a fraud, I am thrilled that I am the one in charge. I know what to do! This job in the hands of someone else would be wrong. I'm super confident every day that I'm the best person for this position.

My knowledge as an actor greatly served this position, because I was joining a team of other actor/producers. With the amount of work we had before us, our main concern was how to protect the talent. How do we best serve the actor, writer, director of the piece? The phrase "Talent comes last" – thrown around freely in production development – does not apply to our business. I've spent decades hearing how replaceable my contribution to a project was, usually accompanied by some effort to satiate my anxiety with "This is good exposure for you." You can imagine, dear reader, how well the "good exposure" line goes over with actors these days. Most actors I know do not have any trouble shedding light on themselves. Social media provides an enormous platform for actors to expose themselves, as it were, in whatever way they choose. The "We'll give you exposure" carrot no longer exists. And my experience as an actor, one would hope, means that I know my fellow actors want to get paid. Pretty simple. The only old phrase that still stands is "Before you win a Tony, you have to eat."

Has sitting on the other side of the table changed how you view yourself an actress in relation to casting directors? Agents? Managers? I'd love to hear a before-and-after story.

Yes, it's not just important for an actor to sit on the other side of the table, it's vital to the actor in his/her learning how not to be a *weirdo* in auditions and meetings. Being on the other side of the table, in my experience, doesn't help me be less needy. Everyone's needy. Every actor needs something. What that need is, is between you and your therapist, but there's no arguing a basic need to want the job or the representation. I continue to study with Bob Krakower in New York. Bob used to be involved in casting and has definitely seen a lifetime of auditions. I love his take on neediness. I'm paraphrasing, but casting directors are human beings. Human beings have an implicit desire to make you feel better if it's perceived that you are nervous and/or at odds with something. An entire day of making actors feel better is exhausting. Casting directors aren't assholes. They're just exhausted with reassurance. *Asshole* would be my word, not Bob's.

> "Say the words. Don't worry about verbatim. Engage the reader. Know the reveal. Know what my character's job is based on the information given. Because word-for-word, perfectly executed dialogue is a rare ask in my world of auditions."

Before-and-after stories imply that I've finally "gotten it," but there are days when all my previous knowledge in front of and behind the table doesn't help me. I would say that I just let the audition go quicker. The beauty of getting older is that I let go of the bad auditions. Wallowing is insane and unproductive and indulgent. There's too much to do. And the "doing" is the key. I can chastise myself into ego mayhem about how often I asked a casting director if I could "begin again," despite their eye-rolling "Sure." Or I could commit to my camera-practice group and develop the skill of the one take – which begins with thinking in pictures, getting the skeleton of the scene down, making sense of what is happening as written. Say the words. Don't worry about verbatim. Engage the reader. Know the reveal. Know what my character's job is based on the information given. Because word-for-word, perfectly executed dialogue is a rare ask in my world of auditions. I have had maybe *two* auditions like that in my life, and the material was Sorkin and they were both for the same casting director. It was her thing that actors be word-perfect. Whatever.

My "after" story is simply to confess that I have leaned into my neediness in auditions, without making the casting director feel uneasy. I put the neediness into the character instead of into my banter with the casting director. I book needy characters. I book nervous, jumpy, judgmental, superior, mean-spirited, cuckolded, neurotic female characters. Leaning in is working so far. I suppose when I start to feel differently about my life, I'll book those characters as well. Pay attention to what other people say about your look, vibe, energy, essence on camera. One person's opinion is different from a bunch of feedback. I love what my mom thinks I look like, but I listen to what my practice group says.

Do you now see content creators differently, now that you are the buyer?
Yup. But I'm also meeting with a wide variety of skill levels. I'm not Netflix meeting with well-established and highly skilled writers. Some of the writers I meet are highly skilled, but most are in a group of talented thinkers who aren't killing it in LA. Plus it's theater content, so it's a specific kind of person who wants to write about and for theater. Someone who *has* to write about theater. From their gut.

I intellectually knew I would receive pitches from predominately male writers. I just wasn't prepared for how little content I'd receive from women and writers of different ethnicities. It's easy to just sort of announce that Stage is seeking diverse content. I've needed to go out and find it and grab it and bring it back to the office. And I've let go of being surprised by this and now I just make it a weekly priority. I seek diversity in content. Not figuratively. Not on paper. I mean, I put my shoes on and seek diverse content.

You are also a content creator yourself who has written a one-woman show as well as a television pilot for yourself. What was the genesis of these projects?

The genesis of the two projects was a direct result of my living a full life and committing to putting certain aspects of my life down on paper. I've read many pitches and scripts where it was obvious, though expertly and sometimes brilliantly written, that the creator was a huge fan of television and movies. And I've read many technically challenged scripts where it was obvious that the writer had experienced an incredible thing or time period or relationship. The latter writer can be taught *Final Draft*. Easy. The former writer, though their taste in film/television is excellent, needs to be engaged in real-life experiences. Not so easy. And I'm not suggesting that one needs to backpack through Europe or bust their ass waitressing to write a good script. Because there's no one I know of who's directly experienced anything dreamed up in a SyFy movie. But even if I'm reading about aliens starting a regional theater company on a distant planet, I can tell if the writer has walked in someone else's shoes, you know?

As far as what my pilot actually is, I've spent many hours with Mary Lou making it all come together. There's no way I'm describing it in her book. Ha.

You also have children and a husband who are active in the performing arts. Can you talk about your philosophy when it comes to them booking jobs? Surviving in the business?

Oh, thank you for not asking how I manage to do it all. I would have politely referred you to the recent *Gazette*/Groff interview.[1]

My husband, Andy Taylor, books stuff despite being ill-prepared, unambitious, and often a sweaty mess. It's both unbelievable and not. He spent his first 35 years working on a specific skill set (accomplished singer, dancer, cellist), and that disciplined training has paid off. He's not lazy; he's just kind of done "learning." And he's a smart, affable dude who genuinely enjoys a wide variety of people. Casting directors like him. His manager scooped him up after watching him be a reader. They had a few laughs. He signed Andy. It happens.

My daughters, Ruby and Lucy, both attend the Professional Performing Arts School (PPAS) in Manhattan. They've booked a few commercials, television spots, one or two short films each, but Andy and I made a decision as parents to wait for them to come to us about the business. We don't spend any time taking them to auditions. Our family rules are the following: learn a language other than the one you speak, learn to play one instrument, get off your phone and read a book once a day. The girls' pursuit of performing comes from them. They brought PPAS to our attention, they auditioned, they're managing their grades and their dance/singing/acting classes. They're driving the boat.

My son, Dash, is a musician and came into his own style and tone after high school. Again, he creates music based on his experiences. He writes lyrics from what he knows, not what he doesn't. We help when we're able to, but any success Dash has achieved is of his own doing. His survival instincts are incredible. His failures fuel his creativity. Wanting to shield and protect Dash did not serve him. Beyond our basic common-sense parenting, my kids have needed to learn from their mistakes in the business. It's heartbreaking but ultimately makes them kinder.

We talk to them about perseverance, grit, resilience, having a thick skin, learning other skills, etc., but they'll need to figure out survival as they go. We'll be there, we'll be the net, but they have to experience it themselves. We'll just provide the ear and the hugs and the ice cream when the shit hits the fan.

You do it all: sing, dance, act, produce, write. What satisfaction do you get from each, or a combination of doing it all?
There's a deep hole inside of me that I try and fill with applause, attention, and validation. It's like I haven't evolved from being 13 years old. It's unproductive, crazy-making, and bottomless. Why was I wired this way? How do I censor these shortcomings so I don't actually ruin my kids' lives? Is there an app that can fix this?

So I write about the ugly, immature, snarky aspects of myself. My chest burns with the above-mentioned shortcomings and then I write about them, and then the feeling in my chest melts away and what ends up on paper is good and funny, and I decide that being transparent about the undesirable parts of my personality might help someone else. I mean, that's satisfying. But I have a feeling I'll be writing about my need for attention the rest of my life. It's okay. There are worst things.

> "I determine my own level of success. My goal is to be kind and honest about the process. And eat ice cream. My goal is to spend my life eating ice cream."

And helping emerging writers at Stage Network is extremely satisfying. Meeting a wide variety of people, both young and old, and listening to their responses on what I've determined is funny or profound or sad or scary is extremely satisfying. It's both wonderful to hear "I totally agree" as well as "I have no idea what you're laughing at."

Mary Lou posted something on Facebook a while back about creating a life that makes you want to jump out of bed in the morning. I did. I have. I determine my own level of success. My goal is to be kind and honest about the process. And eat ice cream. My goal is to spend my life eating ice cream.

Note

1 Kozelsky, Kristin. 2018. "Alienation proves fertile state of mind for Lauren Groff". *Harvard Gazette*, July 17. https://news.harvard.edu/gazette/story/2018/07/lauren-groff-on-florida-as-a-state-of-mind/.

INDEX

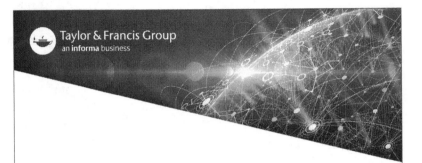